LEADERS DON'T HAVE TO YELL

LEADERS DON'T HAVE TO YELL

NATIONAL TEAM COACH ON LEADING HIGH-PERFORMING TEAMS

James Kwasi Appiah
with Kyei Amoako

Spotlight Publishing
Columbus, Ohio

Copyright © 2019 Spotlight Publishing

All rights reserved. No part of this publication may be reproduced, distributed or transmitted in any form or by any means, including photocopying, recording, or other electronic or mechanical methods, without the prior written permission of the publisher, except in the case of brief quotations embodied in critical reviews and certain other noncommercial uses permitted by copyright law. For permission requests, write to the publisher at SpotlightPublishing@mail.com.

Ordering Information:
The book is available for purchase at various online outlets, the publisher's website and at various retail locations. See **CoachKwasiAppiahBook.com** for more information. Special discounts are available on bulk purchases by corporations, associations, and other groups. For details about bulk purchases, please email the publisher at **SpotlightPublishing@Mail.com**.

Cover Photo: Kwame Appah
Cover Design: Adam Hayman
Interior Design: Ryan Magada
Clothing for Cover Photo: JayRay Ghartey FashionHauz
Back Photo of James Kwasi Appiah: Emmanuel Offei
Inside Photos: Emmanuel Offei, Ghana Football Legacy, and Appiah Archives
Leaders Don't Have to Yell/ James Kwasi Appiah with Kyei Amoako. - 2nd ed v2.
ISBN 978-0-9998312-2-9 (Hardback)
ISBN 978-0-9998312-3-6 (Paperback)
ISBN 978-0-9998312-4-3 (eBook)

JAMES KWASI APPIAH'S DEDICATIONS:

To President J.A. Kufour, Coach E.K. Afranie, Ambassador Ayisi Boateng, and Mr. Kwabena Aidoo for their exemplary leadership.

KYEI AMOAKO'S DEDICATION:

To the legacy of Rev. Paddy Brew, a teacher and pastor who impacted many lives.

CONTENTS

Foreword 1
Introduction 5

PART I: FROM BOY TO MAN

1. From Humble Beginnings 11
2. Opoku Ware School 19
3. Turning My Passion into My Profession 31
4. Fabulous Kumasi Asante Kotoko 43

PART II: A LEADER OF MEN AND TEAMS

5. Becoming a Coach 79
6. Becoming the Black Stars Coach 85
7. Win Now, or Forever Lose Your Peace 101

PART III: CHAMPIONS ALWAYS PLAY TO WIN

8. Black Stars: Libya 1982 133
9. Kumasi Asante Kotoko: 1983 Africa Championship 141
10. Black Stars: Senegal 1992 153
11. Black Stars: South Africa 2010 World Cup 165
12. Black Meteors: 2011 All-Africa Games 175

CONTENTS

13. Black Stars: Brazil 2014 World Cup 183

14. Al Khartoum Al Watani (Sudan) 205

15. Black Stars: The Road to AFCON 2019 243

16. Black Stars: Going for Glory at AFCON 2019 273

17. Black Stars: Biggest Lessons from AFCON 2019 295

PART IV: LEAVING A LEGACY

18. Making Money and Investing Wisely 321

19. Ghana's Best XI... 337

20. The Future of Ghana Football 347

21. Closing Thoughts 367

Afterword 373

Appendix 377

Index 383

AUTHORS' NOTE

Due to the limitations of memory recall and the varied spelling of names in the available historical records, please note that we made a good-faith effort to use the correct spellings of the names mentioned and also the specific dates of events referenced.

If any corrections are necessary, please contact the publisher and such corrections will be addressed in future editions of this publication.

FOREWORD

by Kwabena Yeboah
President, Sports Writers Association of Ghana (SWAG)

Renowned achievers are often indulgent, tender-hearted and of a gentle disposition. That is because success in most areas of life does not necessarily come about through squealing and howling your point across.

James Kwasi Appiah is a fine example of success made in Ghana, and I have the singular honour to script the foreword to his book, which I believe will inform and inspire those who read it.

Having been closely associated with Kumasi Asante Kotoko since 1974, first as a young "ball boy" (during the days of Dan Oppong, Yaw Sam, and Kuuku Dadzie, to name a few) and later as a sports journalist, I have been privileged to be associated with several footballers with varied characters and disposition within the Kotoko fraternity.

Foreword

When I met Kwasi Appiah in 1982, my instincts suggested that I had met a real gem of a person because he was different in many ways. He had an unassuming nature and displayed an utter lack of pretence. He exhibited a let-it-all-hang-out honesty and proved to have a highly-relatable personality. Additionally, his humility and prodigious talent suggested that he was destined for greatness.

During his playing days, I observed Kwasi become everybody's idol. His adorers transcended Kumasi Asante Kotoko with many Ghanaians falling in love with not only his luminous career but also his highly affable character.

As the captain of the Black Stars, he earned the respect and admiration of many Ghanaians. That was largely the reason fans across the nation utterly rejected the decision to strip him of the captain's band in 1992 on the eve of Ghana's participation in the Africa Cup of Nations in Senegal.

Made of a heart of gold, Kwasi Appiah harboured no ill-feeling towards his colleague and captain Abedi Pele nor the authorities who took that injudicious decision. Rather, he showed fine leadership alongside Abedi, often leading prayer sessions with the entire playing body. I personally witnessed a few of those sessions.

It was no surprise that after ending his playing career soon after the Senegal 1992 tournament, he became a Kotoko coach, and then a national team coach years later.

Kwasi Appiah embodies selflessness and a commitment to focusing on the bigger picture, which makes him an example worth emulating. Known widely for diligently serving as the assistant under Ghana's foreign coaches, who were often disproportionately much better paid than he was, Kwasi often insisted that a service to one's nation couldn't be about pecuniary gains. Eventually, his patience and forbearance led to his assuming the headship of the Black Stars. And in this role, he's been an exemplary leader despite many obstacles.

Those who know very little about him are quick to judge him as docile and lame. How wrong they are! And I hope this book reveals to many what some of us have known for many years. Beneath that seeming docility is a solid character of steadfastness, persistence and total resolution.

His quiet nature does not dilute his intense focus and unmistakable candour. And there is a line everyone who deals with him knows not to cross. That couldn't be lost on his Black Stars players who secretly nicknamed him "The Silent Killer" in acknowledgement of the resolute actions he took managing the team. Indeed, calm waters can be deep.

In Ghana where most football fans have a notorious penchant for only foreign coaches, the constant bastardizing of indigenous coaches have unfortunately been commonplace. However, I admire how gracefully Kwasi has handled the many unfair criticisms and insults rained on him by people in high and low places.

Not many believed a Ghanaian helmsman could superintend the qualification of the Black Stars to the World Cup. But Kwasi Appiah did, demonstrating a competence that his critics often fail to acknowledge.

Kwasi has lifted hearts in distressing times, has given hope to those in despair, has refined the characters of his players, and has given courage to the youth. In consonance with that character, he brought more youthful players into the Black Stars than any coach in the history of Ghana's football.

Foreword

I feel eternally blessed to have known Kwasi, a friendship that spans more than 37 years. As my brother from another mother, he earned my respect with his candour, independence and self-belief. He earned his place in the annals of Ghana's history by dint of hard work and by being his own man. And considering his impressive achievements in life, his story is worth sharing with all.

I am extremely pleased about the opportunity this book will afford many people - both young and old - to be inspired by a true Ghanaian success story.

Even though I was present during most of the events highlighted in this book, it has been insightful following along as Kwasi Appiah retold them from his point of view. I hope every Ghanaian and every African takes the time to read this book, particularly his thoughts on the future of Ghana football.

Kwasi has been a gift to Ghana, and that is an opinion many in Ghana's football circles share. Thankfully, this book will shed more light on his illustrious career and personality, which many Ghanaians only know about through the news headlines.

Good Lord! Thank you for the gift that is Kwasi Appiah - a selfless leader and a true gentleman.

INTRODUCTION

In most of my public and private life, I have been a man of few words. Even when I have strong opinions on a matter, I have often preferred to share them when I found it absolutely necessary to speak out publicly. That approach has worked well for me in my private and public life. Many of the conversations that needed to be had around the topics I have an interest in discussing, have been had. Therefore, I resisted suggestions over the years from friends and colleagues to write a book.

In a recent conversation with a close friend, he brought my attention to the fact that sharing my experiences and perspectives in the form of a book would not only be for the benefit of the people alive today, but also for the benefit of future generations. That got me thinking.

I realise that very few people have had the opportunity to walk the path that my life has taken. Very few people have risen to the position of responsibility that my professional life

Introduction

has provided me. As a result, I have seen things that only a few people have seen; I have had experiences that only a few people have had; and I have perspectives that only a few people have. Until now, the stories about the things I have seen, the experiences I have had and my perspectives on issues have been shared with only a relatively small group of people. So, as I thought about what purpose a book from me will serve, I became convinced that the time to commit my experiences and ideas into writing is now.

I owe it to my generation and to the many generations that will come after me to document my experiences and my account of history. I owe it to present and future generations to pass on any insights that will help them do greater exploits than I will ever accomplish. My reason for writing this book is to share my professional experiences and my account of major events that have shaped me into the man that I have become.

Most of my public life has been in the area of professional football in Ghana and around the world: as a member of Prestea Mine Stars and Kumasi Asante Kotoko, as a player in Ghana's junior and senior national teams, as a captain at both club and national team levels, as a coach at the club level, as an assistant coach at the national team level and as the head coach of Ghana's senior men's national team, the Black Stars. In each of these positions, whether on the local or international stage, I have learned valuable lessons about making decisions, working with people and leading high-performing teams. I believe these lessons are worth passing on.

Ghana has a special place in my heart. Ghana has given me many opportunities and I am fortunate to have had opportunities to serve the nation in many different capacities. Every time I have represented my country anywhere, I have done that with pride.

It has never been lost on me that football is an important aspect of the nation's pride, economy and culture.

My greatest motivation whenever I take on any task as a coach and as a leader has always been to make Ghana and Africa proud. And in my line of work, I have experienced "the good, the bad and the ugly" of Ghana football. The good times were great. The bad times were painful. The ugly times were unfortunate. But through all of those times, I learned. Whether quietly observing from my corner or standing in the middle of the action, there were useful lessons that have helped me, as a player and as a coach.

I have learned from my victories and my defeats. I have learned in secure times and in uncertain times. I have learned from the praise and the appreciation, and I have also learned from the resistance and the criticisms. Above all, I have learned how to live with and work with people, and how to lead people gracefully through normal and difficult times.

While my stories and perspectives are mainly from the world of football, I hope that the lessons and the inspiration they provide will be useful to footballers, coaches, and administrators, as well as to the fans and those who have little or no interest in football.

It is true in most areas of life that talent alone cannot make anyone successful in most areas of life. Effort is necessary and the discipline to continue, even when things get tough, is very important. If a person does not develop leadership qualities, his or her talent could go to waste. So, I hope that my experiences and my perspectives will be helpful to readers.

Introduction

Leadership is about having the appropriate influence over people, as well as about having the respect of the people you lead. In some parts of the world and in some professions, leaders are often characterized by their intimidating and domineering methods. I am not one of those types of leaders, and I have no interest in that style of leadership. Different leaders get their influence and respect through methods that are unique to them.

In my humble opinion, leaders don't have to yell in order to get their points across. For me, leadership is about putting my best foot forward at all times, and always looking for ways to help my team win. That is what has served me well, and I hope my story inspires the leader in you, and encourages you to be the best leader you can be – regardless of your profession or your leadership style.

At the time of writing this book, many of us are hard at work trying to restore Ghana football to its former glory. It is my hope that each of us will take advantage of this defining moment in the nation's history, and use that as motivation to do the right things to help us fulfill our destiny as one of the greatest football nations in the world.

Together, we have celebrated our successes. Now, let us reflect on our shortcomings, explore our opportunities, and look for ways to consistently do better. And I hope you don't have to yell, just to get your point across.

PART I:
FROM BOY TO MAN

· CHAPTER 1 ·

FROM HUMBLE BEGINNINGS

Before I could take the helm of Ghana's national senior football team, I had to prepare for that moment. That preparation took many years and some growing pains. All those experiences helped to shape me into the leader that I have become. My experiences from the field, from the sidelines and from the dressing room are what I hope will inspire others to believe in their abilities and always strive to be the best at what they do.

The story of my professional life represents what is possible. It represents what is possible if an African professional footballer, or a professional in any other field of work, develops his or her talents and applies him or herself to become the best in their field of work. My story also represents what can happen when a capable person is given the opportunity to prove himself or herself, and is also provided the necessary support to succeed.

I was born on 9th August 1959 in Sunyani, the capital of what was then Ghana's Brong-Ahafo Region. Brong-Ahafo was one of Ghana's 10 regions, and it was known for its agricultural activities and tourist attractions. In 2019, the region was divided into three: Bono Region, Bono East Region, and Ahafo Region. For simplicity, I will refer to the region as Brong-Ahafo Region in most of this book since most of the events took place at a time when it was called Brong-Ahafo Region.

My father, Joseph Emmanuel Appiah, is a native of Kokotro, a village near Bekwai in the Ashanti Region. He was popularly known as "Ten Ninety." One of his cars at a point in time was a Peugeot with a license plate GE 1090. That is how he became known by that nickname. My father was originally a teacher but he became an auctioneer. He became an auctioneer before I was born and I never asked him why he stopped being a teacher to become an auctioneer. I suppose he did that because he knew he could make more money as an auctioneer than he did as a teacher. Or maybe he wanted to settle in one place to raise his family. As a teacher, he was often transferred from one town to another.

My mother, Martha Ama Kyeremaah, is a native of Dormaa-Yaakrom in the Brong-Ahafo Region. Antie Ama, as my mother was called by most people, was a business woman involved in small-scale trading of beverages and foodstuffs.

At the time my parents met and married, my father had five children from previous relationships and my mother had two children from a previous marriage. My mother's children did not come with her into her new marriage. My father, on the other hand, brought some of his children to come live with us. Together, my parents had five children of which I am the eldest. My three sisters, Sophia, Rose (Obroni), and

Grace, and my brother Kwabena Appiah (Cobby) were born in a span of ten years.

I grew up in Sunyani starting out in a neighbourhood called Nkwarbeng. My parents had rented part of a private house that belonged to one Mr. Brobbey, a very rich businessman who had a "provisions" store in the neighbourhood. A "provisions" store is the neighbourhood shop where we would buy essential household supplies like soap, sugar, sardines and other things that one would usually have had to travel to a bigger city to buy from a departmental store.

As my younger siblings and I grew older, Mr. Brobbey's house was no longer large enough for our family. We had outgrown the space in the home so our family moved to a new residence in a neighbourhood called Sunyani Area 4, which was located near the Sunyani Regional Police Station. That was when my father brought two of my half siblings from his previous marriage to live with us. In addition, he brought my brother Kwaku Appiah, whom he had from another relationship, to come live with us. At that point, there were eight of us living with our parents, making it a total of ten people in the household.

My father was doing well financially in his auctioneering business, so he bought several cars. There was a time when he had seven cars – one car for each day of the week. He often wore an outfit to match the color of the car he drove on a given day. He also had a farm in Nsuatre, a village near Sunyani, where my brothers and I would go with him on Saturdays to help out. He drove us there in his white Peugeot 404. As was typical during that time, the sons went with their father to the farm while the daughters stayed at home with their mother to do household chores like cooking and cleaning.

My parents were always kind towards each other, and they treated each other with respect. Both of my parents were quiet and reserved people, even though my father had a tendency of initiating and engaging outsiders in conversations. Maybe it had something to do with the fact that he worked as an auctioneer. He was very conversational towards strangers, even more so than he was with people who were part of his household.

In those days, a father seeming emotionally distant from his children was typical. A father's role was often seen as the one who provided financially and maintained discipline in the house, and my father did those. Frequent conversations with his children was not something he seemed too excited about. My mother, on the other hand, was very welcoming even though she was quiet. She embraced all of us warmly, and we grew closer to her.

My father was a devout Catholic and my mother was a passionate Presbyterian. My siblings and I attended the Roman Catholic Church with my father. That was mainly because my father would insist that we attended church every Sunday, and we chose to go with him to the Roman Catholic Church because it was right there in our neighbourhood. The Presbyterian Church was a long walking distance away, and walking that far to attend church didn't appeal to us.

I started my primary education at the local Roman Catholic school, where I attended for four years, and then transferred to Sunyani Ridge Experimental School. Like other experimental schools at the time, Ridge Experimental placed a strong focus on academics in order to prepare the students to take the Common Entrance Examination and then go on to attend secondary school. My parents moved me there because they wanted me to have the best education, and they had high expectations of me.

During my early days at Ridge Experimental, I owned a ball that I received as a gift from my father. I took the ball to school almost every day and played with my classmates during breaks. Because I owned the ball, I had a major say in who got to play and who didn't. Furthermore, if someone did something that upset me, I angrily picked up my ball and left.

Even though I was nice to my friends most of the time, I was very sure to enforce my ownership powers as far as my ball was concerned. As a result, my playmates were very accommodating of me to make sure that I did not end the game abruptly because someone made me angry. I eventually grew out of that behaviour as I realised football was more fun when played with others.

As a young boy, I played a lot of football largely because I enjoyed playing the game. The more I played, the better I became. The better I became with my ball-handling skills, the more confident I became. And the more confident I became, the more I wanted to play.

In Class 5, I was selected to join the school's football team. Most of the players on the team were in Class 7 and were at least two years older than I was, but I was able to hold my own. I played in Class 6 and also in Class 7, and played in the attacking midfield. Gradually, I earned a reputation among the kids around town for being good at football.

My father knew I was playing football in school and he was not very happy about that. He wanted me to focus on my education and someday become a lawyer or a doctor or practice another profession that he believed would give me a secure financial future. He viewed football as a hobby that should not take too much of my time.

In Class 7, my school team qualified to play in a tournament that was to be held in Cape Coast in the Central Region. My father was so much against my playing football that he refused to let me go with the team. My headteacher at the time had to come to my house to beg my father before he reluctantly agreed to let me go. In Cape Coast, we were victorious in that tournament but I knew better not to attempt having a conversation with my father about what happened there. So, I kept that story to myself.

Also, in Class 7, I was selected for the Sunyani District team that played in the regional tournament. It was a big tournament played in front of my hometown crowd at the Sunyani Coronation Park.

During our first game, I was on the attack with the ball when the opposing goalkeeper somersaulted after he caught the ball. In the process, he rolled over my knee and hurt my knee badly. I laid on the dusty field, in severe pain, and wondered what was going to happen next. I didn't know how severe the injury was. I was helped to the sideline, got my knee tied with a bandage, and sat out for the rest of the game. I limped home after the match.

When my father returned home later that evening to find out that I had been injured while playing football, he was visibly upset. He unleashed his anger on me.

"*M'anka? M'anka?*" my father said in Twi. That translates into, "Did I not say it? Did I not say it?" and that was him justifying why he did not want me to play football.

Fortunately, I sustained that injury at the beginning of my three-month break from school. Therefore, I was able to spend that time getting better and did not have to miss school. I underwent treatment in the care of a herbalist who wrapped my knee in herbal concoctions. I had limited mobility for about two months during which time my knee successfully healed. Even though the injury scared me, it was not enough to scare me from continuing to play football. I returned to playing like nothing ever happened to my knee.

During most of my childhood, we had no electricity, let alone a television. Many of the fancy devices that many people take for granted these days had not even been invented yet or were rare in Ghana. That was the 1960s, and we entertained ourselves by sitting around in the compound of our house and sharing stories. We shared Kwaku Ananse stories. Kwaku Ananse is the cunning villain in many Ghanaian folk tales. In each story, Ananse tries to outsmart his family or neighbours but is ultimately exposed for his mischief. No matter how many times I heard an Ananse story, it felt fresh each time. My siblings and I also shared other stories that we had heard from other people. It was a very simple life but it was a happy childhood.

In the 1970s, the Brong-Ahafo Region saw a lot of infrastructural development. Electricity had been extended into Sunyani and we had street lights in our neighbourhood for the first time. An interesting past-time for the young people around that time was to take strolls at night under the illumination of the street lights. Under the street lights was where all the popular kids in the neighbourhood gathered at night. That was the place many young people came to hang out if they had nice clothes or anything with which they wanted to grab people's attention.

Upon completing Class 7, I gained admission to Opoku Ware School in Kumasi. At the time, Opoku Ware and Prempeh College in the neighbouring Ashanti Region were two of the best secondary schools in the country where most young people in Sunyani dreamed of attending. Many parents in Sunyani were obsessed with getting their children to Opoku Ware or Prempeh College because those schools were known to have produced many prominent people in the country. I wanted to attend Opoku Ware because I had heard good things about the school. I had in mind to become an accountant because I was good in Mathematics.

So, I entered Opoku Ware determined to take my academics very seriously and believed I had left my competitive football days behind me in Sunyani. My father thought so, too. Little did we both know that the story of my football life had just begun.

· CHAPTER 2 ·

OPOKU WARE SCHOOL

Most people who attended a secondary school in Ghana believe that their particular school is the best in country. It is very reasonable to expect that the school that helped to shape a young person into an adult will be so special to him or her. While most people think their secondary school is the best in the country, I think my secondary school is the best in the world. I am not the only one who believes that. You can ask anyone who attended Opoku Ware about which secondary school is the best in the world. And they will gladly tell you.

Opoku Ware School, or OWASS for short, is an all-boys boarding school located in the Santasi suburb of Kumasi. Named after Asantehene Nana Opoku Ware I, the school was founded in 1952 by Catholic missionaries. It is the alma mater of many people who went on to play prominent roles in the affairs of our nation. That is the school I had chosen for my secondary education. My father, being the ardent Catholic that he was, fully supported my interest in Opoku Ware.

Moving from Sunyani to Kumasi to live away from home came with some anxiety. Kumasi is a much larger city than

Sunyani, and I had been there only once before coming there for school. After I gained admission to Opoku Ware and before I was to start there, I visited Kumasi with my father. We went to see some of his uncles and other extended family members who lived in the Ashtown suburb of Kumasi. I was impressed by how developed and busy Kumasi was compared to Sunyani.

When I arrived in Kumasi to begin my secondary education, I was glad about leaving home to spend most of my time in a boarding school. At the same time, I was anxious about the routine bullying that most first-year students like me were going to have to deal with.

Together with my father, we came to Kumasi from Sunyani by bus to the main State Transport Corporation (STC) bus terminal. My clothes, my books, my non-perishable food items (my provisions), and my other personal belongings were packed into my trunk and my chop box. Trunks, the metal suitcases, and chop boxes, their wooden equivalent, were standard luggage for all secondary school students. My father hired a taxi, helped me carry my trunk and chop box into the taxi, and then we made our way to the school.

It was a little after midday when we arrived on the campus. My father knew a staff member at Opoku Ware. The man, who I think was an extended family member of his, worked in the school's bookshop. My father had given him money to purchase my school uniform and other items I was required to have.

Most of the students at the school lived in the cluster of dormitories called houses, and I was assigned to St. Mark House. The dormitories were large rooms lined with bunk-beds, and a mix of students from Form 1, Form 2 and Form 3 were assigned to each dormitory. Each house had several dormitories with about fifty students in each. The older students were often in charge of running the dormitories and the houses.

When I brought my belongings to St. Mark, I was shown to my dormitory and to my assigned bed. From that point on, I was going to be in the care of the school's staff and my father was free to leave. Before he left, he reminded me that Opoku Ware was a very good school because the students there are good students, and that I should take my studies seriously. He bade me good-bye and then departed.

OWASS students are known as Akatakyie, the plural form of Okatakyie, which means a conquering hero. That was the title Asantehene Opoku Ware I was known by. Appropriately, Opoku Ware students proudly carry the name of that prominent Asante king. Having fully settled in as a student of the school, I was officially an Okatakyie. Every Okatakyie has a student number, a unique identifier assigned to each student at the time of enrollment. Mine was O123.

Lawrence Okyere was the only person I knew prior to arriving at Opoku Ware. We both came to the school from Sunyani where we had known each other. Coincidentally, Lawrence and I shared a bunk bed. I had the bottom bed and he had the upper bed.

On my first night at the school, I was nervous just like most of the other Form 1 students (the freshmen). The older students were picking on Form 1 students and subjecting them to all kinds of interrogations. That kind of behaviour was the standard practice in boarding schools. The older students, we called them seniors, made it a point to put fear into the younger students, who were called juniors. Sometimes, a senior may detain a Form 1 student for no reason and demand a gift from the younger student before that younger student could be set free. Sometimes, the senior may grab the junior's nose in between two fingers, and then squeeze and yank the nose. That was a very painful experience and could easily make the junior cry. All those were forms of bullying generally referred to as *homoing*.

While the school authorities did not endorse homoing, they turned a blind eye to it unless it became excessive or a parent complained. To avoid being the victim of any such stressful experiences, I tucked myself away in my bed on that first night and stayed there till the next morning. On most days during my first few weeks, I often pretended to be sleeping to avoid the bullies.

As the days went by, I made a few new friends. Together, we endured bullying at the hands of the older students and we found ways to outsmart them. The senior students who had "123" in their student numbers, just like me, drew me closer to them and protected me from bullies.

Anyone who ever attended Opoku Ware has a student number, and that unique combination of characters is as unique as that person. Opoku Ware is the only school I know of in the world who take their student numbers so seriously. A student's number remains with the person for life. Mine is O123, as in the letter "O" and the number "123", and I will always be Okatakyie O123.

Student numbers for each year group are distinguished by the letters they start with. At the time I enrolled, my group of

Form 1 students had student numbers that started with the letter "O". I don't know how they decided on the other part of my student number but it was "123". Therefore, James Appiah was "O123".

You would think the Form 2 students at the time, who came to the school the year before my group, would start with "N" but they didn't. Theirs started with "X" and the Form 3 students' numbers started with "T" and the Form 4 students' numbers started with "H". As such, there was someone in Form 2 with student number X123, another in Form 3 with T123, and another in Form 4 with H123.

After a few weeks in the school, most of our routines became established. That routine included attending classes for most of the day during the each weekday, hanging out with my friends in the afternoon, and then attending evening church services almost daily. The church services were Catholic services, and they were compulsory for all students. As part of our daily routines, each of us had housekeeping duties such as cleaning the dormitories and the bathrooms, and sweeping the compound.

To the best of my knowledge, nobody, other than Lawrence Okyere, knew anything about the fact that I had played football for my school before arriving at Opoku Ware. When we played football among ourselves at St. Mark, some of my peers observed that I was a little more skilled than the rest of my peers. I, however, downplayed their praise of my skills. When the time came for St. Mark to select a team to represent us at the school's inter-houses football tournament, I was selected.

We did not have the best team, and it was not surprising that we did not win the inter-houses tournament. However, many people noticed my playing abilities, including the teacher in charge of the school team who later invited me to join them.

On the school team, I played at the right midfield position as an attacking midfielder. Even though most of the students on the team were much older and more experienced than my 14-year-old self, I got playing time right away. My competitive action from playing in games around Sunyani had given me enough confidence to go against opponents, some of whom were the best young players in the Ashanti Region at the time.

My first match on the Opoku Ware school team was against Obuasi Secondary Technical (SecTech) School, where we won by one goal to nothing. Obuasi SecTech was a very good football school at the time, so beating them that year was a really big deal. Playing on the school team made me known to many of the seniors and they became hesitant about bothering me like they did to other Form 1 students.

My father had no idea I was playing football actively and that I was a member of the school team. As long as I maintained good grades and never got into trouble, he didn't have to know what else I was doing in addition to my studies. Whenever my parents asked how things were going at school, I always told them that everything was fine. And everything was indeed fine.

In addition to playing football for my house and for the school team, I represented my house in table tennis, 100-meter and 200-meter races, volleyball, and field hockey during inter-house sports competitions. In field hockey, I was selected for the school team when I was in Form 4, and remained on the team through the following year.

James Appiah is my formal name, and I started out at Opoku Ware known simply as that. In Form 3, a teacher who did not know my name called on me to answer a question. He said to me, "Hey, Yaw B, answer the question." I answered the question and I didn't think much of the name he called me. Not long after that incident, my classmates started calling me Yaw B and would not stop even when I told them that was not my name.

Most students in secondary schools in Ghana create nicknames for themselves. At Opoku Ware, some students picked up nicknames for themselves because that's what they wanted to be called. Others got theirs because they used a word or made a statement that other students thought was funny or unique. There are many more ways students gained nicknames. I have no idea how my teacher came up with the name Yaw B.

My classmates continued to call me Yaw B. Students in my house started calling me Yaw B. Slowly, that name made its way across the school and almost everyone was calling me Yaw-B. Even though I was slightly concerned that people would confuse me for a Thursday-born (Yaw) instead of a Sunday-born (Kwasi), I didn't resist the name much. The sound of Yaw B had a natural ring to it when students were cheering me on during sports competitions. The name remained throughout most of my secondary school days. Years after we left school, some people were confused by why I was called Yaw-B in school but was called Kwasi Appiah when I became well known as a footballer.

For me, one of the greatest benefits of attending a boarding school was the opportunity I had to develop strong friendships with my peers. Living in the same dormitory for the greater part of each year and doing so for five years was a special experience that helped us develop a brotherhood. By spending most of our teenage years together and figuring our way into adulthood, we developed a friendship that remained long after we left the school. Some of the friendships that I developed in secondary school remain part of my closest friendships till today.

When I was in Form 4, a new set of dormitories called St. Andrew House was completed. It was scheduled to be occupied by students who were to be hand-picked by the school staff. Each of the other houses were to select its most troublesome students and send them to St. Andrew. I had a group of friends, about ten of us, and some of them were picked to move to St. Andrew. The rest of us quietly gathered our belongings from St. Mark and also relocated to St. Andrew. Nobody asked us to return to St. Mark so my group of friends stayed together at St. Andrew. By the time the school staff discovered what we had done, we had settled in and they weren't that motivated to kick us out of St. Andrew. So, we stayed and enjoyed its newer facilities.

St. Andrew was divided into chambers. My friends and I occupied our chamber and the other students occupied their respective chambers. Nobody bothered us and we didn't bother anybody. More importantly, my group of friends remained together.

One of my closest friends was Godfred Graham, whose nickname was Olele. His mother worked at Kinsgway Stores in Accra and Godfred always brought with him all kinds of provisions including canned milk, sardines, and Milo chocolate powder. Godfred was a very generous guy and he freely shared his food with all of his friends. He gave me a second pair of keys to his chop box and welcomed me to have anything I wanted at any time. There came a time when I stopped bringing any food items from Sunyani. Godfred brought enough for me and for our group of friends. Godfred, who is now one of the biggest lawyers in Ghana, was like a brother to me. He didn't only share his provisions with me but he sometimes brought me shirts from Accra.

Most of my friends and many of my classmates from Opoku Ware, even the troublemakers, grew up to become prominent and successful people. Techie Menson went to France to study to become an electrical engineer. Maxwell Brobbey left for the UK not long after we left Opoku Ware, and he stayed there until we reunited decades later. Bonah (Joe Poti), who was also from Sunyani, became very close to me. He earned a PhD in Agriculture. Kofi Nsiah, who was my classmate, now operates Kinapharma, a prominent pharmaceutical manufacturing and distribution company in Ghana.

Our time at Opoku Ware was eventful because we had some students who were well known as troublemakers. Danny Kyei and Ntim Mensah (Black Moses), for example, were famous for the troubles they caused. If anybody had told us in secondary school that those guys would become pastors someday, I am sure we would have laughed at that person. But it has come to pass. Danny Kyei is now Bishop Danny Kyei. Black Moses is also a bishop. Looking back at those years brings fond memories. Those friendships were crucial to my development into a young adult. I am honoured to know many of these men I have known since secondary school. I do the best that I can to maintain close contacts with as many of them as I can.

Even though our school team's success during my five years there was modest at best, I made a name for myself as a member of the school team. We did not win any regional tournaments but made it to the regional semi-finals one year. We competed against schools like T.I. Ahmadiyya and Konongo Odumasi who sometimes fielded players who were already playing in the Premier League. T.I. Ahmadiyya for instance had Kumasi Asante Kotoko players such as Kofi Badu, Albert Asaase, and Opoku Nti playing for them. Those guys were some of the best from around the country. So, for our school, which was focused more on academics and not sports, to make it to the semi-finals against teams with such experienced players was satisfactory.

Every time I was on a long break from school, beginning from when I was in Form 3, I trained with Rainbow Stars. That was a Second Division team based in Sunyani. Even though my interest and confidence in the game had grown significantly by the time I completed secondary school, I was sure I was going to only pursue football as a hobby. I was thinking about furthering my education and becoming an accountant.

Rainbow Stars invited me to play for them during a friendly match against Wenchi Tomacan Stars, another Second Division team. We lost that match against Tomacan Stars. Tomacan Stars, who were getting ready to play in the Middle League, asked if I would play for them in the Middle League tournament. The Middle League was a tournament featuring the nation's top Second Division teams. The two top teams from the Middle League got promoted to the Premier League.

At the time, the national Under-23 team, the Black Meteors, was being revived after having been inactive for a while. Coach E.K. Afranie was in charge of building that team and he was there watching the Middle League matches. I did not know at the time about the Black Meteors connection to the Middle League and played as well as I could. Tomacan Stars did not qualify for the Premier League but I was invited by Coach Afranie to join the Black Meteors.

My progress in competitive football had been relatively fast – from playing in the Middle League to playing on a national team all within a few months of graduating from secondary school. Playing alongside some of the very best players from around the country, it was beginning to sink in for me that I was one of the best players from around the country at my age level. It was around then that I started thinking seriously about pursuing football as my exclusive career.

From the young boy whose father dropped off at a boarding school in Kumasi, I had grown into a young man who had come to believe he is talented enough to pursue a career as a footballer. During the time, the examples of people who had built successful livelihoods from playing football were very few. Even though my father wanted something else for me, I seriously considered following a path where I knew my passion and my talent could make me successful.

· CHAPTER 3 ·

TURNING MY PASSION INTO MY PROFESSION

In Ghana, football is a national passion.

The passion a majority of the Ghanaian population has for football can be rivalled only by their passion for religion. Just like most people in Ghana identify with a particular religion, most people in Ghana, both adults and children, have a favourite player and/or a favourite team. And with that kind of passion throughout the country, it is very natural for a majority of the people to be actively interested in football. That has been the situation for me for as long as I can remember.

Football made me come alive, and I wanted to play anytime I had the opportunity. And when I played, I imagined myself playing alongside the very best players, and winning all the time. Like most of the children I grew up with, I had no idea whether the future I was imagining would come true.

I don't remember a time when I was not interested in football. Even before I could play very well, I was interested. Football was the one activity in which almost every young boy in my neighbourhood participated. My interest in football went to a higher level when I owned my first ball, a plastic ball with a hard outer shell. My father gave it to me and I cannot remember if it was a Christmas gift or just because it was typical for a man to buy his son such a thing. It could be that my father bought me a football because he saw that was something I liked to play with. If only he knew I would become as interested in the sport when I grew older, I am sure he would not have given me that ball.

Organised youth football was very popular around Sunyani, like it was in most places around the country. Saturdays were the big match days. Many boys from around age nine till about fourteen, who were good at football, spent most of their Saturdays playing football in various neighbourhoods throughout the town. Other kids gathered on the sidelines to watch the matches and cheer on the players.

My father was not interested in my going to the neighbourhood park to play football. That was because many of the boys who played football on the parks spent a lot of time roaming around from one neighbourhood to another, and they didn't seem to have much else to do. My father didn't want me to be in the company of such children because he thought they may influence me negatively. Even when people who had seen me play football told my father that I was good at it, he was not moved. He believed that there were other more important things for me to do with my time than to play football.

When I was selected to play on my school team at Ridge Experimental, I was a part of the Starting 11. Even though I was a Class 5 student and there were Class 6 and Class 7 students on the team, my teammates were comfortable with my ability to play so they enthusiastically welcomed me onto the team. Our squad was not the most impressive when compared to the schools we played against. Our team needed all the help they could get and I had what it took to help the team do a little better. So, we did the best we could and managed a modest success.

As I grew older and stronger, I became more competent and a more integral part of the school team. During my three years on the team, we got better and became more confident, won more games and even qualified for a tournament in Cape Coast in the Central Region of Ghana. That was the tournament which my headteacher had to plead with my father for his permission before I got to travel with the team. In addition to playing, I often watched older people play.

Brong-Ahafo Region had two Premier League teams: Tano Bofoakwa and B.A. United (Brong-Ahafo United). My favourite of the two was B.A. United. Premier League matches were huge in Sunyani. The whole town came to a standstill as the attention of almost everyone in the town was focused on these matches. Entering the stadium to see Premier League matches required tickets and I did not have money for tickets. At the time, the stadium was fenced with aluminum sheets and some of the fencing was loose. When a policeman was not looking, one of those loose spots served as a convenient entrance which I used to get in to see the games.

Rainbow Stars was the local Second Division team that trained on the local park on most weekday afternoons. A friend of mine named Chubby was a member of the team, and it was through him that I was invited to join them during their training sessions. Most of them were much older and

Turning My Passion into My Profession

more skilled than I was, and that provided an opportunity for me to learn and to get better at playing.

Occasionally, when my father was out of town, I got to play in some of their competitive games. While playing in the school team was a big deal to me, my father was not amused by that. When my father was at home, I would have to sneak out if I wanted to go play with Rainbow Stars. By that point in time, my brother Cobby was old enough to come along with me. So, together, we sometimes jumped across the wall separating our house from that of out next-door neighbour, and then quietly made our way to the park. We usually played till it was dark outside.

Dinner preparations, especially the pounding of *fufu*, took place in the late afternoon. Fufu is a meal made from pounding cooked cassava in a mortar with a pestle to produce a doughy ball that is eaten with soup. The pounding of the fufu often coincided with the time for playing football. At such times, Cobby and I disappeared before my mother would even know we were gone. My other brother, Kwaku Appiah, who was not as interested in football, was left to pound the fufu alone.

My mother was a quiet woman but she was very principled. Unlike my father, she was not as bothered by the fact that I liked to play football. However, my mother did not take kindly to the practice of leaving home to go play football even though we knew we should have been at home helping to pound fufu for dinner. Instead of having Kwaku Appiah and my sisters pound the fufu for everyone in the family, my mother found a way to teach my brother and me a lesson.

On occasions when we sneaked out to go play football, our dinner ended up being cooked, cold cassava – not pounded into fufu – and cold soup. My brother and I got used to that type of dinner and considered it a small price to pay for the opportunity to play football – instead of staying at home to pound fufu.

Realizing that we were not as bothered by the lesson she was trying to teach us, she made it harder for us to enjoy our dinner. Instead of leaving us the cooked slices of cassava with soup (to eat like *ampesie*), she resorted to leaving us slightly-pounded cassava and soup. Ampesie is the cooked slices of cassava, which is type of meal in itself. Well-pounded ampesie becomes fufu but slightly-pounded ampesie is neither fufu nor ampesie, making it almost impossible to eat. On evenings when we returned home to find the cooked cassava in that semi-fufu state, we had no option than to throw it away and have only the soup and meat for dinner.

As unpleasant as that experience was, that too felt like a small price to pay for the opportunity to go do something I had become very passionate about. Despite of the possibility of getting yelled at by my father, the appeal of being on the football field was strong enough for me to find a way to get there almost every time there was a match to be played.

It was not lost on me that most of the Rainbow Stars players were not playing football as their careers. People on the team were either unemployed or had blue-collar jobs. I knew that furthering my education by going to secondary school was an important step in my preparation for my future.

While many of the young players in the Ashanti Region aspired to play for Kumasi Asante Kotoko, I didn't think seriously about playing football professionally, let alone think of playing for Kotoko.

Turning My Passion into My Profession

When I left Sunyani for Kumasi to attend Opoku Ware, I knew I was heading into a bigger city and anticipated that there was going to be more to discover. I didn't know much about Kumasi Asante Kotoko at the time of starting Opoku Ware, and I wasn't too interested in what was going on in Kumasi outside the walls of my school.

However, the sequence of very distinct events – starting with the friendly match for Rainbow Stars against Tomacan Stars, to my playing in the Middle League for Tomacan Stars, and then on to the Black Meteors – got me to seriously think of football as a possible full-time career for my future.

On the national Under-23 team, there were about twenty of us. Those were some of the very best players in that age category from around the country. Coach E.K. Afranie appointed me the captain of the team. In my role as the leader of the playing body, I had the responsibility of helping lead team activities and also keeping my colleagues focused when we were on the field. My experience from training with the Second Division side gave me a fair idea of the routines of a semi-professional team during training. So, I was knowledgeable enough for Coach Afranie to find me reliable.

During camping sessions, I would sometimes respectfully point out to my peers some of the expectations the coach had of them. Other times, I would make suggestions about the way a particular situation should be handled, and what we should or should not do. And my colleagues listened to me. In return, I made sure I spoke up on their behalf if they needed something.

Our Black Meteors team played in a WAFU (West African Football Union) tournament in Ivory Coast and won a medal

– it may have been a silver or bronze medal. I don't remember exactly which one it was. The team disbanded and the players moved on to their respective teams or back to whatever they were going to do next.

Prestea Mine Stars was one of the teams that qualified from the Middle League into the Premier League that year. They hired Coach Afranie to become their head coach. Coach Afranie invited me and several of the guys from the Black Meteors team to play for him at Mine Stars. The core of the Meteors team essentially became the core of Coach Afranie's Mine Stars.

I realised that my talent had opened doors for me to be able to compete at the highest levels in football. I had excelled at the opportunities I had been given. I had developed more confidence in my abilities and had earned Coach Afranie's confidence to come play in the Premier League. At that moment, I had very good reasons to choose football as my career and to give it my best effort.

When I left home to play in the friendly match for Rainbow Stars, and then in the Middle League matches, I did not inform my father. He found out after I had left. When I returned, I told my mother I had been selected for the Black Meteors. She told my father. He did not oppose my going to play for the Meteors, even though he was not entirely happy about me continuing to play football actively.

My playing for the Meteors was to take place during my long break from school so I had time on my hands, which somewhat justified my doing the one thing I loved. I knew, however, that relocating to Prestea to play football professionally was not going to sit well with my father who was expecting me to return to school for Sixth Form and then on to a university.

Coach Afranie came to my house to meet with my father to obtain his permission before I could leave for Prestea. He impressed upon my father that he (Coach Afranie) was going to be the coach of the Preastea team, and that I would be under his care. My father reluctantly gave his permission.

Prestea is in Ghana's Western Region, about 300km from Sunyani and about a five-hour drive. It is a gold-mining town that was riding high on the excitement of its local team's promotion to the Premier League. Mine Stars' squad was rejuvenated with the young players Coach Afranie brought with him from the Meteors.

Playing in Prestea for the Mine Stars was the first time I earned money as a footballer. It was not much but it was enough for me to help my parents with their living expenses. By that time, things were tough financially for my father. His auctioneering career was not generating enough income due to changes in the Ghanaian economy. With the money I made from playing for the Mine Stars and also for the Black Stars, I became more confident about making a decent living pursuing football as my profession. So, I stuck with that career choice.

For Tomacan Stars and for the Black Meteors, I played as a central defender. At Mine Stars, I started out as a central defender and Coach Afranie moved me to the left-back position ahead of a match against Kumasi Asante Kotoko.

Emba Owusu Sekyere was a winger for Kotoko, and he was a very fast dribbler. Kotoko had played most of that season unbeaten, and the secret behind their success that season was

Emba. Coach Afranie determined that if we could shut him down, Kotoko wouldn't have many other options. I was assigned the task to contain Emba, and I shut him down that afternoon. We won against Kotoko, and Coach Afranie kept me in the left-back position from then on.

Word about me and how good I was started spreading around Premier League circles. Within a year of playing for the Mine Stars, I was invited to play for the senior national team under Coaches C.K. Gyamfi and Osam-Duodu. That was in 1981, and they were preparing for the 1982 African Cup of Nations final qualifiers. The team was loaded with the very best from across the Premier League teams. Some of the players were veterans whom I admired and respected very much. It was extremely exciting for me to be in the company of those accomplished players and their two legendary coaches.

Even though being called to the national team in itself felt like an accomplishment, I was determined to justify my inclusion in the team and become an active member. The Black Stars squad was very focused on winning the upcoming qualifiers and therefore took their training very seriously. During training, we played against each other and I held my own against my senior colleagues.

My chance to earn a spot on the team came in a friendly match against Accra Great Olympics, then a Premier League side based in Accra, Ghana's capital city. Yaw Mark, Great Olympics' celebrated right winger, had to be taken out before the end of the match because he could not get the ball past me and his team struggled as a result.

Turning My Passion into My Profession

The final qualifying games for Libya 1982 were against Congo Kinshasa, now Democratic Republic of Congo. Together with Abedi Pele and Ben Kayode, the other newest members of the team, we watched the Black Stars draw 2-2 at the Accra Sports Stadium. Congo Kinshasa's right winger was a player named Mayele. He scored both goals for his side in Accra with Offei Ansah playing at the left-back position. Hesse Odamtten replaced Offei Ansah in the second half but he too could not contain Mayele satisfactorily.

In Kinshasa for the second leg, all that the Congolese needed was a goalless draw that would take them to Libya for the tournament. We needed to score at least one goal. We also needed to prevent the Congolese from scoring since conceding a goal would be detrimental to our chance of qualifying. Mayele was the problem.

When I was called on to start the Kinshasa match as the left-back, I was told I had a specific task – to shut down Mayele. That was a breakthrough moment and I performed that task with distinction.

With my success at rendering Mayele ineffective, my colleagues started calling me Mayele. That is how I earned that nickname, which is what many colleagues called me for many years.

We won that Kinshasa match 2-1, both Ghana goals were scored by George Alhassan with crosses from Abedi Pele. Abedi came on for Adolph Armah who got injured about halfway through the first half. We qualified for Libya and were poised to ride on the momentum from our final game in the qualifier.

Libya was extremely cold, and that caused stiffness and pain in my knee. Even though I was not going to be able to play, the rest of the team was ready and determined. We participated in the tournament, taking on some strong opponents such as Algeria in the semi-finals, and then Libya in the finals. With goals from George Alhassan and Opoku Nti, we beat Algeria, and drew 1-1 with Libya. On penalties, we beat Libya 7-6 to win Ghana's fourth African Cup of Nations title.

Joining the senior national team that early in my career boosted my confidence and exposed me to some of the very best players whom I was able to learn from.

Albert Asaase, a Kotoko player, was my roommate at the Black Stars camp. He treated me with respect and made me feel welcome at the camp. Opoku Nti, also a Kotoko player and one of the biggest stars in the country at the time, was also very welcoming and easy to talk to. He introduced me to several other players at the camp.

There were many Kotoko players on the national team, including Opoku Afriyie, Papa Arko, Kofi Badu, and Francis Kumi. They all spoke highly of Kotoko and encouraged me to consider joining them. They all spoke of the incentives Kotoko players enjoyed, which included cash gifts from their rich supporters, the opportunity to play with many Black Stars players on a consistent basis, and the opportunity to play in international tournaments.

In the span of three years, I had been exposed to the highest levels of competition, played under the guidance of coaches who helped me to grow professionally, and worked with colleagues who were some of the best at the game. As I spent more time around them, Papa Arko and Opoku Nti actively encouraged me to join Kotoko.

My time with Prestea Mine Stars had been a successful one. For a while, I played as an attacker and was the team's leading goal scorer. Understandably, Mine Stars would have liked me to stay with them but the Kotoko opportunity was too good to let go. So, I left Mine Stars for Kotoko.

· CHAPTER 4 ·

FABULOUS KUMASI ASANTE KOTOKO

I made my decision to join Kumasi Asante Kotoko with mixed feelings. On one hand, I was enjoying my time at Mine Stars playing with a team of young, talented players and a respected coach. We had decent success in the Premier League placing sixth out of fourteen or so teams in our first year.

On the other hand, I saw the potential of playing at the highest levels of the Ghana Premier League by joining Kumasi Asante Kotoko. Furthermore, I was likely going to play in the African Club Championships in that year since Kotoko had won the league in the previous year and were going to compete in the continental championship.

The relationships I had developed with the Kotoko players on the Black Stars team contributed to my leaning more towards playing for Kotoko. There was more I could learn from those experienced players. There was more room for me to grow at Kotoko. Kotoko was one of the dream clubs for most Ghanaian footballers and I had an opportunity to become a part of the team.

The more I thought about it, the clearer it became to me that Kotoko was the right choice for my career. Kotoko was going to give me more local and international exposure.

My coach and colleagues at Mine Stars were anticipating that I might join Kotoko having spent time with the national team, which was dominated by Kotoko players.

Kotoko enjoyed immense support from their large fan base which comprised an overwhelming majority of people in the Ashanti Region as well as large groups of people in almost every region in the country. That immense support sometimes was demonstrated through extreme enthusiasm and devotion to the team and its players. In Kumasi, for example, it was very common to see entire households or neighbourhoods or the entire city come to a standstill when there was a major match involving Kumasi Asante Kotoko.

By the same token, fans sometimes lost their appetite for food when Kotoko lost an important match. While that kind of passion for football may be found in most communities in Ghana, the Kumasi version was and continues to be at an extraordinary level. The Kotoko fans were also known for their generosity and their regular practice of giving cash and other gifts to the team's players. And since many footballers didn't make much money by way of salaries or winning bonuses, having a generous fan base who also had a lot of money was always a good thing.

The Asantehene, the overlord of the Asante people, is a life patron of the club. At the time I was considering joining Kotoko, Otumfour Opoku Ware II was the Asantehene, and he took particular interest in the team's wellbeing and its success. Prominent business people in the Ashanti Region and around the country were also passionate about the team and supported the players immensely.

In that era, most of Kotoko's recruits came from the Ashanti Region (from teams like Kumasi Cornerstones and Kumapim Stars), from the Brong-Ahafo Region (from Tano Bofoakwa and B.A. United), and the Western Region (from Prestea Mine Stars, Secondi Eleven Wise, and Secondi Hasaacas). Kotoko looked for the best players from those teams, enticed them with the team's resources and reputation, and then registered the players with the football secretariat as members of their club. At that time, the acquiring team didn't have to negotiate any transfer terms because the players were unrestricted by any contract. All that mattered was the player agreeing to play for a particular team and registering with the GFA at the beginning of the season as that team's player.

Kotoko sent a driver to come get me from Sunyani to meet with the team's chairman, Sims Kofi Mensah, in Kumasi. We met at City Hotel, now Golden Tulip, and he welcomed me warmly. He commended me on my abilities, told me the other Kotoko players who played in the Black Stars had spoken very highly of me, and added that he would like me to join Kotoko.

I affirmed my interest in Kotoko and my willingness to join the team. He then made me an offer – they were going to cover my accommodation and he was going to give me a one-time cash sum of 10,000 cedis. In the 1980s, 10,000 cedis was a very respectable amount. In today's money, that would be the equivalent of about 100,000 new Ghana cedis or about 25,000 dollars. While the financial aspect was attractive, it was more about the prestige of playing for Kotoko and the opportunity to play in the African Cup Championship that drew me to the club.

The Kotoko squad I joined was widely regarded as one of the most impressive in the team's history. The players were very talented and most of them played together at both club and national team levels. They had played together for about four consecutive years and had very good chemistry as a unit. Most of the team's core players had been there since 1980, and had won the league in 1980 and 1981.

The team was under the leadership of Coach Adabie, the legendary coach who had been brought in to help Kotoko rebuild and end their series of loses to their arch rival, Accra Hearts of Oak. Coach Adabie had made a name for himself as the coach of Akosombo Akotex in the 1970s, and was brought to Kotoko in 1979. He coached the team in 1979 and 1980, and then left. He was brought back in 1982, the same year that I joined Kotoko.

Players such as Opoku Afriyie, Opoku Nti, Joseph Carr, Haruna Yusif, Seth Ampadu, Ahmed Rockson, Addae Kyenkyehene, Albert Asaase, Papa Arko, John Bannerman, Akwettey Quaye (Joe Tex), Kofi Badu, Francis Kumi, and Abdul Karim Zito made up the team. They had two very good players for each position. Karim Zito and Charles Oppong were the left-backs at the time, and I had to compete with them for a chance to play regularly, let alone become a part of the Starting 11.

Many of the players were extremely confident in their abilities to the extent that our scorers could predict how many goals they were going to score in a match, and then deliver as predicted. No matter the opponent, they found a way to score crucial goals to secure wins for the team. Those guys played with an unquenchable passion and they left everything on the field every time they played. Their work ethic was superb and it was just the right environment for me to take my game to the next level.

The team had a winning culture. The players were extremely serious about everything they did during training and during matches. The veterans on the team set the tone and everyone else followed. Opoku Afriyie, for example, was our captain and lead striker who played almost every minute of every match with a sense of urgency that inspired the rest of the team all the way till the referee's final whistle. He had no problem screaming at a player if he realised the player was letting the team down. He was a very influential man and he was not shy about exercising his influence.

Another influential person on the team, Kofi Badu, was another example of how leadership on the part of key players contributed to the team's winning culture. Kofi Badu was one of our attackers and he was so competitive that he would confront his colleagues in the course of the match if he thought they were not doing enough to help the team win.

I once made a defensive mistake that almost cost us a goal. From where he was up front on the field, he ran all the way to me in defence to deliver a staunch warning. He made it clear to me that if I made another mistake and cost the team the game, he was going to have a problem with me. I couldn't fault him for being so hard on me. He demonstrated that same intense passion everywhere on the field and he helped the rest of the team develop a sense of seriousness. That sense of seriousness helped to make all of us better players.

Having won the Ghana Premier League in 1981, Kotoko got to play in the 1982 African Club Championship. We won against Togolese club Semassi in the first round and defeated Liberian side Invincible 11 in the second round, We routed Kampala City Council from Uganda 6-0 at home in Kumasi and drew 1-1 away to qualify on a 7-1 goal aggregate to play in the semi-finals. We beat Congolese side FC Lupopo and met El Ahly from Egypt in the final game.

When we went to Egypt to play them in the first leg, they scored three goals against us within the first 35 minutes. One of the tactics they used successfully against us was taking their free kicks very quickly, even before our players would be ready to resume play. We were used to restarting the game at the referee's whistle and didn't know that the referee's whistle was not necessary for taking a free kick. We figured that out after we had conceded three goals. We made adjustments to our game plan.

I was brought on to help shut down El Ahly's attack. We ended the game with the 0-3 final score. With my performance during that game, I cemented myself in place as the team's starting left-back.

In Kumasi for the return match, the 1-1 draw was not enough for us to win the trophy. It was disappointing that our very talented team could not capture the ultimate prize. Fortunately, we won the Ghana league title again in 1982, which meant we were going to play in the African Club Championship in 1983 and have the chance to try again.

Before the start of the next season, many unexpected changes hit the team. Albert Asaase and Kofi Badu left for the Ivory Coast that year. Francis Kumi left for Belgium. Those were some of our key players and their departure impacted the shape of the team. That was not all.

Sims Kofi Mensah had been the club's chairman in 1980 and 1981, and was due to pass on the chairmanship to Yaw Bawuah. At the time, Opoku Afriyie wielded much influence as the team's captain and the son of a sub-chief under the Asantehene. Opoku Afriyie preferred Charles Allen Gyimah, one of the team's major financiers at the time, over Bawuah as the chairman.

Yaw Bawuah prevailed and became the chairman. And as a result of the bad blood that had developed between the two powerful people from their disagreements, Yaw Bawuah sent Opoku Afriyie a letter informing him that he had been retired from the team. Even though Opoku Afriyie was in good playing form and still had a lot to offer, Yaw Bawuah retired him. Essentially, he kicked Opoku Afriyie out of the team. Obviously, that was to make the point about who had more power in the affairs of the team.

Many of the players were unhappy about the management's decision to retire Opoku Afriyie, a key member of the squad whom we couldn't afford to lose. As the Akan proverb says, it is the grass that suffers when two elephants fight. And in that case, the proverbial fight was between our captain and our chairman. In the end, it was we the players who became the grass that was likely going to suffer. Even though we had lost Albert Asaase and Kofi Badu, we knew we had a strong enough core to try to win the cup in 1983. However, losing Opoku Afriyie was a bigger blow to the team.

After several talks with the management to resolve the matter, Papa Arko, who was the vice-captain at the time, went with senior players Opoku Nti, Addae Kyenyenhene, George Kennedy and Sirebour to petition the Asantehene to intervene and help bring Opoku Afriyie back into the team. The Asantehene advised that Opoku Afriyie should apologise to the Bawuah management team and make peace with them. As it turned out, Opoku Afriyie did not think that he had done anything wrong for which he had to apologise to the Bawuah management team. Instead, he wanted the rest of the playing body to boycott the team in solidarity with him.

I was a young player on a legendary club and boycotting the team seemed like a very extreme move given the facts of the situation. And besides, the senior players, who I took my cues from, didn't seem interested in a boycott. To most of us, a boycott was a lot to ask for.

At the start of the season, the Opoku Afriyie-Yaw Bawuah feud remained and the team played our matches without Opoku Afriyie. He went on to play in the Ivory Coast for a little over a year and then joined Accra Hearts of Oak.

After Opoku Afriyie's departure from Kotoko, the players voted Papa Arko as the team's captain. The veterans and the entire playing body seemed unified in their support of Papa Arko's leadership. Even though we didn't have a team as strong as we did during the 1982 championship campaign, we had a cohesive unit and we won some important matches at the beginning of the season. Those victories instilled a sense of confidence in the team. We realised that we could have another very successful year if we stuck together and gave the team our all. Many people feared it was going to take a while for us to return to our winning ways after Opoku Afriyie. But with our early-season winning streak, the Kotoko management felt vindicated about their decision to part ways with Opoku Afriyie.

Some of my teammates lived in one of the team's club houses in Anwiam on the south side of Kumasi while the others lived in another club house at Dekyemso. The club house at Dekyemso, called Kotoko House, was where I lived when I first moved to Kumasi. I later moved from the club house to a private residence I shared with some friends of mine.

Ransford Apraku, popularly known as Gabo, was an ardent Kotoko fan and a very close friend to many of the players. When we became more acquainted with each other, I learned that Gabo was from the Brong-Ahafo Region. That common bond drew us together. With the growth of my friendship with Gabo, I joined him in a house he shared with his brother Baffour-Awuah, and some of the Kotoko players, including George Arthur. That house was located in the Ashtown suburb of Kumasi.

That Ashtown house was owned by a woman named Eno Yaa. Her son built that house and she was the landlady. She was a very nice lady but she made it very clear to all her tenants that she was the one in charge at the house. She had many rules, some of which were ridiculous but it was her house and she had every right to set her rules. For instance, she believed that walking on the cement floor in high heels would damage the cement floor. So, even though she was very respectful and welcoming to us the players, she frowned on females coming to the house. She didn't want any woman living in the house – so, no woman lived there.

It was also in 1982 that I met the woman who eventually became my wife. Angela is a cousin to the wife of my teammate Papa Arko. Through my friendship with Papa Arko, Angela and I became more acquainted. She was not very keen about football at the time we met, and had no interest in coming to the stadium to watch any of our matches. My interest in her grew as I came to know her more and more over the course of about a year. We married in 1983 after she completed her secondary education.

The year 1983 was a big one for me not only because I got married but also because of the Africa Club Championship we were participating in. After the successful start to our season, Kotoko fans had high expectations. The team was also poised to win the championship. The squad had been strengthened with the addition of new players who were playing the game at a very high level. Francis Agyeman joined from Secondi Hasaacas; Ebo Mends and Yahya Kassum joined from Accra Standfast; Kwame Sampson joined from SS74; and Akye Erzuah joined from Prestea Mine Stars. Ernest Appau also joined the team from Kumasi Cornerstones.

We made it to the final of the African Club Championship and faced El Ahly, the same Egyptian team we lost to a year earlier. In the first leg, we played to a goalless draw in Cairo. In the second leg, we beat them 1-0 in Kumasi with a goal from Opoku Nti. We had overcome the early setbacks and we had become champions of Africa. That was Kotoko's second-ever continental championship win, and it was a very big deal to the players, the fans and the entire nation.

Not long after we won the championship, a football agent contacted me about an opportunity in Italy with Serie A side Torino. It certainly was exciting to have been contacted about an opportunity abroad but I was not ready to leave Kotoko to go live outside the country. I felt very much at home with Kotoko. My teammates, the supporters, and the entire city of Kumasi made me feel so much at home with their adoration and their support. The idea of leaving all that behind to go start afresh in a foreign country where I didn't know anybody didn't appeal to me. So, I stayed on with Kotoko.

Chairman Yaw Bawuah left and was replaced by Ofori Nuako. Ofori Nuako was very well-liked by Kotoko fans. He was well known for wearing a big red scarf around his neck and on his wrist every time Kotoko played. Ofori Nuako was the chairman for several years. Former President Agyekum Kufuor also served as the chair of the team's board in the late 1980s.

Papa Arko was the team's captain through 1984. He handed over the captaincy to Opoku Nti. Opoku Nti left in 1985 for Switzerland. Addae Kyenkyenhene became captain and I was appointed vice captain. In 1988, I was appointed captain and remained so until I retired after the 1993/94 season.

In addition to playing for Kotoko, I continued to play for the Black Stars and captained the team from 1988 through 1992. Captaincy at the club level and at the national team level were often based on seniority, the captain's dependability and influence on the players, and the coach's confidence in the captain's decision-making ability both on and off the field.

The unique thing about my appointment as captain, both at the club or national team level, was that I never lobbied anyone for those roles. I did what I needed to do to help my team be productive, and with time earned the respect of my coaches and colleagues to merit the appointment. One important lesson I learned throughout my captaincy at both the club and the national team levels was that we are not leaders because of the titles we carry. We are leaders because we are accountable to the people we lead. I always wanted the people I led to do well, and I did everything I could to ensure that my players were successful and they were treated fairly.

Playing at the left-back position required that I disrupt attacks coming down the right side of the field. My intention was usually not only to dispossess the opponent of the ball but also to gain possession. That boiled down to having a good understanding of the attacker's mindset. Because I had earlier on in my career played successfully as an attacker, that was very helpful in anticipating the way an attacker thinks. I found a way to put fear in my opponents by studying their actions on the field and anticipating their moves before and after they had the ball.

When I went in for an attack, I made sure I was kicking as close to the ball as possible. If I needed to intimidate a player, I made sure I was kicking their foot as closely to the ball as possible. That technique made it almost impossible for a referee to call a foul against me and it was an effective way of closing down an opponent. Even though I had a reputation among referees and fans that I was a clean player at all times, there were several not-so-clean tricks that I used to disrupt an attacker's movement.

It helped to have a reputation among referees that I was a clean player. That also earned me their respect. There were many occasions that I used some of my not-so-clean tricks on attackers and got only verbal warnings from referees. Often, after rough tackles on wingers, referees calmly told me that those types of plays did not befit me. Some of them would softly tell me, "Oh, I don't expect that kind of play from you so please don't do that." I smiled and thanked them and went back to playing like nothing had happened. Meanwhile, the winger would have gotten the message that they better think twice about trying to get the ball past me next time. Even though I was usually calm on the field, my opponents knew I could play tough when necessary. I got away with most things, except on a few notable occasions.

My only red card I received during my playing career was in a game against Accra Hearts of Oak in Kumasi. Offei Ansah was a ruthless right-back and he had a reputation for being a hard guy. He was pretty good at intimidating opponents and I knew his go-to moves having played with him for years on the national team. In that game, we both went in for a bounced ball, and I knew he was likely to raise his leg as he often did in situations like that. I was going to match him and give myself an equal chance of winning possession of the ball. He cleverly brought his leg up briefly and brought it back down. I went in with my leg fully raised. And just like he intended, the bottom of my foot landed in his stomach area. That was a glaring foul.

With that kind of foul, the whole stadium gasped in disappointment. The referee and his linesmen had a clean view of what happened, and there was no way I could explain that my intention was not to land my foot where it landed. The referee blew his whistle and, without hesitation, ejected me from the game. Our team played with one less player and we ended up losing that game 2-1.

Also, most people didn't associate me with rough antics during my playing career but such antics were sometimes necessary. Faking an injury to frustrate opponents or to waste time is a tactic players use all the time to give their team the opportunity to get themselves together. Because I rarely did things like that, I usually got away with it whenever I did. If I fell to the ground indicating an injury, the referees believed me.

In a match against Real Tamale United Tamale (RTU) at the Tamale Kaladan Park, a referee believed me when I faked an injury. The RTU fans, however, did not buy into it and they literally took matters into their own hands. At that time, the Tamale Kaladan Park was a grassless pitch with no stadium-style seating. The fans stood a few feet away from the sidelines and they had very easy access to the field of play.

RTU was down by two goals to one, and time was running out. Their attack was mounting immense pressure on our defence in an attempt to equalize. From the players' feet stomping the ground as they ran around the dusty field, there was a cloud of dust filling the air. Their fans were cheering them on and they were piling on the pressure. The more we pushed back, the harder they pressed. They were determined to score and we were doing everything we could to hold on to our lead.

Fortunately, I made contact with one of their attackers and I fell to the ground. The referee called for a foul. Under normal circumstances, I should have gotten up and kept playing. But the circumstance at that moment was not normal. We needed to maintain our lead at all cost, and the most effective way I thought of was to exaggerate the impact of the contact with their attacker and continued lying on the ground pretending to be seriously injured. That was usually an effective time-wasting tactic.

The referee signaled to my team's medical staff to come on the field to attend to me. That was likely to waste about three-to-five minutes. That was enough to disrupt RTU's momentum.

The RTU fans who were standing close enough to where I was lying saw the contact. I suppose they were convinced that I was not hurt. Even if I was hurt, they were not going to allow me to hold up the game. So, before our medical staff could make their way to where I was on the field, a few of the RTU fans held me by my hands and others held me by my legs. They picked me up, rocked me from side to side like a swing and threw me onto the sideline.

The referee, under pressure to resume the game, blew his whistle and the game was back on. At that point, I realised that I was no longer helping my team by pretending to be injured and staying out of the game. I hurriedly put myself back together and quickly ran back into the game to join the defence. RTU's offense continued to mount pressure on us but we were able to hold them off to win the match. Thankfully, I was neither hurt from the initial contact nor from the RTU fans throwing me off the field.

During my time on the team, Kotoko won league titles in 1986, 1987, 1988/89, 1990/91, and in 1991/92. From 1988, the season officially started in one year and ended in the next year. That is why the season years are written the way they are written (with the slash). We also won the SWAG Cup in 1988, 1989, 1990, 1991, 1992 and 1993. SWAG is the Sports Writers Association of Ghana and that cup named after them was a prestigious championship that was played between the two top teams in the country each year.

My father warmed up slowly to being in total support of my career as a footballer. He eventually became one of my biggest supporters. He even got into the habit of telling people, at any opportunity, that Kwasi Appiah of Kumasi Asante Kotoko and the Ghana Black Stars was his son.

He encouraged me to make it a habit of paying courtesy calls on the Asantehene. I didn't think it was necessary to keep showing up at the palace just because I would be welcomed there. My father on the other hand thought that was something I should do. As my excuse for not making such frequent visits to Asantehene's palace, I told my father I didn't have any appropriate clothes for that kind of visit.

My father was really serious about his idea of me paying frequent courtesy calls on the Asantehene, and he didn't want any excuses. He took it upon himself to travel to Accra to get me some outfits. He returned with two political suits. I took the outfits and agreed to follow his suggestion. After he left, I wore the clothes but I did not visit the Asantehene every morning like he had suggested.

My father was not the type of father who easily expressed his emotions but I knew through his actions that he was proud of me. His enthusiasm, as was demonstrated in several other gestures, showed his pride in what I had accomplished.

By the time I decided to call it quits from actively playing football, I knew I could have kept on playing. However, I did not want to leave I had declined significantly in terms of my playing ability. My career had been filled with good experiences and I was satisfied with what I had achieved. I had given my best effort to the game and to my teams. I knew I always gave the game my very best, and there was nothing more to prove. I was ready to move on to the next phase of my professional life.

By 1994, my daughters Peggy and Audrey had been born. Stepping away from actively playing football was also going to give me more time to spend with my children. Travelling less meant I would be home more. I could also spend more time visiting my parents and my extended family. Moving away from active football was also going to allow me to explore other professional opportunities. So, I hung my boots and closed the chapter of my Kumasi Asante Kotoko playing career.

I wanted to remain in football and to help shape the next generation of players. Malik Jabir was the coach of Asante Kotoko at the time, and he invited me to become his assistant. That was a great opportunity to learn from someone who loved and understood the game of football. Malik Jabir played for about 16 years at Kotoko and was on the team that won Kotoko's first African Club Championship in 1970. His technical brilliance had been beneficial to me as a player and I was more than happy to continue to learn from him.

After working under Coach Malik for a season, Abubakari Ouattara took over before making way for Burkhard Ziese. I continued to serve under both coaches as the assistant. I helped to run training sessions, managed the coaching staff's relationship with the players, and saw to the players' general wellbeing. With very different leadership styles, I learned different things from each of the two coaches. I also grew into my own as I had been building capacity and looking forward to the opportunity to independently coach the team when the opportunity came.

As destiny would have it, Coach Ziese resigned from his post at the end of the 1994/95 season, and I became the interim head coach. By that time, I had participated in several local coaching courses taught by Ghana's senior CAF-licensed coaches. With my training and exposure up until that point, I was confident that I could lead the team to win the league title.

I coached the team for most of the 1995/96 season. With three games to go to the end of the season, we were in first place and leading Ashanti Goldfields (later known as Ashanti Gold) by two points. My players were very motivated and they were playing well. I was confident about the team securing the necessary wins to finish the season at the top of the league.

George Adusei Poku, popularly known as Georgido, was the team's chief executive officer at the time. He insisted that the season had come to a crucial moment and the team needed a more experienced coach to ensure that we finished at the top of the league. So, he brought in Coach Afranie who had coached the team in previous years. Coach Afranie was in charge for the team's three final matches.

Kotoko lost one of the three final matches to Afienya United. Goldfields edged us out to win the league – by one point. That was a painful way to finish an otherwise very successful season but we had to move on and look forward to the next season.

Subsequent actions of the team's management towards my role as the team's coach made it obvious to me that I needed to look elsewhere if I seriously wanted to build a career as a football coach. Kotoko was at the time going through a phase that made the leadership hesitant to embrace a coach who was not widely perceived as a coaching legend. I was sidelined many times by the management from decisions about the team. Under normal circumstances, I would have been invited to participate in such decisions. I turned my dissatisfaction into motivation, and chose to pursue further professional training to prepare for the next opportunity.

Fabulous is a word often used to describe Kotoko – Fabulous Kumasi Asante Kotoko. One of the cheers the supporters often shout out – Fabu-Fabu – is derived from "Fabulous." Kotoko had been a fabulous organization for my football career. And I count it a great honour to have been a member of the Kotoko family. My teammates, the club's leadership, and their supporters have been great for my career. Kotoko was one of the best-run clubs in Ghana during my era, and I enjoyed the stability and leadership of some of the finest football administrators in the country.

If I had to do it all over again, I would not change a thing about the path my career took. I am blessed to have been in the situations I have been in, and I have always looked upon my Kotoko years with great contentment.

 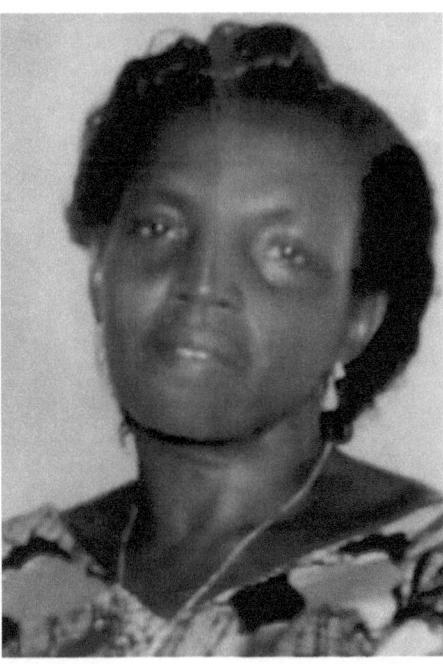

My father, Joseph Emmanuel Appiah. My mother, Martha Ama Kyeremaah.

A family portrait from the 1960s, with me in the front right.

Standing: My siblings Cobby, Sophia and Rose. **Seated**: Uncle Kwaku, me, Uncle Kofi Roger, and my sister Grace.

Playing for Kotoko (#3 jersey) against El Ahly (1982).

Playing for Kotoko at the Accra Sports Stadium during the 1982 league season; in the background is Opoku Nti.

Top (L-R): John Bannerman, me, Kofi Abbrey, Nana Eshun, Sarfo Gyamfi and George Arthur. **Bottom (L-R):** Abdul Razak, Mohammed Odoom, Sampson Lamptey, Ahmed Rockson and Rauf Iddi.

Kotoko squad for the 1983 Africa Club Champions Cup final. **Top (L-R):** Akye Erzuah, Addae Kyenkyehene, Seth Ampadu, Ebo Mends, Yahya Kassum, Joe Carr, Ernest Appau, Papa Arko. **Bottom (L-R):** John Bannerman, me, Kwame Sampson, Ahmed Rockson, Opoku Nti, Francis Agyemang, Joe Tex, and Afranie.

Captain Addae Kyenkyenhene introduces the team to Sports Minister Ato Austin during a ceremonial match at the Accra Sports Stadium in 1986. **(L-R)**: Me, Abdul Razak, Anane Kobo and Kofi Nti.

Kotoko team that beat Zamalek of Egypt 5-1 at the Kumasi Sports Stadium in the quarter finals knockout stages of Africa Club Competition in 1987. **Top (L-R)**: Goalkeeper Salifu Ansah, Kwaku Kyere, George Arthur, me, Asare Boateng, Saarah Mensah. **Bottom (L-R)**: Rauf Iddi, Opoku Nti, Abdul Razak, Addae Kyenkyenhene, Sarfo Gyamfi.

At training with Kotoko colleagues; **(L-R):** Mohammed Odoom, George Arthur, Opoku Nti, Sarfo Gyamfi and Abdul Razak.

Comedian Super OD (second from right) was a huge Kotoko fan. Here, he is pictured visiting the team's camp. George Arthur is on the far left and I am on the far right.

LEADERS DON'T HAVE TO YELL

My life off the pitch in the 1990s.

Kotoko squad that won the 1990/91 league title. **Top (L-R):** Anthony Osei Kwadwo, Ibrahim Tanko, Frimpong Manso, Edward 'Opeele' Aboagye, Kwaku Fori, Emmanuel Ampeah, Samson Appiah, John Benson, and me. **Bottom (L-R):** Bight Obeng, Kwaku Kyere, Isaac Otoo, Thomas Boakye, Isaac Kwakye, Stanley Aboraah, and Ben Kusi.

Kotoko team in 1990/91 pose for the national anthem before a match at the Kumasi Sports Stadium. **(L-R):** Okyere Darko, Ben Kusi, Emmanuel Ampeah, Kwaku Fori, Thomas Boakye, Stanley Aboraah, John Benson, Kwaku Fori, Kwaku Kyere, Sampson Appiah, Opeele Aboagye, Frimpong Manso, Anthony Osei Kwadwo, Isaac Otoo, Bright Obeng, me, Ibrahim Tanko, and Isaac Kwakye.

Receiving a trophy from Flt. Lt. Rawlings, who was the Head of State of Ghana during all of my years playing at Kotoko.

Serving Kotoko as captain came with enviable duties such as receiving trophies.

Top (L-R): Jerry Adjei, Kwaku Fori, Kwaku Menkah, Isaac Kwakye, Frimpong Manso, Emmanuel Ampeah, and Kwaku Adu; **Bottom (L-R)**: Sarfo Gyamfi, Yussif Alhassan, Kwaku Kyere, me, Thomas Boakye, John Bannerman, Mohammed Odoom, and Joe Debrah.

Black Stars (1980s): **Top (L-R):** Owusu Mensah, Emmanuel Quarshie (captain), Isaac Acquaye, unidentified, me, Opoku Nti, unidentified, Isaac Paha, and Joe Carr; **Bottom (L-R):** Mohammed Polo, unidentified, Joe Odoi, Abdul Razak, George Alhassan, Kofi Abbrey, and unidentified.

Black Stars (1990s): **Top (L-R):** Abukari Damba, Mohammed Polo, Bernard White, George Arthur, unidentified, Frimpong Manso, Me, Mohammed Odoom, and Coach John Eshun; **Bottom (L-R):** Ibrahim Gariba, Kwadjo Sumaila, John Bannerman, Alex Donkor, George Alhassan, Sarfo Gyamfi, Edward Opeele Aboagye, and Joe Odoi.

As part of pre-game formalities, I introduce my colleague George Alhassan to a dignitary before a Black Stars match.

Black Stars (1992): **Top (L-R):** Me, Edward Ansah, Sai Coachie, Tony Baffoe, Emmanuel Armah "Senegal", May Kano, Emmanuel Ampeah, Ali Ibrahim, Joe Addo, and Abass Cesar; **Bottom (L-R):** Michael Osei, Anthony Yeboah, Opoku Nti, Prince Opoku Polley, Stanley Aboraah, Frimpong Manso and Richard Naawu.

Squad that qualified Ghana for Senegal 1992. **Top (L-R)**: Edward Ansah, Robert Eshun, Joe Addo, Michael Osei, Coach Bukhard Ziese, Emmanuel Ampeah, Joe Debrah, me, Kofi Abbrey, and Abukari Damba. **Bottom (L-R)**: Frank Amankwah, Frimpong Manso, Emmanuel Armah "Senegal", Abedi Pele, Saarah Mensah, Stanley Aboraah, and Sam Johnson.

Black Stars squad for final of the 1992 Africa Cup of Nations in Senegal. **Top (L-R)**: a team official, Edward Ansah, Nii Darko Ankrah, Frimpong Manso, Sarfo Gyamfi, Tony Yeboah, Opoku Nti, Salifu Ansah, Emmanuel Ampeah; **Bottom (L-R)**: Emmanuel Armah, Prince Opoku Polley, Tony Baffoe, Richard Naawu, Yaw Preko, Isaac Asare, Stanley Aborah, and Nii Odartey Lamptey. Remaining squad not pictured are Abedi Pele, Mohammed Gargo, Kofi Abbrey, Ali Ibrahim, Abukari Damba, and me.

With my teammates in 1992 upon our arrival from Senegal. **(L-R):** Kofi Abbrey, Opoku Nti, Isaac Asare and Sarfo Gyamfi.

PART II:
A LEADER OF MEN AND OF TEAMS

· CHAPTER 5 ·

BECOMING A COACH

Since my earliest days as a player, I have usually been keenly observant of the people and situations around me. I am usually one of the first people to arrive at a meeting but may be one of the last people to offer an opinion. By the time I speak, I would have had the benefit of assessing the situation at hand, and then offer a balanced opinion. As often as possible, leaders should listen more than they speak.

With that approach to offering my opinions, even the people who disagree with me often concede that I am being thoughtful in my submission. That's one of the ways by which I earned the respect of my teammates and coaches, and emerged as a leader. As a player, that respect from my colleagues often contributed to my coaches appointing me captain of the teams I was a member of. Of course, seniority matters but influence and the ability bring people together matter more when it comes to leading people.

As the captain at both club and national team levels, part of my job was to promote cohesion on the team, work closely with administrators in the best interest of the players, and help others develop their potential. As the curtains were getting ready to come down on my playing career, coaching came more and more into focus for me. I wanted to continue to help teams win and to help talented footballers develop their skills to the highest levels. I wanted to do so by passing on my knowledge and experience.

I needed more than the local training and the understudy I had received from the Kotoko coaches as an assistant. At that time, England was the best option I could think of as far as coaching training was concerned. The English teams at the time played the game at a very high level and their coaches demonstrated a mastery of the game.

So, in coordination with Kwabena Yeboah the journalist and publisher of Africa Sports newspaper, I reached out to my former national team colleague, Anthony (Tony) Yeboah, who was then playing for Leeds United in the English Premier League.

Through an introduction from Tony, the team's coach, Howard Wilkinson, invited me to England to pursue further coaching training. I had travelled to many parts of the world as a member of Kotoko and the Black Stars but that was going to be my first time going to the U.K.

When I presented my documentation at the British High Commission in Accra for a visa, I was denied the visa. That was disappointing. I had presented the letter from Leeds along with my passport and my application. They wanted additional supporting documentation, including bank statements, which I didn't take with me because I thought the letter was enough. Somehow, they seemed to doubt the authenticity of the invitation letter.

Tony was on holiday in Ghana at the time. After I gave him the update on my visa application, he went with me to the high commission. With Tony Yeboah affirming in person to the consular that the letter was legitimate, the visa was approved. I left for the U.K. in the summer of 1996.

My wife's aunt, Auntie Kakra, lived in the Stratford neighbourhood of London at the time and she hosted me for about a year. I later lived with my wife's sister, Patricia Adusei-Poku, and her family in the Beckton neighbourhood of London.

Leeds is located north of London and it took about three hours to get there by train. When I arrived there, I put myself up in a hotel and met with the team at their training facility the following day.

My coaching training at Leeds United was a month-long professional attachment designed to expose me to team management at the highest levels of professional football. It was to afford me the opportunity to acquire first-hand practical experience and sharpen my leadership skills to launch into coaching at the highest levels.

I participated in the team's training sessions, both on and off the field, engaged with the coaching staff regarding their game preparation decision-making, observed how the medical staff managed players' health issues, and interacted with various professionals in the discharge of their specific duties. I paid particular attention to how their respective roles impacted the team.

Following the Leeds United attachment, I returned to London and enrolled in a coaching course for my diploma in professional football coaching. That involved classroom instruction, on-field demonstrations and independent coaching practice that needed to be logged and submitted. Along with about 60 other professionals, I carried out the supervised instructions aspect of my training. When the instructors found out about my extensive playing career at both the club and national levels, they took an interest in calling on me to help during the parts of the class that involved the demonstration of key skills and techniques. After a year as a freelance coach and filling up my log book with the required activities, I returned to the classroom for another month-long session to finish up the training.

Training to become a high-level professional football coach requires a lot of personal motivation. Having to independently spend a year putting into practice what I had learned required a high level of discipline and commitment to excellence. It's almost like being an entrepreneur – you cannot succeed by just sitting around and waiting for someone to tell you what to do. You cannot succeed by taking your work seriously only when someone is watching you.

Discipline and commitment to excellence are some of the characteristics that separate high performers from average performers in almost any profession I know of. What kept me on track with my training was the work ethic I had developed as a player and as a local club coach. Also, my focus on becoming the best coach that I could be was another motivating factor.

Having obtained my coaching badges, first the B badge and subsequently the A badge, I had learned many technical and administrative skills. However, there were other skills such as managing player egos, navigating political influences, and helping players through personal issues that a coach needs in order to be successful. The need for those skills presents a layer of complexity to the coaching job, and that requires time and experience to master.

Managing egos on a team requires a leadership perspective that is a combination of self-respect, firmness, and good human relation skills. It is no secret that African players who play in leagues outside of their home countries enjoy a high social status and celebrity treatment due to the large amounts of money they earn. That high social status and celebrity treatment can inflate some players' egos to the point that they fail to submit to their coach's leadership. That kind of dysfunction is even worse when the coach is compromised by money and gifts from his players.

A major part of any coaching job, especially in Africa, is dealing with issues off the pitch. When you're not strong enough as a coach to deal with these situations off the pitch, then automatically, those issues follow the players onto the field. When you need them to deliver results, you will not be able to get results from your players.

Excessive political influences can place a complicated burden on a coach. For an African coach leading an African team, that burden is usually greater. An example of such influences is when political leaders or football administrators take actions that undermine the coach's authority. Sadly, these kinds of actions happen too often in African football, I've had to be strategic enough at handling such influences. The leadership mindset that is required to be successful under such circumstances cannot be taught in a classroom. Those skills are what a coach picks up from professional experience, from watching other leaders lead, and from trusting one's own instincts.

Managing disputes is another leadership skill I developed as a player, which came in handy in my role as a coach. Being the captain of Kumasi Asante Kotoko and of the Ghana Black stars helped me learn how to deal with people, and how to lead. Whenever a player had an issue with the coach or with another player or with an official, I often helped where I could to resolve the dispute.

The threat of a revolt is a common method that players use to get their demands met. It is also destructive for a team in the long run. There is usually a better way to resolve most issues when the people involved can calm down and talk about things like grown-ups.

As a player, I experienced many instances where my colleagues wanted to revolt on an issue. In each instance, I tried to find a means to calm them down and then talk to the management as to how to get to an agreeable resolution. In many of those instances, I was successful in getting a resolution. In other instances, I was unsuccessful. But in every instance, I learned something about managing disputes.

Not every player will become a coach, and I did not become a coach simply because I knew how to play football. I became a coach because I wanted to share what I had learned in order to bring out the best in others.

I had to be patient and determined. I also had to remain a constant learner and a humble leader. More importantly, I had to be a leader at all times.

· CHAPTER 6 ·

BECOMING THE BLACK STARS COACH

In 1999, I came home to Ghana from London to help care for my mother who was sick. My father had passed away ten years earlier. Coach Jones Attuquayefio was in charge of the Black Stars at the time. We had known each other from being around Ghana football over the years and we had a very good relationship.

When he heard I was in town, he reached out to me and invited me to join him as an assistant on the senior national team. I had neither played under him nor worked closely with him previously. However, accepting the invitation to work with him was an honour and a very easy decision.

After a while of working under Coach Attuquayefio, I requested that my work on the national team be formalized by way of a contract. I had been working as an assistant coach of the senior national team and nothing about my appointment was in writing. All that was in place was the coach's verbal invitation and the FA's verbal approval. The FA's response to my request for a contract was neither an outright no nor a direct yes, but it was obvious that my request had fallen on deaf ears.

The FA (Football Association), as the governing body that controls football in the country, hires, fires and oversees personnel decisions for the country's national teams. They told me it was not their practice to offer contracts to assistant coaches, and that they were going to think about my request.

Not having a contract for a coaching job in Ghana at the time was typical, whether at the club or national team level. Ghanaian coaches were appointed and fired at will, and they had very little input in the terms under which they worked. Foreign coaches, however, were offered contracts when hired for national team or club assignments in Ghana. Even though that practice of treating Ghanaian coaches with less professionalism was not right, it was the order of the day.

When a coach and the football administrators formally agree to the terms of the coach's employment, it helps to clearly establish the expectations the two parties have of each other. I expected that having a contract clearly defined, in writing, my job duties, the scope of my authority, salary and benefits, how my performance was going to be measured, and other items a professional coach's contract should cover. However, that was not the case with me or many of the Ghanaian coaches I knew. Coach Attuquayefio had a contract.

At the time, Ghanaian coaches were barely making enough money for their services, and therefore, they had very little leverage to ask for a contract. Coaches were expected to take whatever was offered to them, and many did so without question. Some coaches relied on handouts from their rich players and from people for whom they did favours. Even though that practice of accepting money from players or players' representatives created conflicts of interest for the coach involved, many coaches resorted to that way of earning a living. Unfortunately, that behaviour diminished the respect a player was supposed to have for their coach, which led to a culture of disrespect. Of course, coaches who acted in such ways undermined their own authority but some coaches did that anyway, partly due to Ghanaian national team coaches not being treated with all the professional courtesies due them.

Still without a contract, I continued to work with Coach Attuquayefio and we played some African Cup qualifying matches. That year, we fielded a team made up of predominantly Accra Hearts of Oak players in a World Cup qualifier against Nigeria. He had invited several foreign-based players for the previous match, and the foreign-based players showed very little commitment to the team. They came and played the way they wanted, and then left. They did not listen to him and he was not happy about that.

Hearts of Oak, which he had coached prior to taking over the Black Stars, had been doing very well. They had just won the African Cup. So, I suggested that he should pick the core of the team for the Nigeria match from the Hearts of Oak squad. That was a group of players who played very well together and whom he had a very good relationship with. Ghana against Nigeria was always big game, and therefore, taking a team of players who were not battle-tested was a big risk.

It was going to be a risk anyway if he invited the foreign-based players who had demonstrated that they would not listen to him. He chose to go with the Hearts of Oak players and a few Kotoko and other local players.

From our perspective, inexperienced-but-capable players who listened to their coach made a better team than experienced players who did their own thing and ignored the coach's directions. We were confident that our team would perform well against Nigeria's big-name stars.

During the game, our boys played very well and created many goal-scoring opportunities but could not convert them. That was because some of our players didn't have enough big-game experience, and there were moments that their lack of experience had them wasting good goal-scoring chances.

A win would have been a better outcome but the decision to use the local squad sent a positive signal to all the players, the fans and the FA. We demonstrated that it was possible to build a successful national team around competent and committed local players.

For the players selected to play in that match against Nigeria, it was an opportunity for them to showcase their talents and to let the whole country know what they could do when given the chance to play for the nation.

Even though the willingness to take a chance on local players is vital to the sustainable future of any national team, very few national team coaches will take such a huge chance on local players. Coach Attuquayefio did and I respect him very much for making that decision.

In many aspects of Ghanaian life, there's a saying – do before complain. That means you need to get the work done first before you complain about the part of the work that you're unhappy about.

When I revisited the topic of a contract for my services, I thought that was a reasonable request. Even if that had not been the FA's practice, I believed we needed to start from somewhere. I had done my "obeying" and it was only fair that I got to work under a contract going forward. The FA continued to drag their feet even though they admitted that I had proved myself useful to the coach and to the team.

Being a member of a national team coaching staff is an honour. However, the working conditions at the time did not seem like the best situation for my career. I resigned from my position in 2000, not long after my mother had passed away. I returned to the U.K. and continued to explore other coaching options. It took eight years before the next Ghana national team coaching opportunity came up.

After Ghana's appearance in the 2008 African Cup of Nations, I found out that there was a vacant position on the Black Stars because the coach at the time, Claude Le Roy, had sacked his assistant. I made a call to a few people I knew at the Ghana Football Association (GFA) office to inquire about the vacancy and to apply.

As the first formal step in the process of applying for the job, I presented my CV (curriculum vitae or resumé) to a GFA representative. The person accepted my CV and that was the end of it. Like we say in Ghana, they sat on my CV. They just held on to it and did not invite me in for an interview. Neither did they inform me that I was not going to be considered for the job, even though I was duly qualified.

At the time, Mr. John Agyekum Kufuor was the president of the country. I had a good relationship with him from my days with Kumasi Asante Kotoko where he had served for a while on their board of directors. I contacted the Office of the President to request an introduction to the GFA leaders.

It was my hope that the President's influence could get someone to take a look at my resumé and let me know what was going on with my application. Thankfully, that introduction from the President led to a phone interview, and then I was invited to come for an in-person interview in Accra.

I paid my way to Accra from London, and was interviewed by a panel of GFA executive committee members. We discussed my plans for the role, the GFA's expectations of me, my salary expectations as well as other employment conditions.

I was offered the assistant coaching job but the GFA officials were initially reluctant about offering me a contract, expecting me to work on a verbal agreement. They eventually agreed to a formal contract which included a monthly salary of $3,000.

That salary was extremely low compared to how much they were paying the foreign coaches. That huge disparity in salaries reflected the GFA's gloomy attitude towards Ghanaian coaches. However, the terms of my contract were a significant improvement from what they offered me the previous time I served as the assistant coach of the same senior national team. That seemed like a step in the right direction for my career, and I was hopeful that it was the beginning of bigger opportunities.

I remember President Kufuor reminding me not to focus so much on the money others were being paid but to rather get in there, excel at the job, and see what happened next. That was good advice and I am glad I listened to him.

The President's recommendation helped to move my application along because it is a fact of life that anyone gets anywhere through somebody. It is possible that nothing would have happened with my application without the President's involvement. However, the least they could have done would have been to offer me an interview since I was qualified for the job. That way, President Kufuor's intervention would not have been necessary.

More than the President's recommendation, it was my qualification and experience that earned me the job. And it was my performance that kept me in that job under three successive head coaches.

After finalizing my contract with the FA, I went back to London to get a few things in order before returning to Accra. My wife and kids were in the U.K. at that time, after they relocated there from Ghana in 2000. They remained in the U.K. and I returned to Ghana.

In 2006, Claude Le Roy from France became the Black Stars coach. Before coaching in Ghana, he had coached the national teams of Senegal, Cameroun and the Democratic Republic of Congo. A GFA representative introduced me to him, saying that I was a former national team and Kotoko captain, and a former Kotoko coach who had previously served as an assistant coach on the senior national team. He was very receptive of me and expressed his happiness when he learned that I had been living in London for a while. He then introduced his physical trainer, Herve Renard, also a French man. We started working together not long afterward.

Coach Le Roy was bilingual – spoke both French and English – and was easy to get along with. He preferred to leave it to me to draw up the training programme, and then he would approve or make changes. Some coaches would draw up their programme and hand it over to the assistant coach to execute.

Coach Le Roy, on the other hand, would usually give directions on tactical activities he wanted the team to focus on, and then left it up to me to put the programme together.

Under Coach Le Roy, we played two matches – I believe those were World Cup qualifiers. He resigned from the position about three months after I joined him. He told me it was unfortunate he had to leave Ghana because he had some family issues to take care of at home. Herve did not stay for long. He left for a coaching job with Zambia not long after I joined the team.

After he left, my Ghanaian colleague Sellas Tetteh was appointed an interim coach while the GFA searched for a permanent coach for the team.

In August 2008, Milovan (Milo) Rajevac was appointed the Black Stars' coach. He is from Serbia, where he played his professional soccer and then spent most of his time coaching at the club level. Ghana was his first time coaching a national team and also his first coaching job in Africa.

Milo did not speak English. He came with an interpreter. I was introduced to him at the GFA office and we later made time to sit and get to know each other. Even though the interpreter had to translate my statements and vice versa, we had a fairly good conversation and we hit it off right away. Our first conversation was mostly about family.

On most evenings, we spent time at the Accra Mall just hanging out and discussing the team's progress and planning for what was ahead. Sometimes, we met at his house. When his family was in town visiting from Serbia, I got to meet them.

Milo is the one person I give credit to for a great deal of my development as a coach. He gave me many opportunities to lead, gave very practical feedback, and encouraged me to participate in making key decisions concerning the team. During many of our training sessions, he allowed me to lead the team in drills and to direct the players on what to do. He often called me aside to share ideas he had for the team. He sometimes asked what I would do in a particular situation and why, and then he would share with me his approach and his reasons for that approach.

Working with a coach who communicated mainly through an interpreter was not as cumbersome as it may have seemed from the outside. With much of interpersonal communication is non-verbal, paying attention to what's going on around me and anticipating Milo's reaction was an important key to communicating effectively with him and his interpreter. And besides, Milo is a man of few words. He said what he needed to say and did so concisely. His interpreter also did a fine job translating Milo's statements into English.

Regarding activities on the field, most of that was carried out using what we refer to as football language. Not every instruction was spoken. Being able to use hand signals and gestures to convey ideas was, and still is, fundamental to coaching. So, Milo not speaking English was not a setback to our ability to work effectively together.

Milo didn't learn English, at least during the time I was with him. Neither did he learn any Ghanaian languages. As far as communicating with the players was concerned, we got through the on-the-field communications just fine. Some of the players spoke to him through his interpreter. Those who were more comfortable expressing themselves in Twi explained what they wanted to say in Twi, and then I translated to Milo's interpreter, and he in turn passed it on. Milo responded in the Serbian language, his interpreter translated into English, and then I further translated into Twi.

Milo developed a great deal of confidence in the team as most of the players were playing some of their best football at that time.

Under his leadership, we qualified for the 2010 African Cup of Nations where we were runners-up after losing 1-0 to Egypt. We also qualified for the 2010 World Cup in South Africa. At the group stage of that World Cup, we won 1-0 against Serbia, drew 1-1 with Australia, and lost 0-1 to Germany to finish in the Top 2 to qualify for the Round of 16. We beat the USA 2-1 and lost to Uruguay on penalties to exit the tournament at the quarter-finals stage.

Playing against his native Serbian side put Milo in an unusual position. He had a job to do, which was to help Ghana win against Serbia. He knew the backlash he would receive from the Serbian fans if he led a foreign team to beat Serbia. But being the professional that he was, he focused on psyching our players for a win against a tactically-disciplined side.

After the win against Serbia, I was excited and I instinctively hurried to congratulate him with a hug. But he refused my hug, saying, "Kwasi, please, please!" That brief moment of him resisting my hug was caught on camera and broadcast around the world. It appeared as if he had pushed me away but that's not what happened. Understandably, he was trying to show no reaction to the game's outcome.

I did not take his reaction personally because it was understandable. However, it would have been less awkward for both of us if he had told me going into the game that he would not celebrate if Ghana won. He later explained that he chose not to celebrate out of respect for his home country. At the end of the day, he congratulated the players, we talked about the incident regarding the celebration, and we all got over that awkwardness shortly after.

It was at that tournament where Suarez's antics got in the way of our team becoming the first African nation to reach the World Cup semi-finals. In the late stages of the tied game against Uruguay, one of their players, Luis Suarez, stretched out his hands like a goalkeeper to stop the ball and deny Ghana a goal.

Of course, Suarez was shown a red card and we were awarded a penalty. Asamoah Gyan's penalty hit the crossbar and the game went to a penalty shoot-out, where we lost. We had a very good team and could have gone all the way to the final, and even win the cup. That game would remain on the minds of many people as to what if Suarez didn't do what he did or what if Gyan had scored that penalty.

I was an assistant under Milo for about 27 matches, including the 2010 World Cup. The World Cup ended in July, his contract with the Black Stars expired in August, and in early September, he left to coach Saudi Arabian club Al-Ahli Saudi FC. The GFA had the opportunity to renew his contract before the tournament but did not. With the much bigger offer that came in after the World Cup, he left. Before he left, we talked about how he had enjoyed working with the Ghana players, and he wished me well in my coaching career.

When he expressed his interest in bringing me along to his new job if only his contract allowed him to pick his assistant, I was honoured that he thought that highly of my work. I also wished him well and told him that it could happen someday in the future that we may get to work together again. He received that remark with a broad smile.

With Milo's departure, I was asked by the GFA to coach the team in the interim. I did not apply for the head coaching job at that time because the FA had in mind to bring in another foreign coach. I was in charge from November 2010 till January 2011, during which time we played an international friendly with Saudi Arabia. That match ended in a goalless draw.

Goran (Plavi) Stevanovic, also a Serbian, was appointed head coach in January 2011. Plavi spoke English and he was more outspoken than Milo. He asked many questions and seemed very interested in learning about the psychology of the Ghanaian people.

He led the team to qualify for the 2012 Africa Cup of Nations held in Gabon and Equatorial Guinea. Ghana lost to Zambia in the semi-finals of that tournament, and many Ghanaians blamed him for the team's lackluster performance. He was released from his duties with ten more months left on his contract, even though he wanted to continue. The GFA wanted to go in a different direction due to the immense public pressure they were facing to fire him.

In a statement, GFA President Kwasi Nyantakyi expressed the FA's gratitude "to the general public for their concerns about the national team and their patience so far" as part of the announcement of Plavi's firing.

Under Plavi, the team had an unbeaten run in qualifying for the AFCON tournament. Failing to lead the team to win the tournament was the FA's reason for firing him. Plavi was surprised by the firing but he explained that he was not disappointed, knowing that the FA reserved the right to go in a different direction if that's what they thought was good for the team. I was an assistant under Plavi for 14 matches, and once again, I was appointed interim head coach until a permanent coach was named.

In April 2012, I was in Bechem in the Brong-Ahafo Region watching a match between Premier League sides Bechem United and New Edubiase United. That was part of my routine travels around the country to monitor local players for the national team. It was there that I received a call from the GFA president. He wanted to know if I was interested in the Black Stars head coaching position.

I calmly responded, "Why not? If given the chance, I know I can do it." Mr. Nyantakyi invited me to a meeting in Accra later that week with the GFA executive committee.

Even though I was excited about the FA's interest in me for the job, there were important conversations that needed to happen before I took the job.

The appointment of a permanent coach for the Black Stars was a hot topic across the country, with some insisting that it was about time a local head coach was appointed and others arguing that a foreign coach was better for the national team.

Those who opposed appointing a Ghanaian coach cited reasons such as lack of extensive coaching experience on the part Ghanaian coaches and the players' tendency to disrespect Ghanaian coaches. Those in favour of appointing a local head coach cited the successes of past Ghanaian coaches and the need to give Ghanaian coaches the opportunity to prove themselves.

Obviously, I was in the camp of those who advocated for a Ghanaian coach because many Ghanaian coaches could do the job and deliver results if they were treated with the same professionalism that our foreign counterparts enjoyed. Going into my meeting with the GFA executive committee, I knew it was important for me to think not only about me but also look out for the best interest of Ghana's future with qualified Ghanaian coaches.

To cut to the chase, I asked that we start our discussions from Milo's contract and then negotiate the necessary adjustments. That approach made the conversation fairly straightforward. Even though Milo's contract was about two years old at the time, the salary we agreed on was $15,000 less per month than what Milo was paid. I was not offered some of the perks Milo received but that didn't bother me. More than the money, I was interested in working under a contract that clearly defined the GFA's expectations of me and also allowed me to be successful on the job. At the end of the negotiation, both parties believed the agreement was fair.

On April 11, 2012, I was announced as the head coach of the Black Stars. That was an important moment in my career because I knew the national and social implications of my appointment. With many of the Black Stars' previous successes having been achieved with Ghanaian coaches at the helm of affairs, I knew I was standing on the shoulders of giants like C.K. Gyamfi, Fred Osam-Duodoo, E.K. Afranie and Jones Attuquayefio.

Furthermore, a majority of Ghanaians supported my appointment and I appreciated it. It was going to take time to change the perceptions of those who opposed my appointment, if ever. Above all else, I was pleased to have earned the position on merit.

I don't believe in lobbying for a coaching position by seeking favours from my employers. And I don't encourage anyone to do that. When you do that, you put your hand in their mouths, like we say in Ghana. Automatically, you will be constrained to always acting delicately because of the fear of losing the favour that got you your job in the first place. On the other hand, if you earn your job on merit, you maintain the respect that is due you from your employer.

Of course, in Ghana, there is always someone who is willing to take less money and accept less-than-ideal working conditions just to snatch an opportunity from you. But I also believe that if you are qualified and maintain your integrity, you will be better off in the long run. Somebody once said that you have to compromise to keep what you compromised to get. And that is very true in football and in many areas of life.

Even though I had a solid resumé as a player, my transition into coaching did not happen automatically. As a matter of fact, it took some time and I had to work my way up to the job. Most importantly, I was ready when the opportunity came my way.

· CHAPTER 7 ·

WIN NOW, OR FOREVER LOSE YOUR PEACE

The last time Ghana's Black Stars won the African Cup of Nations (AFCON) was in 1982. Since then, the team came extremely close to winning on two occasions, put up lackluster performances during other appearances, and failed to qualify on other occasions. Even though the Black Stars had been to the World Cup twice as at the time I became head coach, which was a major accomplishment by any standard, the elusive AFCON championship was a major source of frustration for many Ghanaians.

When I took over as the coach of the Black Stars, I knew the trophy drought was the big elephant in the room. I could feel almost every football-loving Ghanaian and supporter of the Black Stars yearning for that important symbol of accomplishment. Most Ghanaians genuinely believe we are one of the best – if not the very best – on the continent, but could not rightfully claim that accolade if we had gone for more than thirty years without winning an AFCON. So, my immediate task was to build a team to qualify for the 2013 African Cup of Nations, and possibly, win the trophy. We also needed to qualify for the 2014 World Cup in Brazil.

I recruited Maxwell Konadu to be my assistant. Maxwell's extensive playing experience at both club and national team levels were particularly important to me. His success as a player and as a club coach made me confident in choosing him. Maxwell serving as my assistant was an important step towards ensuring that other Ghanaian coaches received the needed exposure to enable them coach the national team when the opportunity came.

He was coaching league champions Kumasi Asante Kotoko at the time, and the Kotoko management and supporters were not particularly happy that I took away their coach. They eventually understood the importance of Maxwell serving with me on the national team.

The rest of the technical team remained as it was before, with one exception. I brought on Michael Okyere as a video analyst. Michael, who had been trained in this specialty at English Premier League Club Manchester City in the U.K., was to help with our player monitoring. Due to the evolution of the game and how our players are scattered around the world, detailed data on our players is critical for good decision making. Being able to pull detailed data about each current or prospective player's on-field performance is extremely useful to the process of selecting the very best players to represent the nation at all times. With a video analyst on our staff, we were able to monitor known players and discover unknown players who could be useful to the national team.

Monitoring players is a key part of my job as a head coach. Beyond what we read or hear in the headlines about how a player is doing, there are other key attributes I consider before calling a player to the national team. While media reports and public opinion about a player may reflect a player's form, digging into the data about players reveal a lot more about who is playing at the highest level or who is exhibiting the qualities that we need on the national team.

Ghana has players all over: in Ghana, Europe, Asia, North America, South America, and across Africa. Some of them play in first divisions, some in the second and third divisions. Some play in leagues that are more competitive than others. Some leagues have televised games and some do not.

Regardless of where the player is located, I have a duty to monitor that player. If that player can be useful to the national team, I have a duty to stay on top of where he is playing, what form he's playing in, and how well he can be used on the national team – both now and in the near future. Sometimes, a player may be doing well on a bad team. That should not prevent the player from getting a chance to showcase his talent.

Monitoring players often involve observing the player in action in person, watching the player on video, analyzing key data about the player's on-field activities, or a combination of all these methods. As often as possible, I do all these for each current and potential player of the team so that I get a more comprehensive appraisal of each of them.

With the help of Wyscout, a player data software, we have access to a wide range of video, statistics and reports about players and teams around the world. When we combine the information gathered during player observation and the available data from the scouting software, we are able to make coaching decisions that are both scientific and artistic.

The scientific aspect of football is about the things that you cannot measure with the naked eye. For example, a player's work rate, which has to do with how much movement a player is involved in on the pitch cannot be measured accurately with the naked eye. However, data from the software helps us to objectively measure that kind of performance indicator, and be able to do so consistently for every player.

The artistic aspect of football has to do with experience and intuition. There is a lot of creativity involved in coaching decisions before, during and after a match.

Therefore, a coach needs to apply both the scientific and the artistic assessment methods of football in order to be successful. Adding a video analyst to our technical team brought new insights to the way we made decisions about the team.

We needed to build up our talent pipeline to reduce our overreliance on a few key players, and to make sure we were going to be successful for a long time to come. As such, call-ups included many young and previously-unknown players on purpose. Some of those players were going to, hopefully, go to the 2013 AFCON and 2014 World Cup, and then develop the experience and confidence needed to become key parts of the team for future assignments.

Of course, the experience of our key players was going to be vital in playing against some of the best and most experienced players around the world. My long-term vision was to make a strong showing at AFCON 2013, qualify for Brazil 2014, make a stronger showing there and then have a talented and experienced team for AFCON 2015.

For the AFCON 2013 qualifiers, we didn't have to play in the first round because we were highly-ranked by FIFA. In the second round, we played against Malawi and beat them 2-0 in Kumasi. On their home turf a month later, we won 1-0 and qualified on a 3-0 goal aggregate. That made us one of the final sixteen teams to qualify out of the 47 teams that started the qualifiers.

Our 23-man team comprised goalkeepers Daniel Agyei, Adam Kwarasey and Abdul Fatawu Dauda; defenders Richard Boateng, Mohamed Awal, Jerry Akaminko, Jonathan Mensah, John Boye, and Harrison Afful; midfielders John Paintsil, Anthony Annan, Emmanuel Agyemang Badu, Derek Boateng, Albert Adomah, Mohammed Rabiu, Solomon Asante, Isaac Vorsah, and Kwadwo Asamoah; and forwards Asamoah Gyan (captain), Christian Atsu, Emmanuel Clottey, Richmond Boakye, and Mubarak Wakaso.

We started off with a 2-2 draw with DR Congo, beat Mali 1-0, and beat Niger 3-0. In the quarter-finals, we won 2-0 against an impressive Cape Verde side, but lost to Burkina Faso on penalties in the semi-finals after a 1-1 draw. Nigeria won that tournament after beating Burkina Faso 1-0. We placed fourth after losing 3-1 to Mali in the third-place match.

Considering that many of the players who played in that tournament were young and untested, I was pleased with their overall performance. I was not impressed with our performance in our semi-final game against Burkina Faso, a game we could have won within the ninety minutes of play action. Some of the players lost their concentration during the match and did not perform as well as they had done in previous matches.

Though the final outcome was not what we expected, our AFCON performance offered a good basis for fine-tuning the team to continue with our World Cup qualification campaign. Our young players were developing the experience necessary to be able to play well at such high-level tournaments.

For the World Cup qualifiers, we were placed in Group D with Zambia, Sudan and Lesotho. Zambia was the defending African Cup of Nations champion and we had to emerge at the top of that group to qualify for the next round of qualifications. In Kumasi, we beat Lesotho 7-0. Later, we lost 1-0 to Zambia on their home ground. Some individuals started having doubts about my ability to get the job done after losing in Zambia.

Not only people in the media but certain officials in the FA were very vocal with their doubts about whether I was the right person for my job. What such doubters failed to see was that when building a team, it's not only about winning and losing but also about what the team learns from their wins and losses, and how they use that experience to develop. We were learning from our experiences and we were getting better as a team. I knew that, and I was not paying much attention to the doubters.

In March, we beat Sudan 4-0 in Kumasi. In the return leg played on their home soil, we beat them 3-1. Continuing with our winning ways, we beat Lesotho again 2-0 and won 2-1 against Zambia to top our group.

In the next and final round, we were paired with Egypt in a two-leg qualifier. The winner, on aggregate, was heading for Brazil. The Pharaohs of Egypt, at the time, had won their seventh AFCON championship and they were the only African national team that had won all their World Cup qualifying games for that campaign. Naturally, many Ghanaians became nervous about the Black Stars' prospects for qualification.

Everyone makes decisions all the time. But when you're in a job like mine, where the stakes are much higher because of the extent of public scrutiny that follows every decision I make, you need a high level of mental toughness in order to tune out the excessive noise.

I needed to focus, firstly, on calling up a team that was right for the job against Egypt, and, secondly, on executing tactics that I believed would make us successful. We were focused on winning and we knew we needed to win convincingly to avoid any surprises. Our aim was to win by a minimum of three goals in the first leg in Kumasi.

Studying the Egyptian team ahead of our preparations, I recognised that their strengths were primarily with their two key players up front. Their key weaknesses were on the wings where their defenders did not move quickly. To shut down their two key players upfront, I assigned a quick defender to each of their wingers. Our defenders' jobs were to keep their eyes on the opposing wingers and to move with them at all times. To exploit Egypt's defensive weakness, I chose attackers who could outwit their defenders with speed.

Whenever our two midfielders had the ball, our wingers and strikers knew to start sprinting so as to give the midfielders multiple options for quickly placing the ball behind the Egyptian defenders to create scoring chances. Our players executed the plan brilliantly.

The starting lineup comprised Abdul Fatawu Dauda, Samuel Inkoom, Daniel Opare, Jerry Akaminko, Rashid Sumaila,

Win Now, or Forever Lose Your Peace

Kwadwo Asamoah, Sulley Muntari, Michael Essien, Andre Ayew, Asamoah Gyan (captain), and Abdul Majeed Waris.

By the fifth minute, Asamoah Gyan, who was sprinting forward, received a quick pass from Majeed Waris and got past the Egyptian defender to strike home a powerful shot to open the scoring.

We continued to mount pressure on them and stuck with our plan. Around the twenty-second minute, Andre Ayew won possession of the ball, beat two Egyptian defenders and found Michael Essien. After Essien got the ball away from the oncoming goalkeeper and an Egyptian defender, another Egyptian player came from behind him to clear the ball but that clearance landed in the Egyptian net to give us our second goal.

Around the fortieth minute, we conceded a penalty when our defender, Rashid Sumaila, bumped Mohamed Sallah to the ground during a tackle. Mohammed Aboutrika converted that penalty for Egypt's first goal. And before we went into the half time break, a freekick from Sulley Muntari into the penalty box was converted into a goal through a header from Majeed Waris.

During the break, we tightened up lapses in our defence. We refocused on shutting down their two key guys up front, controlling the midfield, and taking advantage of their defensive weakness.

Around the fifty-fifth minute, Gyan headed in a kick from Sulley to bring the score up to 4-1. At the seventieth minute, Egypt's goalkeeper fouled Waris as he got the ball past him and toward the goal. We were awarded a penalty, which Sulley calmly converted to bring the score up 5-1.

With about fifteen minutes to go, we wanted to maintain the offensive pressure we were putting on the Egyptians. Mubarak Wakaso came on for Asamoah Gyan, Emmanuel Agyeman Badu came on for Sulley Muntari, and Christian Atsu came on for Andre Ayew.

In an offensive push around the eighty-eighth minute, Atsu powered in a left-foot shot from outside the penalty box to add to the tally. In front of the packed crowd at the Baba Yara Stadium, we had beaten Egypt 6-1, a margin wide enough to have one foot planted in Brazil.

Going into Cairo to play them in the return leg, our mindset was to play for a win, even though we knew losing by a margin of less than five would still have us qualifying. Our approach to defensive play, however, was going to be different. We planned to have as many players as possible behind the ball defending every time they had possession of the ball in the midfield.

We were concerned about the security situation in Egypt at the time due to the 2013 Arab Spring. The Arab Spring was a political uprising and a series of anti-government protests that seemed to have made the country unsafe to visit. Additionally, we were also concerned that the officiating may go unfairly against us since the officials may be under the threat of violence if the home team did not win the match. We were assured by FIFA and by the Egyptian FA about our safety. Indeed, the security at our camp was really tight throughout our stay in Cairo even though concerns about the team's safety lurked in my mind.

We knew the Egyptians were going to press us early and push for a goal within the first twenty minutes. I knew they would want an early goal to validate their game plan and also raise their team's confidence. We also knew that if we could hold them goalless through that first twenty minutes, we could shift the momentum in our favour. So, we started off defending well and relying on counter attacks for our offense.

In the twenty-fourth minute, the Egyptians earned a free-kick near the outside of our penalty box, and converted that into a goal. For the rest of the first half, we defended excellently and occasionally pressed forward with an attack.

Mubarak Wakaso came on for Andre Ayew in the fifty-seventh minute, Emmanuel Agyeman Badu came in for Sulley Muntari in the seventy-second minute, and Kevin Prince Boateng came on for Majeed Waris in the seventy-eighth minute.

In the eighty-fourth minute, the Egyptians scored from a defensive lapse on our part. In the eighty-eighth minute, Asamoah Gyan made dash with the ball after a quick pass from Harrison Afful. He found Kevin-Prince Boateng open in front of the post for him to get the ball into the net.

The final whistle followed shortly thereafter and we had beaten Egypt on a 7-3 goal aggregate. We had dominated Egypt convincingly and we were bound for Brazil for the 2014 World Cup!

Before and during the qualifiers, there were two main hurdles we had to contend with. The first of the hurdles was the commitment to doing the right thing, and the second was the need for us all to respect and encourage the abilities of made-in-Ghana coaching talents. Players, FA officials, and members of the general public all contributed to these problems we had to deal with.

The commitment to doing the right thing had to do with many different topics, including player commitment to the national team, player discipline, and leaders being transparent with the players. If each of our individual actions could pass the "Is that the right thing?" test, we would all be much better off as a national team and as a nation.

There were players who, at various points in time, retired from international duty for various reasons. Specifically, Michael Essien, Andre Ayew, Jordan Ayew, and Kevin-Prince Boateng, who were important members of the team, who made themselves unavailable at key moments in the journey. Each of these players were entitled to their decisions, and I gave each player the benefit of the doubt and carried on without them.

With the national team being bigger than any one person, we needed to be able to carry on with the players that were available at any given time. So, we did. However, the reasons some of our players gave to absent themselves from the team raised questions about how reliable these big-name players could be to the future of the team.

It's always been my vision to have at least two solid players for each position so that if a player could not be available for whatever reason, we would not be handicapped severely. For our World Cup qualifiers, we would have failed if we sat around waiting on some of our big-name players to finish working through the issues that made them decide to make themselves unavailable.

Andre had failed to show up in camp ahead of one of our AFCON preparations. When I called to check on him, he explained that he was unable to leave his base because he was getting treatment for an injury. I gave him an extension and asked that he should come for the Ghanaian medical staff to continue his treatment. He still did not show up. We moved on with our preparations without him.

Eventually, I maintained the team that had been available for the qualifier and did not include Andre in the AFCON 2013 squad. As a result, Andre, and his brother Jordan who had also not made my list, decided to temporarily withdraw their services from the Black Stars. Personally, I have known Andre and Jordan since they were infants, and we've always had a very good relationship.

Professionally, I have great admiration for their individual talents and what Andre and Jordan bring to the team. However, it was important that I applied the same standard of expectation to every player on the team. Eventually, we were able to talk it out and for both of them to make themselves available for subsequent call-ups.

Kevin-Prince Boateng cited the toll that the physical demands of playing for both club and country at high levels was taking on his health as his reason for retiring from the national team. He also complained about the conditions of pitches in Africa and how those were not conducive for him. While his reasons did not sit well with me, and with many people in the country, there was nothing much I could do about that situation other than to proceed with the players who were available and ready to play.

For Michael Essien, he took a break from international football to concentrate on his club career stating that he needed time to settle in fully at Real Madrid where he had moved to from Chelsea on loan. As I said in an interview with BBC then, I understood him for making a decision he felt was best for his career. It was unfair that some people in the media and in the general public referred to his decision as disloyal and unpatriotic. I believed he still had a lot to offer to the national team and I was ready to welcome him whenever he was ready and in form to be considered for call-up.

One benefit that came out of the unavailability of four key players was that some younger players had the opportunity to step up onto the big stage. They proved that they could play at a high level when given the chance. They did well when called upon to do so, which earned several of them call-ups to the World Cup squad.

The second hurdle had to do with our Ghanaian officials, the media and the general public who needed to respect and encourage the abilities of made-in-Ghana coaching talents. That manifested itself in various ways. Sometimes it was through the direct and indirect comments of GFA officials who publicly questioned my competence or those who blatantly showed their preference for a foreign coach. Other times, it was through the harsh and uninformed criticisms many people offered in the media.

When we lost a game 1-0 to Zambia in the group stage of our World Cup qualifiers, the GFA executive committee invited my technical team into a meeting about the future of the campaign. Many of the statements from several of the FA officials implied their doubt. One of the FA officials was very direct about his doubts and did not mince his words.

In a demeanour of a person who had his mind made up about his lack of confidence in me, the GFA official asked if I believed in myself that I could qualify the nation to the World

Cup. I told him that I believed we were going to qualify for the World Cup. I challenged him to turn around in his chair and mark my prediction on the wall behind him.

My record as the national team coach up until that point deserved more respect than I was accorded. Some people simply chose to ignore the facts or chose to perpetuate their own bias towards foreign coaches for the Black Stars no matter what the facts said. I let my work speak for itself.

It was years later that someone brought to my attention an analysis by Ghanaian journalist Fiifi Anaman, which showed how my coaching record stacked up against my predecessors ahead of our final match with Egypt. Below is an updated version of that analysis.

	Claude Le Roy (2006-2008)	Milovan Rajevac (2008-2010)	Goran Stevanovic (2011-2012)	Kwasi Appiah (2012-2014)
Games Coached	10	28	14	28
Games Won	6	12	7	15
Goals Scored	13	33	19	61
Goals Conceded	9	29	11	30
Winning %	60%	43%	50%	54%

While the analysis is by no means to questioned the accomplishments of my predecessors, it provided a fact-based comparison that should have informed my doubters' opinions.

In a place like Ghana, where people on radio and TV believe they know as much or more than the coach about what decision is best for the national team, you cannot take things personally when people criticise your decisions.

I certainly did not take the criticisms personally. I had a job to do and could not allow myself to be dragged into unnecessary debates. I welcomed feedback from my players, GFA officials, peers, as well as people in the media in getting ready for Brazil. As for the noise, I did my best to tune that out.

Grouped with Germany, Portugal and the USA, we knew we had an uphill task getting out of that group. Apart from the fact that our group was dubbed "The Group of Death" for how tough qualifying from the group stage was supposed to be, it was safe to assume that every team at the tournament came to win. So, even though the teams in our group were some of the best in the world, we knew the expectations on us were high regardless.

We lost our first match 2-1 to the USA, drew 2-2 with Germany in a thrilling game and lost 2-1 to Portugal, leading to our group-stage elimination. Several on-the-field and off-the-field issues contributed to what later became known to many as the Brazil Fiasco.

The consistency of lies told by our leaders regarding player bonuses, the resulting lack of motivation to focus on game preparations, and the disciplinary issues on the part of some of the players combined to overshadow what should have been a showcase of the Ghanaian brand to the world.

We returned to Accra, where the government set up a commission of inquiry that August to dig into what happened in Brazil. Several key witnesses were called to testify before the

Commission, and I gave my account of what I witnessed. The Commission's inquiry continued and I continued in my role.

We started our AFCON 2015 qualifiers with the cloud of the Brazil events still hanging above our heads. The Ghanaian public's dissatisfaction with the team was evident at the time, and the typical support that the team enjoyed from the fans had diminished significantly.

In September, we played against Uganda in Kumasi to a 1-1 draw. We went to Lome a few days later for a 3-2 win against Togo. It was unfortunate that the FA yielded to the public and political pressure to go in a different coaching direction. Reluctantly, I agreed to part ways with the team.

At the time of parting ways with the Black Stars, I had been in charge of 28 competitive matches, had won 15, drawn five and lost eight. I walked away holding my head high and knowing that I gave my best effort to the job. I had attained a respectable record as a Black Stars coach and had developed a talent pool that placed us in a good position for potentially winning the AFCON 2015.

As for the abundant opinions about my supposed loss of control of the dressing room and the supposed loss of respect from my players, those were and will remain opinions of the people who choose to hold those opinions. The findings of the Commission bear me out that those opinions were not informed by facts. The key fact is, I have high disciplinary expectations of my players and I will not accept habitual indiscipline from a player. If one bad apple will spoil the lot, I choose to remove the bad apple for the greater good of the team.

And on the subject of players refusing to train in Brazil, it was unfortunate that it came to that. Our players are professionals and expect to be respected. Promises made to them about their money should be paid as promised. Period. Typically, the coaching staff does not get involved in financial issues between the FA and the players. However, on more than one occasion, I had to convince my players to call off their threats not to train or to boycott the matches in Brazil. While I was unhappy with the training boycott ahead of the Portugal game, I could not in good conscience fault my players for their actions, given the many times the promises made by high-profile government officials had not been kept.

As I moved on from the Black Stars, I was optimistic about my future as a coach. I planned on taking the next few months to explore my options and rely on God to guide my next steps. In a few months following the end of my Black Stars tenure, I received a call from a representative of a Sudanese club. He said the team's executives were interested in engaging my services and invited me to come over for discussions. The representatives made the travel arrangements and sent over a ticket for me to travel to Khartoum.

The Sudan discussions were fruitful. Their intention was to rebuild their team that hadn't been very successful for a while due to their aging stars. I welcomed the challenge and signed on. The job with Al Khartoum Al Watani was going to pay me about twice what I was earning with the Black Stars. Even though the money was attractive, what drew me most to the team was the challenge and the receptive nature of our pre-contract discussions.

In my two years with the team that had consistently placed a distant fourth behind Sudan's powerhouse teams, we placed fourth twice in the Sudanese Premier League. What was different that time was how much Al Khartoum closed in on the top teams. We finished both season with a handful of points separating the top-four teams, and we replenished the team with young, fresh talents.

The team's profile had been elevated and they were in a very good position to be league title contenders for several years to come. As an example of how much the team had improved, nine of their players made it onto the Sudanese national team for the first time.

When I told them I was returning to coach the Black Stars, after the FA parted ways with Avram Grant, my Sudanese employers were saddened. They wanted me to stay and even take on their national team as well. I was honoured by their desire for my services but I viewed the Black Stars job as a national assignment that deserved my priority attention. I left Al Khartoum and became the coach of the Black Stars in April 2017.

Since becoming the Black Stars coach in 2017, I have led the team in playing AFCON 2019 qualifiers, World Cup 2018 qualifiers, and in AFCON 2019. In the latter two of the three circumstances, we did not experience as much success as I would have liked. The team had fared poorly in the World Cup qualifiers prior to my taking over and there wasn't much else left of the qualification opportunity.

With the AFCON 2019, we were confronted with the reality that many of the players we had relied on for years were not in their prime. Our lack of continuity in planning had caught up with us, and we needed to make the most of what we had to give ourselves the best chance at winning the tournament. So, I pulled together a team that blended experience and youth. About a third of the team were playing for the

Black Stars for the first time. We played well against our opponents and topped our group which comprised Benin, Cameroon and Guinea Bissau.

We suffered consequential on-field setbacks such as tournament-ending injuries to two of our key players, an unnecessary red card that had us play about half of a match with ten men, and our inability to fully execute our tactical plans.

We played Tunisia to a nail-biting 1-1 draw and lost on penalties. We were eliminated from the tournament. With the performance of the team, managing through major setbacks to top our group, and to be eliminated on penalties, I was satisfied with where the team was on our journey back to prominence on the African continent.

A basic desire of every football team's players, coaches, fans and administrators is to win important matches and trophies. That desire, when not fulfilled, could be the source of much frustration for all stakeholders. A coach, however, is often handed the ultimate responsibility for a team's success or failure. Fairly or unfairly, that is the reality, especially in high-level professional football. I take ultimate responsibility for outcomes, whether good or bad, and I am thankful for the opportunities I've had to lead the teams.

In my pursuit of coaching success, there are some things that I have total control over, there are some that I have some control over, and there are others that I have no control over.

One of the biggest lessons I have learned is to control the things I can, influence the factors that I have some control over, and not stress myself over things beyond my control. That principle has guided my approach to leading teams, and I hope it continues to serve me well for years to come.

With Coach Goran Stevanovic, who managed the Black Stars at the 2012 AFCON.

My brother Kwabena Appiah and I pose with coach Goran Stevanovic and his interpreter.

With Coach Milovan Rajevac.

With Coach Milo (right) and his interpreter during the playing of the national anthems at the 2010 World Cup in South Africa.

The Black Stars team visited President John Evans Atta-Mills (front row sixth from left) at the Castle after the 2010 African Cup of Nations in Angola. I'm third from right in the middle. Milo is sixth from left in front row.

Victorious Black Meteors squad at 2011 All African Games.

Victorious Black Meteors squad pose with then-Vice President John Dramani Mahama.

With 2011 All African Games trophy; Maxwell Konadu on the left and Sabaah Quaye on the right.

Appointed head coach of the Black Stars and charged with qualifying the team for Brazil 2014, I helped the team get ready for a World Cup qualifier.

At a Black Stars press conference (**L-R**): Asamoah Gyan, Dede Ayew, me, John Mensah and Sannie Daara.

At the end of the our final match in Egypt, my technical team carried me on their shoulders as part of the celebration of our qualification to the 2014 Brazil World Cup.

With former Black Stars players Eric Addo and Matthew Amoah who were visiting the team during a training session.

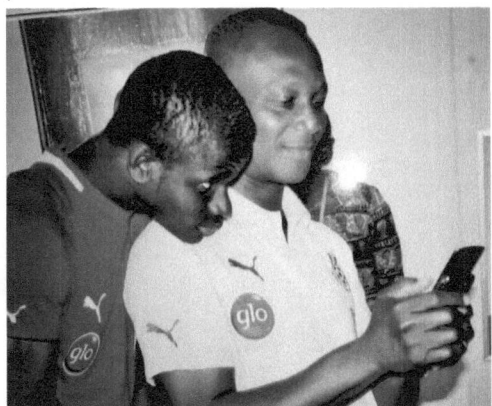

Top-left: With Jonathan Mensah; **Top-right:** With Kwadwo Asamoah; **Middle:** With Dede Ayew; **Below (L-R):** With Asamoah Gyan, Kwadwo Asamoah, Mubarak Wakaso, Michael Essien, Emmanuel Agyeman Badu, Daniel Opare, Jerry Akaminko.

Visiting Ghanaian players at Columbus Crew in the USA. **(L-R)**: Lalas Abubakar, Harisson Afful, me, Mohammed Abu, former Black Stars defender Joe Addo, and Jonathan Mensah

Fond memories from Sudan.

Receiving the Coach of the Year honour in Sudan.

Fond memories from my stay in Sudan. This was after my final game with Al Khartoum. My players celebrated with me after my final match with the team.

PART III: CHAMPIONS ALWAYS PLAY TO WIN

· CHAPTER 8 ·

BLACK STARS: LIBYA 1982

Within three years of completing secondary school and deciding to make football my profession, I was playing for the top club in the country and also on Ghana's senior national football team.

For both Kumasi Asante Kotoko and the Black Stars, I became the starting left-back. After qualifying for the Libya 1982 African Cup of Nations tournament, all the players returned to our respective clubs for a brief while. We were to be called back to camp when it was time to begin final preparations for the tournament.

During that break from the Black Stars camp, I played in a cup match for Kotoko against Accra Great Olympics in Kumasi. After jumping to head away a cross from the opposing team, I landed badly on one leg. Unfortunately, I suffered a fracture in that knee and had to leave the game. Following the injury, I started receiving medical treatment and looked forward to being fully fit for the Libya tournament.

When the Ghana team was leaving for Libya, my knee had not healed but the coaches decided to take me along. Under the care of the Black Stars doctors, we were all hoping that I was going to be in good playing shape before the tournament started. I was making progress with the treatment. I even started jogging and was on track to making a full recovery, and I was looking forward to playing in the tournament.

The Black Stars was one of eight nations to qualify for the tournament but we were unfortunately going to have to miss the tournament for political reasons. At the time, during the Limann administration, Libya was having issues with the international community and countries had been urged to boycott the tournament they were hosting. Dr. Hilla Limann had decided that the Black Stars would not participate in the tournament.

On December 31, 1981, President Limann was overthrown in a coup d'état by Flt. Lt. J.J. Rawlings. That was about three months to the start of the tournament. President Rawlings had a more positive view of Libya's president, Muamar Ghaddafi, and was not in favour of the boycott. He decided that Ghana was going to participate in the AFCON. So, we resumed camping and eventually left for Libya. Naturally, the players were grateful for the opportunity to play in the tournament, even though most of us were a little anxious about the political climate back home in Ghana.

It was winter when we arrived in Libya's capital, Tripoli, and it was very cold. The cold weather did not help my recovery. It rather worsened my pain.

The Ghanaian medical staff took me to a Libyan doctor to check on my knee, and discovered a patch of fluid in the knee. A day after the fluid was drained, another patch of fluid was discovered in the same spot. The fluid was drained again and I continued to receive treatment. Unfortunately, I had to be ruled out of the tournament because it was unlikely that I would recover fully in time to play in the tournament.

Unlike some of the participating countries' players who had been motivated with promises of money and other gifts, the motivation among the Black Stars players was purely out of national pride and the conviction that we were the best in Africa. That shared motivation created a strong unity among our players as we set out to win Ghana's fourth continental championship.

The 1982 team comprised Joseph Carr, Owusu Mensah, Haruna Yusif, Sampson Lamptey, John Baker, Kwame Sampson, Isaac Paha, Emmanuel Quarshie (captain), Albert Asaase, John Essien, Kofi Badu, George Alhassan, Opoku Nti, Seth Ampadu, Kofi Abbrey, Abedi Ayew Pele, Opoku Afriyie, Hesse Odamtten, Acquaye McClean, Ben Kayode, John Bannerman and me.

We played our first game against the host nation and drew 2-2, with Ghana's goals coming from George Alhassan and Opoku Nti. We drew goalless against Cameroon, and beat Tunisia 1-0 in a goal by John Essien. We qualified from our group behind Libya, and played Algeria in our semi-final match while Libya played Zambia in the other semi-final match.

Algeria was a very tough opponent. George Alhassan put us in the lead through an early goal but the Algerians equalized and took the lead halfway through the second half. We struggled to score until the ninetieth minute when Opoku Nti scored to bring the score to 2-2. The game went into extra time of play, at which time George Alhassan scored again to give us our ticket into the final with a 3-2 win.

President Rawlings sent a telegram to commend the team and encouraged us to strive to win the final match. The message, which was delivered by the then-sports minister Zaya Yeebo, also conveyed a promise that if we won the trophy, our children and their children would come to enjoy the reward that we were going to receive upon our return. The minister left for Accra before the final, supposedly to prepare our winning package.

That exciting promise from the President of the nation set our imaginations running wild. Was the President promising us cars? Would we be receiving a huge amount of money? Maybe houses? We didn't know, and we couldn't ask.

With the uncertain times of a new military government, it was common practice that civilians didn't ask too many questions of our political leaders. It was unclear what we could receive but it was still exciting to think about what the nation would give us in appreciation of our efforts if we won the cup.

Meanwhile Libya, had beaten Zambia 2-1 in their semi-final match, and were as poised as we were to win the trophy. They were playing in front of their home crowd and their national pride was at stake.

Libya was an oil-rich nation at the time, and each of their players had been promised a winning bonus of $50,000, a house and a BMW. That was $50,000 in 1982, a lot of money, in addition to a house and a car!

We found out about the promises that had been made to the Libyan players through Opoku Afriyie. He was friendly with some of the Libyan players and had been having conversations with them. Even though Opoku Afriyie was not the star of the team, he was very influential especially in the dressing room. He was very good at finding out information that was limited to very few people. And when he found out information that was useful to the team, he often passed that on to the players or sometimes confront the people in charge of the team.

It was also Opoku Afriyie who found out that every player at the tournament had been given a bag containing slippers, sneakers or trainers, towels and other items. The Black Stars players had not received any such bags. Upon seeing other players at the tournament carrying similar bags, Opoku Afriyie started asking them how they all happened to be carrying matching bags. He found out that the Black Stars had been given bags too but someone in the Ghanaian delegation had "forgotten" to give them to us. Thanks to Opoku Afriyie, we too received our bags.

He also found out that the tournament organisers had given each player an amount of money for participation. We eventually received the money, which might not have been given to us if Opoku Afriyie had not found out and raised the question.

We were in the final with the Libyans whose government had put so much money into their preparation and promised then an enviable winning package. The money for our team's preparation was mobilized through private donations and from gate proceeds of special tournaments played among our local league teams because Ghana's participation in the tournament had been a last-minute decision. Even though we knew the Ghana government's resources were unlike those of the Libyans, we were confident that the government would honour us if we made history by winning the trophy.

In that final match, we scored first through George Alhassan in the first half. The Libyans equalized midway through the second half. Even with extra time, the game ended in a draw. The winner had to be decided on penalties.

Our goalkeeper Owusu Mensah made two crucial saves during the penalty shoot-out to give us a 7-6 win. We were champions of Africa!

At the Kotoka International Airport, we arrived to a cheering crowd of fans. Our team captain, Emmanuel Quarshie, held the trophy and we followed him joyfully like conquerors arriving home from war. From the airport, we were escorted to the Gondar Barracks to meet with Flt. Lt. Rawlings.

He praised us for making Ghana proud and admitted that he didn't know much about football. His passions were carpentry and boxing but he had followed our participation in the tournament, and he was proud of what we had accomplished. He added that the nation was going through difficult times and there was not much that could be given to us in terms of monetary reward. However, he offered us a salute in appreciation of our accomplishment.

While the President's salute was appreciated, it was disappointing to learn that the thing that was promised, which our children and their children would enjoy, was a salute from the President. The disappointment among the players was obvious but no one dared to question President Rawlings. We were living in politically uncertain times and almost everyone was scared to get on the wrong side of the people in power. We left the barracks and returned to our regular lives. Later on, we were given half pieces of cloth each from Akosombo Textiles. That was it.

The 1982 squad was not the only history-making team that had not been honoured in a way that was befitting of the accomplishments they achieved for Ghana. The 1978 team, for example, did not receive the estate houses that were promised to them. President Kutu Acheampong, who made the promise, was overthrown before he could fulfil the promise. The government that took over from him had other priorities that did not include the promise President Acheampong had made.

Years later, a popular belief emerged among Ghanaians that the Black Stars' inability to win another trophy since 1982 was the result of a curse that had befallen the nation because of how poorly the previous continental champions had been treated.

It was in 2014 that the John Mahama administration allocated 1.7 million Ghana cedis (approximately $750,000) to be shared among the 71 living members of the 1963, 1965, 1978 and 1982 African Cup of Nations championship squads. Even though the gesture was too late for some the players who had passed away, it certainly was the right thing to do. It was important to honour the players with the money because some, especially the much older players who did not make any meaningful amounts of money during their playing days, were not in good financial situations. Furthermore, it was not befitting of us as a football-loving country to watch our national heroes die in poverty.

My participation in that AFCON tournament, even though I could not play, was an important moment in my career. Getting to represent Ghana internationally was always a moment to cherish. Getting to experience how the senior players prepared for big matches and how the players relied on each other for moral support was a very helpful learning experience.

When I became the coach of the Black Stars more than 30 years later, I was determined to lead the team to a similar glorious moment by winning another AFCON for Ghana. It was my long-term game plan to build a team for AFCON 2013, keep that team together for Brazil 2014, and then take that team to AFCON 2015, by which time I expected the team to be at their best. Even though I was not around to lead them to the 2015 AFCON, that team did very well but unfortunately lost in the final on penalties.

Fortunately for us in Libya in 1982, things turned out as we had worked so hard for. We were a capable and determined side, and we defied all the odds to carry the trophy home. We had a lot to be proud of as a team and as individuals. For some of us, our careers had just begun and winning that tournament was a major confidence booster. With many of the players being Kotoko players, most of us channeled that same championship mentality into our club matches.

The year 1982 was an uncertain year for Ghana politically. However, it was a shining moment in terms of football. It was a moment that almost did not happen. I am grateful that things worked out for us to participate. I am also honoured that my colleagues and I made the nation proud.

· CHAPTER 9 ·

KUMASI ASANTE KOTOKO: 1983 AFRICA CHAMPIONSHIP

The African Cup of Champion Clubs is what evolved into the CAF Champions League. It is organised by CAF, Africa's football governing body. In the 1980s, it was simply known as the African Cup. It featured African teams who won their local Premier Leagues the previous year. The teams played in a series of home and away matches, with the winners in each round qualifying to play in the next round until a winner emerged.

Kumasi Asante Kotoko had won the championship in 1971 and we came close to winning it in 1982 but lost to Egyptian side El Ahly. That 1982 finals loss, where we lost 3-0 in Cairo and drew 1-1 in Kumasi, was a major disappointment. Our 1983 campaign, therefore, was more like coming back to take care of unfinished business.

By the start of the 1983 African Cup, three of our best players were no longer with the team. Kofi Badu, Albert Asaase and Opoku Afriyie had left. Francis Kumi had left the team in the middle of the 1982 campaign. We replaced the departed players with a group of young, talented players from around the country. The core of the team had been together for about three previous years, and the new players quickly integrated into the team.

As a cohesive unit, we found our stride and continued to dominate in the Ghanaian league as well as in our continental championship matches.

Ibrahim Sunday was the coach, having taken over from Coach Adabie. Malik Jabir was the team manager. The squad comprised Joe Carr, Ernest Appau, Seth Ampadu, Yahya Kassum, Addae Kyenkyenhene, John Bannerman, Papa Arko, Ebo Mends, Opoku Nti, Isaac Afranie, Francis Agyemang, Ahmed Rockson, Abdul Karim Zito, Akwetey Quaye (Joe Tex), Akye Erzuah, "Old" Gyabaah, Kwame Sampson, Sulley, and me.

After we lost our captain Opoku Afriyie, the players voted overwhelmingly to select Papa Arko as the next captain, and Opoku Nti became the vice-captain. Papa Arko had a leadership style that brought the players closer together, and that was an important ingredient in combining a group of seasoned players and young players to play against some of the best teams across the continent. With our leading striker now gone, Ebo Mends stepped up to play at the Number 9 position.

Adversity can bring people closer together when they have a clear focus. Even though losing the key players was a big blow, the reconstituted team had a hunger for winning. Winning the African Cup that year became our singular focus. With that, the unity in the team grew stronger and we became a more closely-knit team.

The management of the team was a group of competent and dedicated people who did everything they could to motivate us to win. Yaw Bawuah was the chairman at the time and he formed a committee that was in charge of the team's general administration. They made sure the players had everything they needed in order to win matches. Antwi Gyamfi, who was a key part of that committee, was a really good administrator. Bawuah also had Charles Allen Gyimah as one of the team's main financiers. All these guys were serious people. When they made promises to players, they honoured the promises and the players liked that. Without a doubt, there was a very high level of mutual respect between the players and the team's management.

Businessman Assad Mallah was one of Kotoko's staunch supporters and financiers at the time. Businessman Simone David, a timber merchant in Kumasi, was another huge Kotoko supporter. Those individuals and others like them were very helpful in addressing financial needs of many players.

There were other people who contributed to the team's success in various other ways. For example, A.O. Lawson, who was an old-time national athlete and who was known for organizing keep-fit trainings for the public at the Kumasi Sports Stadium, was the team's physical trainer. He was influential in getting us to take good care of our physical condition through a consistent habit of eating healthy meals and resting after our morning physical training sessions.

We played most of our matches on Sundays and were off on Mondays. And then beginning on Tuesdays, our weekly routine involved physical training sessions in the mornings and on-field activities in the afternoons. We sometimes trained at Aheneboboano Park at the Kumasi Officers' Mess Park, and at other times at the Kumasi Sports Stadium. Because we were playing in both the Premier League and the African Club Championship, our season was as busy as it had been the year before. We played several matches and travelled extensively.

We started our 1983 African Cup Championship against FC 105 from Gabon. That was one of the toughest opponents we played against. I remember they had some Ghanaian players on their team, including George Alhassan. Apart from they being a very good team, the Ghanaian players on their team were very familiar with the strengths and weaknesses of many of the Kotoko players. As a result, we had to work extra hard to overcome them. We won 2-1 in the first leg and won 2-0 in the second leg to qualify to the next round on a 4-1 goal aggregate.

In the second round, we played Congolese team CARA Brazzaville, lost 3-2 in the first leg and won 2-0 against them during the second leg to qualify for the quarter-finals. AS Bilima was from the Democratic Republic of Congo. We beat them 3-0 in the first leg and lost the second leg 2-0. AS Bilima was a really tough opponent but we overcame them.

In the semi-finals, it became likely that we could play El Ahly if we made it to the finals. While we were playing against Senegalese team ASC Diaraf, El Ahly was playing in the other semi-final game against Zambian side Nkana FC. After losing 2-1 to ASC Diaraf on their home grounds, we beat them 2-0 in Kumasi to make it to the final. El Ahly won their semi-final match and the stage was now set for a rematch of the 1982 finals.

In the 1980s, it was common for a prominent Kotoko supporter or management team member to bring in someone who they believed could help give the team an edge through their spiritual ability. Even though the entire team may not believe in such spiritual gurus, the polite thing to do as a member of a prominent team like Kotoko was to comply with the spiritual guru's directions but then focus on what we had practiced in training when we got on the field.

Football is a game of skill and psychology. At a very high level of play, almost every player is very skilled so it is the best execution of tactics that wins the game. The psychological aspect can significantly affect how a player or a team executes the game plan. That psychological aspect has to do with players' emotional state and also the things that the individual believes in.

In Ghanaian and African football, many people believe in spiritual influences. Sometimes, the spiritual influences are given more prominence than is necessary. While some pray by themselves, it is a common practice for the team to pray together. Apart from that being a spiritual exercise, it helps the players bond and unite around a common purpose.

In addition to that, some people consult pastors and spiritual guides who pray with them. Some wear their lucky socks. Some wear special amulets. Others do specific things in hopes of getting an edge over their opponent.

While it is debatable that any of these rituals can bring the individual or the team the desired results, it will be presumptuous of me to dismiss these activities as ineffective. At the minimum, it has a psychological impact on some players, whether for good or for bad.

Ahead of the 1982 finals, one of Kotoko's influential supporters brought a spiritual guru from the northern part of Ghana to help us win the final. That old man gave the team a dove to take with us to Cairo, and to let it out at the airport. He said the bird was going to fly back to him in Ghana, and that event was going to provide the spiritual momentum that would propel us to victory.

During the flight, "Old" Gyabaah held the bird. He released it onto the tarmac when we arrived in Cairo. With the cold weather and the gust of wind at the airport, the bird refused to fly. Several attempts to get the bird to take flight were unsuccessful. I am not sure about what happened to the dove afterward but I am certain it did not fly from Egypt to Ghana.

That was a lesson we learned in 1982 and brought with us into 1983 – to focus on overcoming the on-field tactics of our opponents and not to count on supernatural forces to win the match for us. Today, we can look back and laugh at that story but it has a lesson that is relevant to players and teams currently playing the game. There is no amount of prayer or spiritual influence that can help a player or team win if they are not tactically prepared and tactically disciplined.

Going into the first leg of the 1983 final in Cairo, there were spiritual gurus brought in, once again, to help us win. Out of respect for these spiritual gurus and the people who introduced them to the team, we received the help they were offering but discarded their help shortly after they had left. A section of the players had always been skeptical about such spiritual help, especially being that we had won many games up until then without any such spiritual help. The players who believed in things like that did their own things privately.

When we arrived in Egypt, our focus was squarely on our opponents. We arrived there on a Tuesday and decided to stay at the Ghana Embassy in Cairo instead of at the hotel the Egyptians had arranged for us. We chose to stay at the embassy because home teams in that era had the tendency of creating unfavourable situations for the visiting team as a way of getting an upper hand. There had been instances where some fans had been reported to have gone to the visiting team's hotel to intimidate them.

There was too much at stake and we did not want to leave anything to chance. At the Ghana Embassy, some of the players slept in the available bedrooms and the rest of us slept on mattresses laid on the floor in the hallway. We felt more comfortable in the Ghana Embassy than we expected to feel in an Egyptian hotel. At the embassy, we were also catered for with Ghanaian meals prepared by people we felt comfortable around. We took as much precaution as we could, and spent most of our time within the embassy compound.

Every morning, after training, we spent hours watching video tapes of El Ahly's previous games to study their strengths and prepare accordingly for them. El Ahly had a star player who was new on their 1983 squad, and he posed a bigger threat than what we were confronted with in 1982. Because of what we saw El Ahly do to their opponents, we had to make a change in our lineup. Akwetey Quaye (Joe Tex) was one of our main starting midfielders. Our coach opted to go with Yahya Kassum instead so that we could stop El Ahly's danger man early in the game. Even though Joe Tex lost his spot in the starting lineup for that game, he understood that change was in the best interest of the team. Yahya Kassum had a reputation for tough physical play and that was needed to intimidate El Ahly's star player.

We also remembered some of the tactics they used against us in 1982 – their quick restart of the game when there were free kicks or throw-ins, as well as counter attacks – and we prepared for that. In Cairo, we held them to a goalless draw.

We had two weeks to prepare for the second leg in Kumasi. Upon our return from Egypt, we did not want to lose the momentum and the focus the team had developed. The team camped together at a house near the Bekwai roundabout. That house was owned by City Foods Supplies. It was a dormitory-styled living space with the players sleeping on bunk beds, frequently talking to each other about football-related matters.

When we were not training or doing a team activity, the players would be in their beds sleeping or sitting round listening to music. The idea was to minimise distractions and also maintain the sense of togetherness needed for the players to operate as a unified team. Even on the nights that we went out to the movies, we went together and returned as a team.

Soon enough, the two weeks had passed and it was time for the second leg. It was December 11, 1983. By 10 o'clock in the morning of that Sunday, the stadium was full for a game that was scheduled to start around 3 o'clock in the afternoon. That early and massive attendance was not surprising for a crucial Kotoko match.

That match against El Ahly held a special significance for Kotoko fans, and there was an overwhelming optimism about we winning that second leg. I could almost feel that positive energy which filled the 50,000-seat stadium.

Our starting line-up comprised Joe Carr, Ernest Apau, me, Seth Ampadu, Addae Kyenkyenhene, Albert Asaase, John Bannerman, Papa Arko (Captain), Ebo Mends, Opoku Nti, and Isaac Afranie.

We had purposed in our hearts and minds not to lose the final, especially to the same team we lost to the previous year. As my team's left-back, I was extremely determined to stop one of El Ahly's top players who played on the right wing. Our whole team was consumed by determination and a willingness to leave everything on the field that day. And, of course, the fans remained loud with cheers for us.

We started the game determined to get a goal early and to maintain the momentum of being the home team. Several minutes into the match, we made a mistake in defence that almost cost us a goal when a back pass to Joe Carr unfortunately went to one of the El Ahly attackers. Fortunately, Carr was able to shut the Egyptian down before the ball could find its way into the back of our net.

We regrouped and pressed for a goal. Around the 20th minute, Opoku Nti scored through a pass from John Bannerman. Confidently, we pressed on to extend the lead. We knew that teams from North Africa had a tendency of using delay tactics and dirty tricks to cause surprises. If we unfortunately conceded a goal, they were definitely going to use delay tactics to waste time because a 1-1 draw on our home soil was advantageous to them. Therefore, we were leaving nothing to chance. We made sure to prevent El Ahly from scoring while at the same time pressed for another goal.

The Egyptians, on the other hand, were unrelenting as they tried to equalize. In the late stages of the game, they mounted serious pressure on us. As a result of their aggressive attempts to score, we conceded seven corner kicks back to back. We felt the immense pressure but we remained focused. None of their chances turned into a goal.

After ninety minutes, the score remained at 1-0. At the referee's whistle, we had defeated El Ahly and we were champions of Africa.

I was extremely excited. I joined my teammates as we jumped around and celebrated on the field. Winning that final game and the trophy was one of the best things that happened to me as a player. The team's name was forever written in the history books as continental champions. The honour we brought to the team, the city and the country was a big deal. That victory elevated the already-high profile of many of our players. Opoku Nti, for example, came in second in that year's CAF vote for African Footballer of the Year.

A parade was held in Kumasi in our honour where we showed the trophy to our supporters while celebrating the accomplishment as a community. Thousands of people lined the streets of Kumasi and cheered as we came by on a bus and waved at them through the windows. The excitement in the city was at an all-time high with some men and women dancing in the streets. Some women even spread their cloth in the streets for the bus to ride on – a classic Ghanaian version of a red-carpet welcome. The parade wrapped up at the Manhyia Palace where we presented the trophy to Otumfour Opoku Ware I, the Asantehene and the team's owner.

In 1983, Ghana went through one of the most difficult periods in the country's history. With a severe dry season and rampant bush fires, there was a drastic shortage of food grown in Ghana. There was a shortage of petrol, and there was a shortage of imported goods. People had to queue in long lines for almost anything because of the shortage. To even get something as basic as a ball of *kenkey*, people had to queue for hours to get an uncooked one.

Before then, there had been several years of political turmoil and corruption, and the military government of the PNDC was strong-handedly trying to turn the country around. It wasn't an easy time in Ghana. Furthermore, several Ghanaians had been forced out of Nigeria back to Ghana, adding to the already-tense situation.

Our victory was a welcome relief for many in the country. That victory gave many people something more cheerful to talk about and forget our national economic challenges for a while. And even though those were times of shortages and scarcity, the Kotoko supporters and the management made sure we didn't lack most things we needed.

One of the good things about being a Kotoko player in Kumasi, especially after we won the trophy, was the fans' generosity and how readily they showed their appreciation to us. I rode in taxis and the drivers refused to accept the payment from me. I went into shops to buy things and the sellers either let me have the items for free or gave me extra for free – simply because I was a Kotoko player and they wanted to show their appreciation.

As part of the honours we received, a leading Ghanaian musician, Pat Thomas, recorded a hit song for us. That 15-minute song called "Asante Kotoko" became a big hit on radio and is still popular among many music fans. It celebrated Kotoko's leaders and key supporters at that time, the players who won the championship, as well as the legendary players who brought glory to the team in previous years. Upon hearing the song, I realised my name and those of a few other players were not mentioned. Even though that was a glaring miss, I did not take it personally. Before I could bring that up to Pat Thomas, who I was very friendly with at the time, he acknowledged the miss. I told him not to worry about it.

Throughout my years in Kotoko, we strived to win another African Cup. We came close to winning on at least one occasion. That was in 1993. I started the season with the team but retired before they made their way to the finals that year. After they played goalless draw games in the first and second legs of that final, Kotoko lost 6-7 on penalties to Egyptian side Zamalek.

That would have been Kotoko's third title, a sweet victory that would have been on the tenth anniversary of our 1983 win. Unfortunately, things didn't turn out the way we all wanted.

In my young career at that time, I had been a part of teams that had won important continental championships within a short period of time. Realizing how good it felt to win, I was hungry for more.

· CHAPTER 10 ·

BLACK STARS: SENEGAL 1992

Going into the 1992 African Cup of Nations tournament in Senegal, the Ghana Black Stars was one of the favourite teams to win the cup. We had some of the best players and we were eager to bring home the trophy.

It had been ten years since we last won the trophy, and the years following that 1982 victory had been rough. We were at the tournament in 1984 but did not make it past the group stage. We did not qualify for the 1986, 1988, and 1990 tournaments.

The early 1990s saw a resurgence of the Ghana Black Stars. Abedi Pele was in his prime playing for French team Marseille, and was one of the best in the world. Anthony Yeboah was playing at a very high level in the German Bundesliga. Other Ghanaian international players like Opoku Nti, Tony Baffoe, Prince Opoku Polley, Stanley Aborah, Ali Ibrahim and Richard Naawu were playing in Europe and were playing very well.

The local players, mainly from Kumasi Asante Kotoko and Accra Hearts of Oak, were playing very competitive and exciting football. Players like Emmanuel Armah "Senegal," Frimpong Manso, Emmanuel Ampeah, Kofi Abbrey, Edward Ansah, Abukari Damba, and Nii Darku Ankrah from the local league were members of the team.

As the team's captain, I was very optimistic about our ability to qualify and then win the cup. German Burkhard Ziese was our coach and he had been in charge since 1990. To qualify for the tournament in Senegal, we started off with a 1-0 win over a very strong Nigerian side. We then beat Togo 1-0, beat Burkina Faso 2-0, and routed Benin 4-0.

For the second leg matches, we played Nigeria to a goalless draw, lost 2-1 to Burkina Faso and played Benin to a goalless draw. In July 1991, we qualified at the top of our qualification group, along with Nigeria, to join 10 other teams at the tournament.

In August of that year, Ghana's Under-17 team had won the FIFA Under-17 World Cup. There was a lot of excitement in the country. The coach of the Under-17 team, German Otto Pfister, was appointed the coach of the Black Stars to take the team to the African Cup. Burkhard Ziese was a very good coach who had successfully qualified the team to the tournament. He had the competence to lead the team to win the tournament. However, he was replaced before we would go for the tournament. I was surprised by that change. However, with the way the GFA administration at the time handled their affairs, I was not completely surprised.

Burkhard Ziese was the type of coach who vehemently resisted GFA officials interfering with how he did his job. That stance did not make him a favourite of the GFA officials and their relationship with him was not a smooth one. Otto Pfister, on the other hand, had become the darling of Ghanaians after winning the Under-17 World Cup. Furthermore, there was an arrangement between the Ghanaian and German governments that made Otto Pfister available to Ghana for little-to-no cost. Replacing Burkhard Ziese with Otto Pfister, therefore, was an easy decision for the GFA.

Otto Pfister made some changes to the Black Stars team that qualified for the tournament. He brought on Nii Odartey Lamptey, Mohammed Gargo, Yaw Preko and Isaac Asare, all key members of the Under-17 championship team. Given the excitement in the country at the time and the caliber of players we had on the team, Ghanaians had very high expectations of the Black Stars winning the trophy that year. We, the team, had high expectations too because we were a very solid squad.

After one of our training sessions during our pre-tournament camping in Accra, some members of the GFA management team and the coach called me into a meeting. They informed me that since the tournament was going to be in a French-speaking country, and I did not speak or understand French, it was better that a player who understood French captained the team. As such, they had decided to make Abedi Pele the captain of the team so that he could speak on behalf of the team.

The reasons the GFA officials gave for their decision left me questioning their real motive for making the change. Making Abedi the captain of the team was never an issue for me because I knew I was not going to be captain forever. Abedi was one of the senior players on the team at the time and I believed he could do the job. So, if the GFA leaders had been direct about their reason, it may have been less of a scandal than it turned out to be.

The French-speaking reason they gave was laughable to many people because it meant we were going to need an Arabic-speaking captain when we played a tournament in an Arab country, a Spanish-speaking captain when we played a tournament in Spain, an Italian-speaking captain when we played a tournament in Italy, and so on and so forth. Meanwhile, in the previous four years with me as the captain, we successfully played in French-speaking countries and I competently interacted with referees and officials who were not native English-speakers.

Not surprising, many Ghanaian fans and media people were upset by the reason given for the captaincy change. On the team as well, the reason they gave created a rift between the players. That controversy could have been avoided with a little bit more transparency.

As had been the norm with captaincy changes on the national team, a team captain is made the general captain if he is still an active member of the team when the coach decides to appoint another player as the substantive captain.

The substantive captain is the leader of the playing body responsible for encouraging his colleagues at all times, and also for advocacy on the players' behalf before, during and after matches.

The substantive captain also serves as an extension of the coach by reinforcing the coach's instructions during the match. During a match, the players look up to the substantive captain to lead any interaction with the referee and other officials in case of a misunderstanding.

The general captain role is that of a patron who uses his leadership experience to help the team be successful. Having performed the team captain's role in the past, the general captain is often a valuable resource the substantive captain and the coach can count on.

On the eve of Senegal '92, the leaders of our national team could have simply moved me into the general captain role and make Abedi the substantive captain, and then leave it at that. Even though the way they handled it was not the best, I did not dwell on the issue. Others did.

We arrived in Senegal in January 1992 and we were based in Ziguinchor, the country's second largest city. We were grouped with Egypt and Zambia. The other teams in the tournament were based in the capital, Dakar.

At that time, it was clear the team was not united. That was partly due to the manner in which the captaincy change had been handled by the GFA. Most of the senior players had expressed their dissatisfaction among the players so it was common knowledge that some of my colleagues were still upset.

During our free time following team activities, most of the senior players gathered and did activities together while the rest of the team were floating around not really concerned about the main group. Sometimes, after dinner, we sat outside having group conversations. The was often a larger group, which comprised senior players and some of the Starlets players.

The gathering usually started with a few people sitting around chatting, and then others joining from time to time.

It wasn't a case of Abedi leading one faction and I leading another. As the conversations went on, some of the players would vent their frustrations.

It became very obvious that some of my colleagues had not been happy with some decisions the GFA had taken in the past, and the captaincy issue added to their frustration.

Realizing that the division was not going to help the team, I suggested to Abedi that one way to bring the team together would be to meet every evening for a prayer session, after which he would speak to the players and then I would also speak to the players. So, we started those evening sessions in my room.

Abedi's message and my message to the team was that we were at the tournament to represent the nation, and that we needed to put all other issues behind us and concentrate on the important mission at hand. Gradually, the disunity among the players started disappearing and that reflected in the improved performance of the team as the tournament progressed.

We won our first game 1-0 against Zambia through a goal by Abedi Pele, and then won our second game 1-0 against Egypt through a goal by Anthony Yeboah. We qualified to the quarter-finals where we beat Congo 2-1.

I played in all our games until halfway into the semi-final match against Nigeria. I pulled a muscle and could not continue playing. Isaac Asare replaced me and the team finished that game with a 2-1 victory. We were going to face Ivory Coast in the final.

Abedi Pele, who was having a great tournament, received his second yellow card during the semi-final match. That second yellow card automatically disqualified him from playing in the final game. Sarfo Gyamfi, who was on the field at the time of the incident that led to the yellow card, told a story of how it came about.

He said Abedi approached the referee to complain about a foul play on Stanley Aborah. Unhappy with the referee's reaction to his complaint, Abedi angrily said something under his breath as he walked away. The referee, unhappy with Abedi's conduct, showed him that yellow card. It was unfortunate that he got a yellow card for stepping up in defence of his colleague. Abedi's absence from the final game was a major blow to our team and we had to adjust our game plan quickly.

It was the norm that another senior player would captain the team with substantive captain due to miss the match. Anthony Yeboah was next in line as far as seniority went, and he was the obvious choice in most players' minds. On the day of the match, Anthony Baffoe was announced as the captain to the shock of almost everyone on the team.

Apart from the traditional role a captain plays, being appointed a captain is often a recognition of a player's immense contribution to the team. It's also a public acknowledgement of that the player's remarkable value to the team.

At that time, Tony Baffoe had played about four or five matches for the national team. Since he had not been around the national team long enough to take over as captain, many of us were shocked by his appointment.

Abedi shared a room at the tournament with Anthony Baffoe, and that fed into the speculation among the players that Abedi had convinced the coach to appoint Anthony Baffoe instead of Anthony Yeboah as the captain.

Yeboah was often very calm and rarely showed it when he was upset. When he was leaving that pre-match meeting room, it was clear that he had been angered by the situation. We had a big match ahead of us and that was our chance to win the African Cup for Ghana. That chance was being threatened by a management decision that upset many of the players.

Opoku Nti and I followed Yeboah to his room to attempt to calm him down. Opoku Nti had been the team's captain before me and it was instinctive for him to join me to go and see Yeboah after we noticed Yeboah's demeanour following the captaincy announcement.

Yeboah was very candid about how upset he was and he was even considering boycotting the match. The three of us spoke at length, after which he resolved to play and to do what he could to help us win.

Even though most of the players seemed to have gotten over the issue of Yeboah being passed over for the captaincy, the atmosphere within the team was not the best. A cloud of disunity was hanging above the team when we moved to the field for the final match. That situation could have been avoided with a little more transparency and open communication with the senior players. There was too much at stake for which reason such a major decision needed to have been made and communicated more thoughtfully.

We played well against the Ivorians and came close to scoring a few times but could not score. The Ivorians were equally dangerous and they came close to scoring a few times as well. In the final minutes of the game, one of their players broke away in a counter attack and was in a one-on-one situation with our goalkeeper, Edward Ansah. The masterful goalkeeping by Ansah denied them a goal and the match ended in a 0-0 draw.

For a tournament as big as the African Cup, penalties seem like an inadequate way to choose a champion. But we had 120 minutes to decide a winner and we couldn't. So, we had to go into the penalty shoot-outs.

The Ivorian player went first and scored, and then Tony Baffoe scored. The next Ivorian scored and then Nii Odartey Lamptey scored. Another Ivorian scored their third penalty and then Richard Naawu scored. The pressure, which always accompanied penalty shoot-outs, was mounting. The Ivorian scored their fourth penalty and then Isaac Asare missed. The Ivorians missed their fifth penalty and then Anthony Yeboah scored. That brought the score to 4-4 and the shoot-out had to continue.

The pressure at that point was at an all-time high because if one team missed and the other scored, it was over. That was the "sudden death" rule. Even for those of us watching from the sideline, the pressure was intense. So, I could only imagine what it felt like for each of our players when it was their turn to take the kick. The Ivorian scored and then Frimpong Manso took his turn. He scored. Emmanuel Armah took his turn and scored. Stanley Aborah took his turn and he scored. Emmanuel Ampeah took his turn and he scored. Prince Opoku Polley took his turn and he scored. The goalkeepers took their turns against each other. The Ivorian goalkeeper scored and then Ansah scored.

For every player on the field to have taken a penalty kick and a winner still not decided, that had never happened in any tournament I know of. The score at the time was 10-10 and we had to start over. The "sudden death" rule was still in effect.

The Ivorian player scored and then Tony Baffoe missed. It was over. We had come so close but lost after a marathon penalty shoot-out. That was a painful loss. Everyone on the team looked extremely disappointed and the Ivorians celebrated while we sadly walked out of the stadium.

On our way back to our hotel, the mood inside our bus was a very mournful one. Everyone was quiet, supposedly reflecting on what could have been if we had won the final match and won the cup. Emmanuel Armah "Senegal" broke the silence with an angry rant toward Anthony Baffoe.

"When did you come to the national team, to pick up the captain's band? Do you think we wear the captain's band just like that? You played only a few matches and you want to be a captain. You see we've lost the match and the cup because you lost the penalty?"

That was Armah essentially blaming Anthony Baffoe's captaincy in the final match as the reason we could not win the cup. While I understood Armah's frustration, it was quite a stretch to blame one person for the outcome. Baffoe played a good game and even scored his first penalty. It was unfortunate that he missed the second time around.

According to Anthony Baffoe, the captaincy wasn't something he asked for but he welcomed it when it was offered. He thought he was being called on to lead the team at a critical moment and probably didn't realise how much his appointment as captain upset his colleagues.

Armah finished expressing his frustration and sat down. The mournful quietness resumed. The loss was painful.

Upon arriving at the hotel, we dispersed into our respective rooms and almost everyone stayed in their room for the rest of the evening.

We departed for Accra the following morning where we were received humbly by the officials who met us at the airport. There were supporters at the airport to receive us. Even though the supporters obviously would have loved for us to bring home the cup, they were still appreciative of the good fight we fought in Senegal.

The Black Stars had a great team in 1991 and in 1992. The Senegal tournament was the big stage for us to prove to everyone that we were the best on the continent.

We showcased our great talents and winning the cup would have been an excellent way to finish the tournament. We were just one successful penalty kick away from winning, but we unfortunately had to settle for a painful second place.

· CHAPTER 11 ·

BLACK STARS: SOUTH AFRICA 2010 WORLD CUP

Ghana qualified for the World Cup for the first time in 2006. That was after many years of trying and failing in spite of having good teams. The Black Stars team that finally qualified featured some of our all-time best players and they represented Ghana well at the tournament in Germany.

I was living in the U.K. at the time and I travelled to go and watch the matches in person. I visited the team and spent time with them at their camp. As determined as they were to make Ghana and Africa proud, it was no surprise that they did as well as they did at that tournament by qualifying to the knockout stage.

Four years later, we qualified for our second appearance at the World Cup. I was then the assistant coach working with Milovan (Milo) Rajevac. Several of our players were returning from the 2006 squad, and were in their prime. The team had been impressive through the qualification so expectations from fans were high. Furthermore, the tournament was taking place on the African continent – in South Africa – and that put the spotlight on African teams.

The qualifiers for the 2010 World Cup also served as qualifiers for the 2010 African Cup of Nations, and the qualifiers were played in three rounds. The top team in each of the five groups in the third round automatically qualified for the World Cup along with the host nation, South Africa. The top three teams in each of the five groups in the third round of the qualifiers participated in the African Cup held in Angola in January. The World Cup was in June.

The first round of the qualifiers was a series of knockout games among the ten lowest ranked teams on the continent. For the second round, the five first-round winners joined 43 countries, and the 48 teams were put in 12 group of four. The four teams played each other two times. At the end of all the matches, the top team from each of the 12 groups and the 8 highest-ranked among the runners-up advanced to the third round. For the third round, the teams were divided into five groups of four, with the winner of each group qualifying for the World Cup, and the top three teams from each group qualifying for the African Cup.

We started our campaign in the second round and were grouped with Gabon, Libya and Lesotho. For our six matches, we lost 2-0 to Gabon and won 2-0 against them; we won 3-2 against Lesotho and then won again 2-0; we won 3-0 against Libya and lost 1-0 to them. We had won four out of our six matches. So had Gabon and Libya. They had the same number of wins and losses as we had. All three nations were tied with 12 points. Goal difference became the tie-breaker. We had +6 goals, Gabon had +5 goals and Libya had +3 goals. So, we qualified as the group winners. Gabon also qualified for the next round because they were ranked high enough to be one of the eight runners-up.

For the third round, we were grouped with Benin, Mali and Sudan. We won 1-0 against Benin and then lost 1-0 to them; we won 2-0 against Mali and then drew 2-2 with them; we won 2-0 against Sudan and beat them again 2-0. With four wins, one draw and one loss, we topped our group three points ahead of the runner-up, Benin.

Representing Africa at the 2010 World Cup were Ghana, Cameroon, Nigeria, Ivory Coast, Algeria and South Africa. For any coach, the World Cup is a major moment in your career. And for my first time at such a major tournament to be on the African continent, that made the moment even more special. I knew we had very good players and that we were going to do well in the competition.

Several of our players had played in the previous World Cup, and their experience was going to matter very much to the team. That was football's biggest stage and we were there because we were as good as any other team in the world. Even the younger players who had never been to a tournament that huge were psychologically tuned to believe that they were as good as any player at the tournament. We all believed that our team was at the tournament to win. And we were going to win it one match at a time.

Almost everyone on the team understood the moment that was upon us. That awareness reflected in how seriously the players took our preparations. Some of the experienced players were motivated by the opportunity to make history with a solid performance. The younger players knew they would have bigger opportunities at the club level if they gave off their best at the tournament. I was motivated by the opportunity to help guide a talented group of guys to make history.

Milo's trust in me was very clear. He asked my opinion on issues and empowered me to make decisions. With that very cordial relationship, I was determined to do everything I could to support him in preparing the team for the biggest tournament that both of us were yet to experience.

With the language barrier that existed because of Milo speaking through an interpreter (who spoke only English), several of the players counted on me to explain his instructions to them.

Understandably, Twi, and not English, was the more comfortable communication medium for several of the players. During training sessions, I often clarified what Milo needed from them as well as gave them feedback on things they were doing well and things they needed to improve upon. Likewise, being able to communicate in Twi enabled some of the players to confidently explain their perspectives or ask follow-up questions when communicating with Milo.

Additionally, I visited the players in their respective rooms to check on them and to reinforce the coaching staff's confidence in their individual and collective ability to win at the tournament. Those one-on-one conversations with players were important because they were opportunities to be specific with each player about a compliment or correction that cannot be shared in the presence of the other players. They were also opportunities for the players to open up if they had any private concerns.

Before going to the World Cup, we played in the African Cup of Nations that January and made it to the finals but lost 1-0 to Egypt. On our way to that final, we beat Burkina Faso, Angola and Nigeria. That loss in the final match was a painful one as the lone goal came around the 85th minute, and we couldn't equalize before the referee blew his final whistle. We had to quickly put that tournament behind us and begin preparing for the World Cup.

About a month after the African Cup, the team was back together for the first of four international friendlies arranged to help us with our World Cup preparations. When selecting opponents for such friendlies, the coach would make the GFA know what types of teams he wanted the Black Stars to play against, and then the GFA would contract a match agent to arrange such matches.

Such series of friendly games often started with an opponent that is not very strong, and then we subsequently played against stronger teams. With that graduated approach, the players got the appropriate levels of competition to help them improve gradually and be at their peak performance by the time the competition came around.

In March, we played against Montenegro and lost 1-0. In May, we played against Bosnia-Herzegovina and lost 2-1. In early June, we lost 4-1 to Netherlands and won 1-0 against Latvia.

By the time we arrived in South Africa in June, we were feeling very confident about the team's ability and knew we could hold our own against any of the teams at the tournament. We had been grouped with Germany, Australia and Serbia, Milo's home country. That group was considered a

"Group of Death" because each of the teams had about the same chance of qualifying. We won 1-0 against Serbia, played a 1-1 draw with Australia and lost 1-0 to Germany. Germany topped our group and we had the same number of points as Australia. We had conceded fewer goals than Australia and had a better goal difference. So, we qualified to the Round of 16.

We played the USA to a 1-1 draw during the first 90 minutes. In extra time, we scored a second goal to win the match and qualified to the quarter-finals. That was the farthest an African team had ever reached in the tournament (Cameroon in 1990 and Senegal in 2002 reached the quarter-finals stage, too). We were one win away from getting to the semi-finals, and one more win to being in the final. We faced Uruguay, a star-studded and two-time World Cup winner.

We were on the verge of making history, and we played one of our best games ever. Just before half-time, Sulley Muntari scored for Ghana using his signature left-foot. He shot the ball from the middle of the Uruguayan half. Not long after we returned for the second half, Uruguay equalized. The 90 minutes of regular play came to an end with the score at 1-1.

We went into extra time and kept the same composure as we had in the first 90 minutes. We were determined to score but the Uruguayans were a force to reckon with. In the dying minutes of the game, however, Uruguayan player Luis Suarez stopped a header from Adiyiah with both of his hands. The ball was destined for the net, after it had almost gone past the last defender who was standing on the line. Suarez was in the air right next to the last defender and he punched the ball out like he was the goal keeper. Suarez was shown the red card and we were awarded a penalty.

Asamoah Gyan was the key focus of our team's attack, and was our best penalty taker. He had been at the 2006 World Cup and was instrumental in our qualification for the 2010 World Cup. His experience and confidence had been a delight to watch at the tournament. He stood behind the ball to win the game for us. Unfortunately, the powerful shot from Gyan hit the crossbar and went wide.

Gyan was our best penalty taker and he had scored many times. There was no reason to suggest another player had to take that penalty. As with every game, we went in having decided in the dressing room who would take penalties if such an opportunity came up during the game. Gyan was our man. I know many Ghanaians were upset with him but there is no doubt that he wanted to win that game just as much as anyone of us, if not more.

That moment of the penalty miss was a devastating one for all of us on the team. Gyan had been instrumental in getting the team to that point in the tournament and then missed a decisive penalty kick. Unfortunately, that was one of the events most people were going to remember him by anytime the story of the 2010 World Cup is told. The players, especially Stephen Appiah, were phenomenal in rallying around Gyan to help him keep his focus on the game.

A few minutes after the miss, the referee whistled for the end of the match. The penalty shoot-out was one more opportunity to make it to the next stages.

Gyan scored Ghana's first penalty after the Uruguayan scored. Stephen Appiah scored the second penalty after the

Uruguayan scored. John Mensah missed his penalty after the Uruguayan scored. Fortunately for us, the next Uruguayan missed. If we scored our next two and they missed one, we would be through to the next stage.

In taking a good penalty kick, a player's aim is to direct the ball in the opposite direction of where the goalkeeper is likely to dive. In the event that the goalkeeper correctly guesses the direction of the ball, the power behind the ball should be enough to still beat the goalkeeper. John Mensah's penalty was not one of the best I have seen from him, and it was easily saved by the Uruguayan goalkeeper. Mensah kicked the ball from only two steps away from the ball. It was a low ball and it lacked power.

The Uruguayan player who took his turn after John Mensah fired his shot wide over the bar, giving us a chance to score and catch up. Dominic Adiyiah took his turn and went in the same direction as John Mensah did. The Uruguayan goalkeeper went in that direction too and saved the ball. With their next penalty, the Uruguayan player scored and that was the end of the match.

The heartbreak of that moment was real. We were all devastated by the loss. Even though our players were crying and consoling one another, I knew they had fought a good fight but had lost. That's the nature of football - one team is sometimes luckier than the other. Uruguay was luckier that day.

Uruguay went on to play Netherlands in the semi-finals, and lost 3-2. Netherlands played Spain in the final and lost 1-0. Uruguay lost 3-2 to Germany to finish the tournament in fourth place.

The Black Stars' performance at that tournament affirmed for me that the future of Ghanaian football was bright, and that we are capable of winning the World Cup.

The World Cup came to our continent for the first time and we hoped to win it for Africa. It didn't turn out that way. Even though we did not win the ultimate prize, the Black Stars represented our country well and made Africa proud.

· CHAPTER 12 ·

BLACK METEORS: MOZAMBIQUE 2011 ALL-AFRICA GAMES

Before I was appointed the head coach of the Black Meteors, national Under-23 team, I was the assistant coach of the Black Stars working under Goran Stevanovic. I took over from David Duncan who had been relieved of his position after the Meteors failed to qualify for the 2012 Olympic Games in London. In my new role, I was to qualify the team and to lead them to the All Africa Games in Maputo, Mozambique.

In the Black Meteors' previous appearances at Olympic Games and All Africa Games, they achieved good results. They won a bronze medal at the 1978 All-Africa Games in Algiers, Algeria. They won bronze at the 1992 Olympic Games in Barcelona, Spain. They won bronze medal at the 2003 All Africa Games in Abuja, Nigeria.

I had been working under Goran for about two months when the GFA leaders asked me to leave my position as an assistant with the Black Stars and take on the Black Meteors job. I was not very happy about the reassignment. The Black Stars were getting ready to play against England in an international friendly match. That was a major friendly match and I was looking forward to being a part of that historic game at Wembley Stadium. With my new role, I was expected to leave my Black Stars post soon after my appointment, which meant that I could not be a part of that historic Black Stars match.

Part of why I was not happy with my reassignment was that the Ghana-England friendly was in March whereas the All-Africa Games was in September – six months away. I could have remained the Black Stars assistant coach through March and then take on the Black Meteors job after the England match. But that was not going to be the case.

Goran brought with him someone he introduced as a physical trainer. For the time that I worked with Goran, I realised that the person was a coach and Goran kept him closer and relied on him more for activities that were typical for me to handle as the assistant coach.

Having noticed Goran's indirect way of pushing me out of my assistant coaching responsibilities, it was not lost on me that the decision and the timing of my Black Meteors appointment had something to do with Goran wanting me to be reassigned so his guy could be his assistant. Even though I grudgingly accepted the new position, it worked out for my good.

With Maxwell Konadu as my assistant and Sabaah Quaye as the team manager, I took responsibility of the Black Meteors team and we started preparing for the qualifiers we needed to play. That final two-leg series of matches was against Nigeria.

With the special football rivalry between our two nations, the stakes were always high. Furthermore, the Nigerians, whose team had the nickname "Dream Team," wanted so badly to qualify so as to live up to the hype surrounding their nick name. Our team was also under pressure to qualify after they failed to qualify for the London Olympic Games a few months earlier.

In the first leg, we lost 3-1 to the Nigerians after scoring first. That match was played in the Nigerians' home. For the second leg, we needed a 2-0 win at a minimum in order to qualify on goal aggregate.

Having learnt from our mistakes in the first leg, we made the necessary adjustments which allowed us to effectively exploit the Nigerians' weaknesses. Through an early goal by Emmanuel Agyeman Badu and another goal by Richard Mpong, we beat them 2-0 at the Baba Yara Sports Stadium in Kumasi to qualify for the tournament in Mozambique.

Of the 20 sports featured at the All Africa Games, men's football was one of the most prominent sports due to its huge popularity across the continent. The six countries represented were South Africa, Mozambique, Senegal, Cameroon, Uganda, and Ghana. Egypt and Madagascar qualified for the tournament but withdrew.

I made few changes to the squad and we started camping in Accra for the tournament. The 20-man squad was made up mainly of locally-based players and comprised goalkeepers Joseph Addo, Daniel Adjei, and Collins Addo; defenders Augustine Sefa, Mohammed Sabato, Edward Kpodo, Ahmed Adams, Rashid Sumaila, and Lawrence Lartey; midfielders Malik Akowuah, Mumuni Abubakar, Richard Mpong, Francis Morton, Sarfo Gyamfi, Alhaji Sanie, Prince Baffoe, and Uriah Asante; forwards Gilbert Fiamenyo, Mahatma Otoo, and Benjamin Acheampong. I had invited four foreign-based players but I was unable to get any of them to join the squad so we were going to make do with the best talent that was available to us.

For that tournament, like any other tournament, it was important to me that we went with players who were versatile, and could play at two or three positions. That was the main reason behind the changes I made to the qualifying squad. The final squad had several players who possessed the qualities I was confident could make us successful.

After a brief stay in South Africa, the team arrived in Maputo to compete.

The six teams were put in two groups of three, and each team was going to play the other once. That meant two group matches for each team. We had South Africa and host nation Mozambique in our group. Mozambique lost 3-1 to South Africa in the first match and we lost 1-0 to South Africa in a very physical match. With that, South Africa qualified for the knockout stage leaving Ghana to battle with Mozambique for a chance to get into the qualifying stage.

Determined not to leave the tournament without a victory, we started the game with the intention of piling on the pressure early to build enough momentum to quiet the home crowd. That worked as Mahatma Otoo opened the scoring eight minutes into the game.

Seven minutes later, Otoo scored again. Ten minutes later, he made it a hat trick to put us ahead by three goals halfway past the first half.

Even though the Mozambicans settled down and found their way back into the game, we held them from scoring for the half.

In the second half, we continued to hold them from scoring until the sixty-second minute when they scored a goal. By that time, the fatigue and the injuries from our previous matches had set in. Our defence had become exposed. We conceded two more goals before we scored a fourth goal through Gilbert Fiamenyo to finish the match with a 4-3 victory.

In the semi-final matches, we won against Cameroon through a lone goal by Prince Baffoe.

We faced South Africa in the final match. Both teams came close to scoring several times, including a Ghana attempt that hit the cross bar. We remained scoreless until the 84th minute when South Africa scored. The Meteors pressed for an equalizer until Fiamenyo was brought down in the penalty area. That was in the 90th minute. Mahatma Otoo converted that penalty kick and the game ended in a 1-1 draw. After a goalless extra time of play, the winner was going to have to be decided by way of penalties.

Otoo converted the first penalty. The South Africans scored their first attempt but missed their second kick. Goalkeeper Daniel Agyei took the second kick and scored, putting us up by 2-1. Both nations scored on our respective third kicks bringing the score to 3-2. Daniel Agyei saved South Africa's fourth attempt. After Ahmed Adams calmly converted Ghana's fourth kick, the Meteors players burst into celebration. We had won gold!

The all-local squad, who at times struggled due to lack of tournament experience, had persevered to win glory for

Ghana. I was very proud of the boys for their accomplishment and for making history. For many of them, their performance at the tournament opened new doors for them and I was excited about what they were going to contribute to the future of Ghana football.

When we returned home to Ghana, we went through the regular celebratory activities, which included visiting the President at his office. The president at the time was Professor John Evans Atta-Mills.

While we were away in Mozambique that September, the Black Stars went to London again to play an international friendly against Brazil. When the Black Stars returned from London, I resumed my duties as the team's assistant coach and helped the team prepare for the final group qualifier for the 2012 AFCON in Gabon. We won that final qualifier 2-0 against Sudan to secure our spot at that tournament.

In all sincerity, I would not have chosen to take on the Black Meteors job at the time I did. I had my plans but God had a different plan as far as my coaching career was concerned. Because I took on the Meteors job and did it to the best of my ability, things worked out for my good.

The team winning the gold medal under my leadership enhanced my profile as a national team coach. It also quietened some of the skeptics who doubted Ghanaian coaches' ability to deliver results.

Working as an assistant on a national team is somewhat different from being a head coach of a national team. As the head coach, the weight of most of the decisions rests on your shoulder and everyone on the team looks up to you for leadership and direction.

The series of events before and during the tournament helped to develop my coaching instincts and expertise. Also, taking a locally-based squad to a competitive international tournament, and getting them to play to win was another confidence builder.

When I returned to my post as the Black Stars assistant coach, Goran still had his physical trainer (coach) on the team. Goran still had a tendency of turning to the physical trainer for help with things he should have allowed me to do. I got the impression that Goran was still more interested in grooming his physical trainer than he was in me working with him. That notwithstanding, I made myself present and stayed close by so that I could know what was going on, and did what I needed to do to be successful in my role. Of course, the two of them sometimes intentionally left me out of their conversations by strategically communicating in their native tongue, which I could not understand. But I had a job to do and I found a way to do the best job I could.

Again, because some of the Black Stars players were not fluent in English and Goran only spoke in English, I sometimes translated what he was saying into Twi because such translations often generated positive responses from the players. They often nodded enthusiastically when I explained Goran's statements to them in Twi.

Goran and I got along fine, for the most part, when I rejoined the team. He often relied on me to explain complicated ideas or give feedback to many of the players. I did not take it personally when he made decisions that I did not agree with. Even though the level of our collaboration was unlike what I had with Milo, I managed to work well with him.

One of the most important lessons I took with me from my tenure with the Black Meteors was that no matter how skilled or experienced the players are, winning starts with psyching up the team such that each player believes that he is the best at what he does. A lot about winning has to do with the players believing that they can do it.

With that mindset comes a willingness to fight till the final whistle even when our backs are against the wall. In Mozambique our back was against the wall many times but we persevered till the very end.

In addition to getting them to play effectively as one team, my job is also to help the players believe in themselves.

When it became clear that none of our foreign-based players was going to be available, each of the local players selected for the team heard from me time and again that they were the ones representing the nation because they were the best. They did not just listen to those words – they believed in those words.

And because they believed, that team became the 2011 All-Africa Games men's football gold medalists.

· CHAPTER 13 ·

BLACK STARS: BRAZIL 2014 WORLD CUP

Leading the Black Stars to qualify for the World Cup in Brazil has been one of the milestones in my career. It was an uphill battle that required a lot of mental toughness and superb teamwork to accomplish. Certain unfortunate events leading up to the tournament and other events at the tournament, overshadowed what should have been a showcase of Ghanaian football mastery. Nevertheless, there is a lot of professional pride and gratitude that I feel about the Black Stars' participation in the 2014 World Cup in Brazil.

The Black Stars qualified convincingly against Egypt in our final round of games and made it to the tournament. At the group stage, we lost 2-1 to the USA, played a 2-2 draw with Germany and lost 2-1 to Portugal. We were eliminated from the tournament at the group stage.

Shortly after the tournament, the government of Ghana set up a commission of inquiry to look into matters relating to the Black Stars' preparations for the tournament, events in our camp during the tournament, and other issues related to the fans who went to Brazil to support the team. As was made evident at the four-month inquiry, an overwhelming majority of the Brazil issues were related to money. The main issues were about inflated budgets, expenses that could not be accounted for, and the payment of appearance fees to players. Appeals Court Judge Justice Senyo Dzamefe chaired the Commission. Renowned lawyer Moses Foh-Amoaning and businessman Kofi Anokye Owusu-Darko were the other members of the Commission.

I categorize the Brazil 2014 issues that directly involved me into two: 1) the money issue, and 2) the conduct of two specific players.

The issue with the payment of the players' appearance fees could have been resolved long before we got to the tournament, as had been the practice during previous tournaments. Unfortunately, the Ministry of Youth and Sports leadership, and consequently the Ghana Football Association leadership, allowed this money issue to escalate into an unfortunate distraction.

As a practice, I do not get involved in money matters between players and the GFA. As a matter of fact, the coaching staff typically does not get involved in money matters and logistics related to the management of the Black Stars. The GFA is tasked to do that work.

So, after I selected the final squad and presented the list of names to the GFA, it was up to them to determine the budget for the tournament, arrange for sponsorship, coordinate the logistics for the team's preparation, and to make sure that the team had everything we needed to be ready to perform when the time came.

The discussion between the players and the GFA about the World Cup appearance fees started in Accra. The players wanted to be paid $120,000 each and the management team wanted them to accept about $82,500 each. Two presidential staffers were present at that meeting, and those discussions were inconclusive.

We left for Montenegro to play a friendly match. The money issue came up again and neither side changed their stance. While the players collectively insisted on the amount they wanted to be paid, most of them were careful in their approach. I suppose that had something to do with the fact that it was unclear who was eventually going to Brazil and who was not. At the time, there were 25 players on the team and two players were going to be dropped.

On the evening of May 31, after our friendly match with Netherlands, I finalized the list of 23 players and gave it to the GFA to be submitted to FIFA. Shortly after then, the players requested their appearance fees of $120,000 each, and they wanted it in cash. They haggled with the management team over the amount and the form of payment but could not come to an agreement. We left for Miami, Florida for the next phase of our preparations.

Historically, the practice had been that the national team players were paid their appearance fees in cash. For the 2014 tournament, the Government of the day decided to move away from cash payment to using electronic payments when paying the players their appearance fees. The players insisted they wanted their money in cash.

At our hotel in Miami in the US, the players held a meeting with the management. At that point, the players were firmer in requesting for their money, citing previous tournaments where they received their money in cash before arriving at the tournament. The management assured the players that the money would be waiting for them by the time they arrived in Brazil.

When we arrived in Brazil and the money was still not available, the players were upset by the sequence of "promise-and-fails." By that time, there had been about three instances of "the money is coming" that never materialized.

All this while, the players were still insisting on being paid $120,000 but the management team maintained that $82,500 was what had been approved by the parliamentary committee overseeing the World Cup expenses as well as the President's Cabinet. The $82,500 included a 10% increase over the appearance fees paid to the players who participated in the previous World Cup.

For a tournament of this nature, teams received money from FIFA for participating. The amount of money was increased based on the stage of the tournament a team reached. So, the money the Government was making available for the payment of the appearance fees was going to come back to the government when FIFA made its payments after the tournament.

Every team appearing at the tournament was going to receive a prize of $8 million from FIFA. If we qualified to the Round of 16, that amount would increase by $1 million. Making it to the quarterfinal would have increased the prize money by $5 million. The fourth place, third place, runner-up and winner prize amounts were $20 million, $22 million, $25 million and $35 million respectively. For starters, each of the 32 qualified teams was given $1.5 million to help with preparation costs.

So, even if each player received $100,000, that was $2.3 million. Adding the amounts for the technical team was going to bring the total payout to about $3 million, which was about a quarter of the $9.5 million Ghana was guaranteed to receive just for qualifying and appearing at the tournament. The remaining 75% was more than enough to cover our expenses and even make a lot of money available for the nation's coffers.

Even if money for appearance fees was not available ahead of the tournament, I am sure the players would have understood and waited for their money after the tournament.

As one player said during one of the meetings, if they had been told the money was not going to be available until after the tournament, they would have come to that agreement and then waited till after the tournament. But the promise-and-fail pattern that had emerged made it difficult for them (the players) to trust any more promises from the management team. The players demanded their money before they would play our first match against the USA.

Threatening to boycott appearances at the World Cup was not unique to the Black Stars. In 2014, Cameroon players refused to board their plane to Brazil because of disagreements over appearance fees, and they arrived one day late for the World Cup – and it was after their money had been paid. At the 2006 World Cup, Togo's players went on strike over bonus payments until FIFA intervened.

In our case, I impressed upon the management team to promptly see to the resolution of the matter since the money issue was beginning to threaten the team's readiness for our first match. In fairness to the management team, they had relayed promises they had been given from someone in Accra. They appeared to be out of options, which was baffling.

Luckily, the nation's Vice President arrived in Brazil and the leaders of our delegation updated him on the issue at hand. The Vice President came to our training ground and assured the players that they would be paid $100,000 after the match against the USA. The players cheered up, believing that they could count on the Vice President's word.

We played against the USA and lost 2-1. Our guys played well but lost the game. When they asked for the money after that match, they were told that the people in Ghana were getting the money ready and that the players should be patient. That was on June 16. Our next game, with Germany, was on June 21.

The person in Accra in possession of the money had four whole days for this matter to be resolved once and for all. Two days to the game with Germany, the money had still not arrived.

The GFA leadership and the sports minister could not face the players directly. They wanted me to calm the players down until the money arrived. The players asked that I let them deal directly with the GFA leaders, and I obliged.

Any time I told the players to do something, they did, including previous occasions where I had told them to be patient and wait for the money. I couldn't blame them for asking me to let them handle the issue directly. I was also convinced that someone was not being truthful to me and to the players about the status of the money.

The players were so upset with the sports minister that they did not want to even see him, let alone have any discussions with him. The sports minister had become the last person the players wanted to see because it was the Ministry of Youth and Sports that was supposed to release the money to the GFA but had not. The players had heated exchanges with the GFA leadership but they could only relay what the sports minister was telling them.

The players grudgingly participated in our scheduled training sessions. Ahead of the match against Germany, our nation's President spoke to the players by phone. He encouraged the players to give of their best and also added that the sports minister was working on getting their money to them. We finished that thrilling match with a 2-2 draw.

Portugal had lost 4-0 to Germany and finished 2-2 against the USA. Qualification from our group was wide open. We could qualify along with Germany if we won against Portugal and Germany beat USA. If we won against Portugal and Germany lost to USA, the qualification was going to come down to goal differences. So, we were confident that we could qualify to the next round.

The Portugal match was scheduled for June 26, and unfortunately, the money issue remained unresolved. The team and the GFA leaders had one more meeting. The sports minister was conferenced into the meeting by way of a phone call. On the speaker phone, everyone in the meeting could hear him and he could hear everyone who spoke in the room. The players made it clear that if they got to Brasilia, where we were going to play Portugal, and the money was not there they were not going to train. The sports minister promised that the plane would be in Brasilia with the money by the time we arrived there. He said that on the speaker phone and everyone heard him.

When we arrived in Brasilia, there was no plane and there was no money as had been promised. The players stood by their decision. I did not ask that they change their minds because it would have been unreasonable of me to do so. Besides, we had travelled most of that day and the scheduled training session was going to be a light workout anyway. Cancelling that training session was not going to affect our preparation in any significant way. So, I called off the training session.

Mind you, the sports minister had a very good relationship with the players up until this money issue became a problem. Some of the players, I supposed, thought the sports minister was taking undue advantage of his good relationship with them to play games with their money.

Even though it had never made sense to me why this money issue dragged on for as long as it did, there had never been a time during the Nyantakyi administration that players' appearance fees had not been paid. Even if it was delayed, it got paid. So, for the issue to have escalated into what it became was unfortunate.

With the Portugal match two days away, that was when the situation erupted into a full-blown chaos. The players refused to practice until they received their money, and therefore missed two vital training sessions. I can empathize with how the players felt because it was clear that someone was not being truthful to all of us.

But to boycott critical training sessions ahead of a decisive match at the World Cup was short-sighted on the part of the players. Our players losing sight of the fact that being on the national team was a privilege and that they were in Brazil on behalf of the nation was a disappointment. But that unfortunate situation which allowed for the players to behave the way they did had come about because of the lack of honest, open communication that did not happen between the players and leaders of our delegation.

A coach's job is made unnecessarily more difficult when the people who employ these players create issues behind the scenes and the coach is supposed to solve. On my part, I cannot force players to train if they had agreed with their employer that the training was not going to happen if certain conditions are not met.

On one occasion, we were told a chartered flight bringing the money had taken off and two days later, the supposed plane had still not arrived. One player, clearly frustrated, asked the people in the room how long it took for a plane to travel from Ghana to Brazil. We all knew it didn't take 48 hours so it was clear that someone was not telling the truth.

There is so much that happens behind the scenes with the Black Stars that I choose not to discuss publicly. There are many things that happen - on the part of administrators and also on the part of players - that make my job extremely difficult. I have worked through many of those situations and continue to work through some. However, the Brazil situation was playing out on the world stage and the players were spending so much time thinking and talking about their money at the expense of the matches ahead.

The players had a meeting with the GFA leadership that evening. It was around 8pm and I was in my room at the time of that meeting. I heard a lot of loud talking coming from the hallway outside my room so I came out to find out what was going on. I ran into Sabaah Quaye, the team manager, who told me that Sulley Muntari had been in an altercation with one of the management team members.

I went to Sulley's room to find out what had happened. He told me he was trying to explain something to the management team member and that turned into a heated exchange. That heated exchange led to the management team member throwing a blow at him, and he retaliated by fighting back. He showed me a bruise, along with a dab of blood, that he had sustained from the incident. I advised him to cut everything short and let it go, and that I would not like to hear about any further fighting. I left the room, which Sulley was sharing with his colleague Michael Essien.

I was told later by eyewitnesses that Sulley had been angered by the consistent promise-and-fail behaviour of the management team and said at the meeting that they (the management team) had lied and lied to them all this while. He calling the management team members liars did not sit well with one of them, and that escalated into the physical altercation.

Not long after I had left Sulley's room, I again heard people talking loudly outside. I came back outside to find most of the players in the hallway and groups of people trying to separate Sulley and a GFA official. I learned later that after I left Sulley's room, he went to the GFA official's room to resume the altercation.

From the earlier incident, several GFA officials were in their colleague's room and were therefore able to intervene when Sulley arrived there. From what I was told, the GFA officials took their colleague to the adjoining balcony while the other people in the room, mainly players, restrained Sulley from attacking the man.

I was disappointed at Sulley not just because he got into the altercation but because he went to the man's room to fight him and destroy his property, including a laptop and cell phone.

After hearing the accounts of the people in the room about what happened, I asked the players present to return to their respective rooms. I stayed and talked with the management team to hear their account of what happened. They confirmed what I had been told.

The GFA official was relocated to a different hotel the next day, a move that was to prevent any future confrontation between him and Sulley. The Minister of Youth and Sports arrived at the hotel later that day and joined the management team and me in a meeting to discuss the way forward for the team as far as the Sulley incident was concerned.

Before the Sulley incident, Kevin Prince-Boateng had displayed a behaviour that I considered disrespectful and unhealthy for the rest of the team. His consistent use of foul language toward me was troubling because that had become an ongoing public display of disrespect toward me, and also toward my technical team members.

Ahead of our game against Germany, I was officiating a half-field game during training when I did not whistle for what Kevin considered a rough tackle by another player on his partner. Kevin was unhappy with my decision and he angrily uttered a sentence laden with the f-word. I ignored the comment.

Moments later, he hit a powerful shot at goal and scored for his side. I remarked, "Good shot!"

"What the f*** is good shot!" he responded angrily, and I ignored his comment. I carried on with the training session.

In another instance, during a training session after the Germany game, he was upset over something and directed his frustration toward me – again using the f-word. I asked him to take a seat on the sideline until later when we could calmly discuss what was bothering him.

After the training session, he defiantly walked up to me – in the presence of the rest of the players –and verbally lashed out at me with his f-word-filled rant. The sequence of events before then and his disrespectful confrontation made me angry but I was not going to be drawn into a verbal fight with one of my players. I kept calm.

When leading a group of players on a national team, a manager needs to exercise a great deal of maturity in managing the various personalities that make up the team. That includes respecting every player's views and treating each player with respect. Likewise, a manager expects the same level of respect from his players.

I had worked with Kevin since 2010 when he first joined the team. He had been polite in our previous interactions and he had not been a kind of person I knew to be foul-mouthed. As such, I ignored previous instances of him dishing out f-words. However, him continuing to do so in front of our younger players was not an acceptable behaviour for the team.

Part of being an effective leader is knowing that it is not necessary to respond to every utterance by a player. Tempers sometimes flare up and a manager needs to be able to ignore certain inappropriate behaviours from players. Foul language, however, is a slippery slope toward a decline in team discipline, especially when the foul language is directed at the team's head coach.

Some people use the f-word generously in their daily communication and I respect their right to express themselves anyway they choose. However, when on a team and in a professional setting, it is vital for each professional to treat the other professionals with respect, including using language that reflects respect for self and for others. The use of f-words towards a person's manager is unacceptable under any circumstance in any culture.

I was hoping Kevin would later recognise the errors of his ways and apologise for his actions. So, I did not officially report the incidents to the management team. The management team members were at the training grounds and witnessed some of the incidents. However, they left it up to me to handle the situation as I saw fit.

I chose to let some time pass and give Kevin an opportunity to reflect on his actions, and attempt to mend the situation. Otto Addo, a member of my technical team who was fluent in German just like Kevin, tried to intervene but it was to no avail. Kevin did not show any interest in mending what had become a strained relationship between us.

Instead, he would squeeze his face, look away and walk past me every time we met each other in the hallways. That behavior went on for two days, after which time I became convinced that he was well aware of what he was doing. It was then that I officially informed the management team of the behaviours that had made Kevin more of a liability than an asset to the team.

In the best interest of a team, no team should tolerate gross misconduct or a pattern of bad behavior that threatens the mission. For the good of the team, one bad apple – no matter how shiny that apple is – must be removed when it is clear that the single, shiny apple can spoil the bunch.

During the meeting with the GFA management team and the sports minister to discuss the best way forward, I recommended that Sulley and Kevin be suspended for their actions.

That disciplinary action made headlines around the world, even though that was not the first time a disciplinary action had been taken against a Black Stars player at a tournament for a conduct deemed unacceptable.

In 2010, Milo decided to sit Sulley after an incident the coach deemed unacceptable. When the GFA management team pleaded with Milo to rescind his decision due to how critical Sulley was to the team, Milo told the GFA officials they would have to choose between him and Sulley if they disagreed with his decision. Sulley's suspension remained in force, and he played only because Andre Ayew had accumulated two yellow cards and had to sit out for the next game.

In another incident, during a 2014 World Cup qualifier against Lesotho, I called for Emmanuel Agyeman Badu to substitute Sulley around the 60th minute. For five minutes, Sulley ignored my call and would not come off. When he finally did, he angrily headed straight for the dressing room instead of joining the rest of the team on the bench. We finished that game 2-0 and I was congratulating the team in the locker room.

Sulley was still upset and he made a comment that featured inappropriate words. As much as he wanted to play, I did not feature him for the next three games – until he apologised for his actions.

When there is no clear line of respect, it is very likely that the players will not take their coach seriously. Even though I can be very friendly with my players, there is a line of respect that my players are not allowed to cross. Maintaining that clear line of respect is important to maintaining order on the team and for treating all players fairly.

Even though many people believed Kevin should not have been on the team in the first place, I believe including him in the team was the right thing for the team. Even though he turned his back on the national team following the 2006 World Cup, I knew his experience would be useful to the team.

Against the advice and wishes of many respected individuals in the Ghanaian media and general public, I invited him. The media backlash against me for inviting Kevin into the Brazil 2014 squad was severe but I don't regret my decision to include him in the team.

Just as I invited Kevin in the best interest of the team, my recommendation that he (and Sulley) be asked to leave the team was also in the best interest of the team. I don't regret that decision either.

The money issue had become a huge distraction for the team. It was obvious that our players didn't have their full concentration on the upcoming match. Their concentration was on their money and matters arising from the delayed payment. The issue made its way into the international news with journalists reporting that the Ghanaian team was threatening to boycott our next match over appearance fees.

The chartered flight from Ghana finally arrived, and bundles of dollars totaling $100,000 for each player and each technical team member were distributed. As was portrayed in the media, some players were displaying their cash with some even kissing their bundles of money.

It was extremely distracting that the players had that much cash on them during the night before a make-or-break match but that is what it had come to and I had to work through that situation. With the pictures and reports of the players in possession of their money out there for the world to see, the safety and security of the players was now a concern for me.

I kept my money in the safe at the hotel. Most of the players carried their money in their backpacks, and kept their backpacks with the rest of their luggage in the dressing room when the time came for the match. They did not think the hotel room was safe enough.

Without a doubt, the players having their hundreds of thousands of dollars sitting in a dressing room was not going to be helpful to their concentration. Also, not getting a good night's rest was very likely going to hurt us the following morning.

To try and get each player's focus back on course, I asked Stephen Appiah, the team's 2010 captain, and Asamoah Gyan, the team's captain at the time, to visit each player in his room and make sure there were no outstanding issues.

Against Portugal, we suffered an own goal in the 30th minute but equalized at the 57th minute. We conceded a second goal in the 80th minute from a miscommunication among our defenders and our goalkeeper, and ended the game 2-1. With two losses and a draw, that was not enough to qualify from the group stage. The USA qualified along with Germany to the Round of 16.

In the Ghanaian media and at the Dzamefe Commission hearing, the sports minister gave his account of what happened in Brazil. The GFA President also gave his account. Several witnesses told their versions of events before and during our time in Brazil. What was clearly evident was that there was a lot of finger pointing and not enough accountability. The system failed, and that led to the team's unsatisfactory performance.

For a Black Stars team that held Germany to a 2-2 draw, we certainly could have done more at the tournament. Germany, who ultimately won the tournament, beat every other team they played against, including their 4-0 thrashing of Portugal and their 7-1 humiliation of the host nation, Brazil.

If only we didn't have the money issue and the many distractions that came with it; if only our players were fully prepared and were playing every match with full concentration, I am very confident that we would have been more successful at the tournament. But the system failed, and we're left to wonder "What if?"

At the time of my appearance at the Dzamefe Commission, I was the former head coach of the Black Stars. On September 17, 2014, the GFA president, Kwasi Nyantakyi, had invited me to his office for a meeting about my contract.

My contract had been extended by the GFA after the World Cup. My contract was supposed to end on August 31, 2016 but it ended thirteen months earlier. I was disappointed by the GFA's decision but I was not completely surprised considering that the GFA had a tendency of giving in to public pressure. At that time, many Ghanaians appeared more upset with the Black Stars, and not with the GFA management team nor the Ministry of Sports, for the Brazil events. To anyone who was objectively looking at the facts of the circumstances surrounding Brazil 2014, it was obvious that my termination was an attempt by the powers-that-be to shift blame away from themselves.

Kwasi Nyantakyi called me to his office that day and informed me that he had been asked by the President of the nation to relieve me of my duties. When decisions about the national team staffing became that heavily-politicized, it was very clear to me that the political machine was flexing its muscles to make me a scapegoat. The Minister for Youth and Sports, who should bear the ultimate responsibility for the money issue that was at the heart of the Brazil problem, was reassigned to another one job in the President's office but I was rather fired.

Considering that the order for my firing was said to have come from the President, that made it a fight I was not interested in. Discerning Ghanaians knew what was going on and I was not interested in becoming a part of any political drama. I wanted to coach football and I did not want to do so under a cloud of political interference.

Per my contract with the GFA, either party could terminate the contract by providing a three-month written notice to the other party or pay three months' salary in lieu of such a notice. That meant if I had quit the job without giving the

GFA a three-month written notice, I would have owed three months' salary. Likewise, I was owed three-months' salary since the GFA decided to terminate my contract without the advance notice. I finalized the severance discussion with the GFA and moved on.

It is worth noting that the circumstances under which the GFA could have terminated my contract without the three months' salary compensation included the following:
- If I had been found liable by any competent authority for an offense involving dishonesty, possession, use or application of illegal or prohibited drugs or substances;
- If I had been found to have behaved in such manner that my continuous employment was likely to bring the Association into public ridicule or if my had behaviour negatively affected the image of the Association or had brought my job into disrepute;
- If I had been found to have fundamentally breached this agreement by (i) refusing or failing to act in accordance with my obligations under the agreement as directed by the Association, (ii) breaching confidentiality obligations stipulated in the agreement, or (iii) failing to qualify the Black Stars for AFCON 2015.

My lawyer and secondary school classmate Godfred Graham, whom I conferred with regarding the termination of my appointment, was convinced that I had a strong case for further legal action. Even though I agreed with Graham's position, I chose to close that chapter in order to move on. For my appearance at the Dzamefe Commission, Graham helped me prepare and he also sat next to me during my testimony.

Many of my critics had not been fair in their conclusion that should be blamed for the Black Stars' failure to live up to expectations at the Brazil tournament. There were some critics who dialed back on their criticism once they heard the facts of the matter. There were also some critics who held on to their opinions in spite of the facts that suggested otherwise.

At the end of the day, people are entitled to their opinions. The facts, however, remained the facts and that's what the Commission helped to bring to light. The facts showed that the issues that surrounded the team in Brazil were not coaching issues.

At the end of my testimony at the Commission, Justice Dzamefe and Lawyer Foh-Amoaning both foretold my eventual reappointment as the Black Stars' coach. Whether or not I was reappointed was not the most important thing to me when I presented my testimony. Rather, my biggest desire was that the people who had the power to correct the problems that plagued the national team found the moral courage to take the necessary corrective actions.

I hope that the recommendations from the Commission are taken seriously and implemented in the best interest of the nation. I hope also that for future tournaments, the GFA administration, the Sports Ministry and the players discuss and finalize player appearance fees and bonuses before the team leaves for the event. With that, the coach can focus on getting the team ready for the matches and the players can focus on getting ready to play, and play to win.

The Brazil World Cup was a defining moment in my career and a major milestone for me as the first Ghanaian coach to qualify the Black Stars to the World Cup.

Looking beyond 2014, I had no doubt in my mind that there were brighter days coming for Ghana's national team – if only the issues with the system could be fixed.

As we move forward, I hope that each stakeholder will put the interest of the nation first when making decisions regarding the Black Stars. I hope that each stakeholder will do the right thing each time so that the players can focus on playing football and the coach (I or whoever) can focus on coaching.

And with that, the Black Stars will qualify for future World Cups, qualify through the knockout stages and make it to the final, and then win the trophy.

· CHAPTER 14 ·

AL KHARTOUM AL WATANI (SUDAN)

When I was parting ways with the Ghana Black Stars in September 2014, I did not know exactly what was in store for me. I was, however, hopeful that another coaching opportunity was going to come my way. I went about with my life spending my time on personal projects that needed my attention and also keeping up with football in Ghana and around the world.

About a month after leaving the Black Stars, I received a phone call from a man who identified himself as a representative of a Sudanese Premier League club. The club needed a head coach and they wanted to know if I was interested in the job. He answered my questions satisfactorily, and the opportunity seemed worth exploring. He made travel arrangements for me to visit Sudan for a meeting with the club's officials.

I didn't know too much about Sudan before receiving the phone call. So, I checked with some Ghanaians living there about what it was like living and working in Sudan.

Al Khartoum Al Watani (Sudan)

Sudan has a rich football history in Africa. It was a major football force in the 1950s and 1960s, and their national team won the African Cup of Nations in 1970. However, they declined in the decades that followed. As at 2014, Sudan was ranked No. 107 out of the 208 teams ranked by FIFA while Ghana ranked No. 35 in that same FIFA ranking. So, Sudan was just an average national team.

Though their national team was not enjoying much success, club-level football in Sudan was not that bad. Two clubs dominated the local league: Al Hilal and Al Merrikh. The club that wanted my services, Al Khartoum Al Watani SC, had been a successful club in the past but their days of glory had faded away.

Al Khartoum had finished in the Top 4 in the two previous seasons but they finished with a significant difference in points behind the Top 2 teams. Their team was aging and they needed to rebuild it to become more competitive, both in the short term and the long term.

The question about my personal safety crossed my mind due to news reports about a civil war in Sudan. I came to find out that there were two different countries with the name Sudan – Sudan and South Sudan. The fighting was in South Sudan and Al Khartoum was in Sudan.

I visited once to meet with the team's officials and to check out what living and working in Khartoum would be like. Language-wise, the Sudanese speak Arabic and English so we were able to communicate reasonably well. I presented my ideas and how I could do what they needed.

They invited me back to discuss the terms of a contract. We reached an agreement and I became the club's head coach.

Sudan is a very big country – the third largest in Africa after Algeria and the Democratic Republic of Congo. It is probably about the size of Ghana, Togo, Benin and Nigeria combined. With a population of about forty million, most of the people in Sudan are very passionate about football.

Egypt is their neighbour to the north, and one can say that they live in Egypt's shadow when it comes to football, considering how dominant Egypt's club-level and international-level football is across the continent. Nonetheless, Sudanese are passionate about football and Al Khartoum's fans were ready for a revival of their team.

My approach to rebuilding the team was to thoughtfully phase out the older players and bring in new, younger players. It was important to me that there was a transition and not an abrupt change in the team's composition. I started out my first year with the team as it was, with the objective of getting to know the players well and then identifying young players whom I could bring on the team. Halfway through the season, I started making significant changes to the team.

Determining which players to drop from the team was not necessarily by the players' ages. I based that decision on each player's work rate and performance on the field of play. After being with them for about six months, I had a very good idea of which players had what it took to help the team going forward.

The Top 2 teams were fond of buying other teams' already-developed players. Rather than follow that example, I advised Al Khartoum's management that we should develop the youth in our junior teams and not take "short cuts." They accepted my recommendation.

Al Khartoum Al Watani (Sudan)

I arranged a couple of matches between our junior team and the senior side to get a closer look at the younger players. Having the younger and the older players play together was a very transparent process by which each player justified his inclusion in the senior side. The players, the team officials and the fans all got to see the process work itself out as players earned their spot on the team based on performance.

I invited several of the younger players to train with the senior side where they had the opportunity to develop a deeper understanding of the game, improve their ball handling skills, improve their decision-making abilities with or without the ball, gain more confidence, and get better at using their individual skills for the benefit of the team.

For any player, especially young players, developing a solid grasp of fundamental skills is vital for a successful career. So, ball control, passing over short and long distances, where to stand and what to do during set pieces, changing positions during a match, what to do when their player has possession of the ball, and what to do when the opponent has the ball, were some of the important aspects of the game that I emphasised. How a player performed these actions determined the player's level of play and how well that player could fit into the team.

Also, football is as much a physical game as it is a mental game. Even for the people who instinctively know what to do, practicing and getting better at the fundamental skills help them make better decisions during matches.

Many of my players needed to learn the proper techniques and routines of organised football in order to raise the level and quality of their game. My feedback highlighted what each of them was doing well and what they needed to improve upon. The players were eager to learn because each of them wanted to earn a place on the senior side and also to get to play in important matches.

The Sudanese were familiar with who I was at the time I took over the team. In 2013, I coached the Black Stars to beat the Sudanese national team 4-0 in Kumasi and 3-1 on their home grounds during the World Cup qualifiers. They also knew me from my coaching of the Black Stars at the 2014 World Cup. As such, I experienced a respectful working relationship with my players and with the team's management.

Match after match, the players and the team improved. By the end of my second season with the Al Khartoum, the team had been refreshed with younger talent whose future held a lot of promise. Nine of Al Khartoum's players earned call-ups to the Sudanese national team for the first time. Of those nine, six were part of the young players I recruited from Al Khartoum's junior side. That was a testament to the success of the player-development programme we were committed to and also a testament to the players' commitment to their careers.

At the end of my first year, the handlers of the Sudanese national team asked me to take on coaching their national team as well. That was a big job with additional responsibilities. It was also an opportunity to expand my impact on Sudanese football. However, I knew how difficult it could be coaching two teams at the same time.

National team coaching requires extensive travel for player monitoring, which could mean travelling to a different part of the country every week and also outside of the country. Travelling that much on national team assignments and coaching my local club at the same time was not going to be easy for me at the time.

If I chose not to travel as much to see other players, I was going to have to pick mainly my club's players for the national team, which I thought was unfair to other players. So, I turned down the Sudanese national team offer and focused on my job with the local side.

Kamal was my interpreter helping me communicate with the players in Arabic. While many of the players understood English, there were instances where communicating in Arabic helped the players grab a better understanding of what I was talking about. Culturally, it also helped that I had Kamal to learn from. Kamal, who was a former player and a former member of the Sudanese national team, was interested in coaching.

Former footballers with high football intelligence and people-management skills have the potential to become very good coaches. Kamal had a good understanding of the game and valuable experience from playing at the international level. Therefore, while working with me as my interpreter he was also learning his way into becoming a coach. We worked very well together and he eventually became a coach after I left. The last time I spoke with him, he was coaching one of the Sudanese Premier League clubs.

Prince Owusu was the coach of Ghana Premier League sides Tema Youth and Medeama SC, and had also been an assistant on Ghana's Under-20 team. I had known him for many years and thought he would be a good assistant to me. In my second year in Sudan, I brought him on to my Al Khartoum technical team. He was as reliable and helpful as he had always been. He contributed greatly to the development of the players and to the success of the team.

For each of my two seasons with Al Khartoum, the team won more games each year, and also finished the season with much smaller point differences between them and the teams ahead of them. At the end of the second season, for instance, the second-, third- and fourth-placed teams in the league were each separated by a single point each.

Other key indicators of their much-improved form were how efficiently the players handled their roles on the field, the confidence with which they made decisions with or without the ball, and how well they played together as a unit. Al Khartoum became a much-talked about team in Sudan because of how they kept the ball on the ground and built their attack strategically.

Over the course of my stay in Sudan, I promoted about 22 young players to the senior side. The difference in the team when I joined them and where they were two seasons later was like the difference between night and day. We had come a long way, and all that had been possible because each stakeholder remained committed to the process. The future looked very bright.

The revamped team had found their stride and had become well-positioned to compete with the powerhouse teams in Sudanese football. It was even foreseeable that they would do better at the CAF Champions League in the coming years.

Apart from their players who were called into their national senior national team, five of them were called into their Olympic team, and two of them were called into their national Under-20 side.

Whether I continued coaching the team or not, I was confident that Al Khartoum had the right team to win them many successes for years to come.

Leaving Sudan for the Black Stars Job

Around early March 2017, I received a telephone call from the GFA's deputy general secretary asking if I was interested in returning to coach the Black Stars. The GFA had parted ways with Avram Grant who had succeeded me. The Black Stars had finished fourth in the AFCON a month earlier and the team's qualification to the 2018 World Cup was in jeopardy.

While the Black Stars head coaching job is a dream job for many Ghanaian coaches and also for many foreign coaches, I was careful not to make a hasty decision. I was honoured to have received the call but I needed to thoughtfully and prayerfully consider the opportunity. So, I told the deputy general secretary I would give his inquiry some thought, pray about my decision, and then get back to him.

In the two weeks that followed, I thought about the pros and cons of taking the job. I also sought the counsel of a couple of key people I often turned to when making major career decisions. I prayed for direction from God and asked a few trusted confidants to pray along with me.

In as much as taking up the job of coaching the Black Stars seemed like an easy decision, I was mindful of high expectations Ghanaians had of whoever took up that role. If I was not convinced that I could deliver on those high expectations, then staying in Sudan would have made more sense. In Sudan, I was going to continue building on what I had started and would also be making more money than the Black Stars job was going to pay. Also, the extremely political nature of the Ghanaian football landscape gave me reason to think about the opportunity carefully and prayerfully.

I found out that I was one of several coaches the GFA had received CVs from and were being considered for the position. Someone told me that there were eight CVs being seriously evaluated at the time. Subsequently, I was one of the three applicants who were invited to be interviewed for the job.

I was in Sudan then so my interview was held over Skype. That first interview was with a panel of three GFA officials, and we talked about the new ideas that I would bring to the team, what changes I would like to see, and what I learned from my first tenure that would make me more successful in a second tenure. I was candid in my responses and respectfully offered suggestions that I thought would be helpful to the Black Stars.

One of the suggestions I offered was for the GFA to provide all the national team coaches – Under-17, Under-20, Under-23 and the Black Stars – physical office spaces where they could periodically hold meetings to discuss tactical issues and exchange ideas.

There is a wealth of knowledge sitting in the heads of our national team coaches. Without sharing that knowledge among ourselves, each person does their own thing with their specific national team and the nation does not get the benefit of our collective wisdom. I suggested that offices and a conference room should be established, maybe at the Accra Sports Stadium, and the national team coaches be encouraged to hold regular knowledge-sharing meetings to discuss strategy and tactics they use with their respective national teams.

For example, I should be able to hold a meeting with all national team coaches after every tournament and share tactics that worked, and lessons I learned. They could also ask questions about decisions I made. I do share such information informally if any of my peers wants to know. However, formalizing such meetings or making them mandatory is the job of GFA's technical directorate of the GFA, and I cannot take it upon myself to call such meetings and manage the technical direction of all the national teams. Those offices are yet to be created.

I had a second interview. That was in person, after which we finalized the terms of my contract as the Black Stars' head coach. That appointment was to begin in early May 2017.

When I informed the Al Khartoum officials and players that I would not be extending my stay with them, they were initially not happy about that. Eventually, they understood that the Black Stars job, a national assignment, was a big deal. They had been happy with our years together and their disappointment quickly made way for their gratitude. I, however, had to refund $100,000 of the money they paid me upfront.

They were really nice to me even though they were losing me. At the end of my final match, the players carried me shoulder-high to celebrate the end of my tenure. They also threw me into the air a few times and caught me each time.

Later, the team held a formal celebration at the their club house, which was attended by several important people, and they presented me with citations and several gifts. There were two additional events in my honour.

Sudan was the perfect job for the time between my first tenure as the Black Stars head coach and my second tenure. I am convinced that God ordered my steps to Sudan to offer me an opportunity to acquire some new ideas as well as to challenge and develop myself professionally in an unfamiliar territory. I also had a lot of time to study the modern game of football, reflect on my prior decisions, and identify areas where I had room for improvement. With that process came a lot of personal and professional development that strengthened my decision-making on tactical matters. I left Sudan for Accra and began my new role as the Black Stars coach.

My task was to qualify Ghana for the 2018 World Cup in Russia the following year. At the time I took over, the Black Stars were sitting third behind Egypt and Uganda in Group E of the African zone qualifying. Even though qualifying from that position was a tall order, I went in and gave it my all, hoping to wrestle our way into qualifying. Unfortunately, we did not qualify for Russia. We, however, qualified for the 2019 AFCON at the top of our group.

How good I was for the Black Stars can be found in my ability to build teams with depth and longevity; teams that always have about three players competing for each position; and teams that are successful for a long time. The work that I had done in identifying and developing young players yielded dividends even after I was gone from the team.

No matter how good I was during my "first coming," I believe I am better in my "second coming" but I still have to deal with administrative hurdles and the need to rebuild the team.

Being away from the Black Stars and staying in Sudan was a growth opportunity, which I took full advantage of. With that growth, I now have a second tenure to implement my forward-thinking approach to making the Black Stars successful now and for years to come.

Coaches Paa Kwasi Fabian (left) and Frimpong Manso (right).

Receiving a CAF coaching certificate from Former GFA Vice President George Afriyie.

Helping to receive a sponsorship cheque from Guinness for the Black Stars.

With the legendary coach and former Ghana Football Association President Ben Koufie (third from left) as we received a cheque from representatives of Glico Life.

With Former President John Mahama. Former GFA President Kwasi Nyantakyi on the left and several government officials in the background.

With GFA officials George Afriyie and Kwasi Nyantakyi, Youth & Sports Minister Isaac Asiamah and his deputy, Pius Hadzide.

With Asantehene Otumfour Osei Tutu II (in cap) in the company of other dignitaries during a Black Stars training session in Kumasi.

With Asantehene Otumfour Osei Tutu II.

With Former President John Agyekum Kufuor.

With Nana Addo Dankwa Akufo-Addo, President of the Republic of Ghana.

Top-left: With the late Nigerian legend and coach Stephen Keshi, winner of the 2013 Africa Cup of Nations.
Below: With Maxwell Konadu and Stephen Keshi.

Top-left: With Nigeria's Victor Moses, who was then playing for English Premier League team Liverpool FC; **Top-right:** With former Liverpool manager Brendan Rogers **Bottom:** With the Ivory Coast's Kolo Toure, who was then playing for Liverpool. This was during my coaching attachment with the team in 2014.

With Minister of Trade and Industry Alan Kyeremateng.

With Kumasi Asante Kotoko CEO Dr. Kwame Kyei.

With Coach Abdul Razak and Kwabena Appiah.

(L-R): Kwabena Appiah, me, Karim Zito, Coach Malik Jabir, Mr. Akoto and Francis Agyeman at the Kumasi Sports Stadium.

Receiving a national award from President Kufour in 2008.

At the National Awards with friends and family members.

With Opoku Nti at the National Awards in 2008.

With Baffour-Awuah Manu and Kwabena Appiah.

Honoured by Guinness Ghana Limited for my accomplishments in 2014.

In 2014, I was awarded an Honourary Doctorate in Psychology by Day Spring University, Mississippi, USA

Top: In addition to coaching the Black Meteors to win a gold medal at the All Africa Games, I received a Leadership and Lifetime Award in 2011.

Bottom: In 2014, I was voted Coach of The Year 2013/14 by Sports Writers Association of Ghana (SWAG).

(L-R): Audrey carrying my grand-daugther Jirah, MaryPearl, me, Angela, Peggy, and my son-in-law Eric.

Standing (L-R): Our daughters Mary Pearl, Audrey and Peggy; Angela is seated with me.

Top-left: With my sister Mrs. Sophia Amoatin;
Top-right: My sisters Mrs. Grace Oppong and Mrs. Rose Ofosu.

Middle: With Maxwell Brobbey (left) and Bishop Francis Sarpong of CCBC in London (right).

Below: With Kwabena Bambola and his kids.

With Stephen Appiah.

With Sonny Badu and his wife at their wedding in London.

With Jonathan Mensah and his wife at their wedding in Accra.

With Coach David Duncan, his wife Marian, and Kyei Amoako at Jonathan Mensah's wedding in Accra.

Former Kotoko players paid a visit to our colleague Teacher Kusi. **Front row (L-R):** Papa Arko, Teacher Kusi, and me; **Middle row (L-R):** Francis Agyeman, George Kennedy, Ernest Appau, Opoku Nti; **Back row (L-R):** Maxwell Brobbey, Kofi Badu and (unidentified).

With former Kotoko players **(L-R)** Opoku Nti, George Kennedy, Kofi Badu, and Ernest Appau in Kumasi.

With former Kotoko teammates at the funeral of former Kotoko chairman Sims Kofi Mensah. **Standing (L-R):** Joe Carr, Yaw Oduro, Ibrahim Gariba, Ntow Gyan, Ahmed Rockson, me, Yahya Kassum, Sampson Ampeah, Godwin Ablordey, and Papa Arko; **Seated (L-R):** Opoku Nti, John Bannerman, Coach Malik Jabir, Karim Zito, Ernest Appau and George Kennedy.

With senior former Black Stars players including Rev. Osei Kofi (seated) and Ibrahim Sunday (right).

At a CAF Awards event with Laryea Kingston to my right.

L-R: Asamoah Gyan (left) and John Paintsil (middle) and me.

With Daniel Amartey.

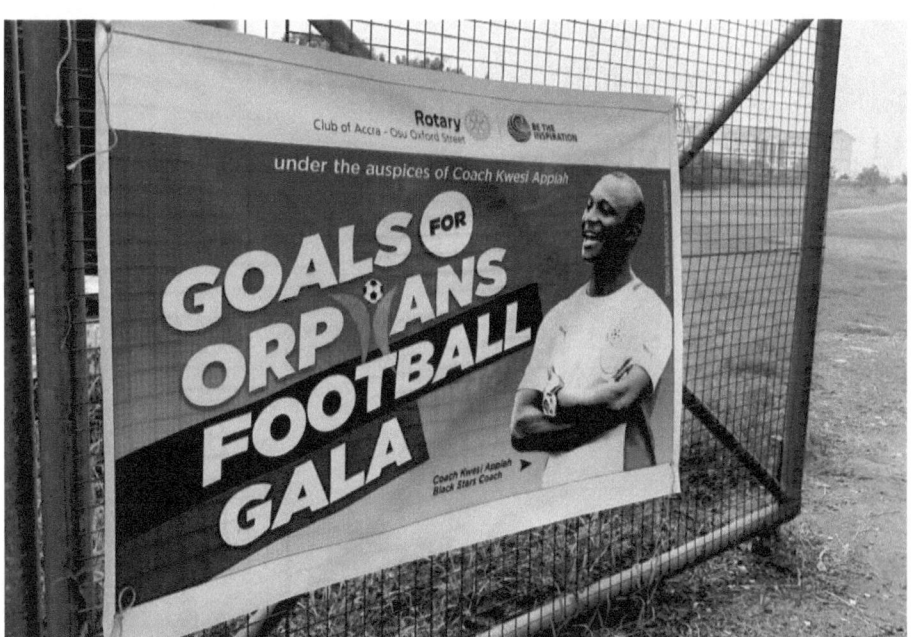

Supporting community development through football, I joined hands with the Osu Oxford Street Rotary Club of Accra to raise funds for the needy.

With my colleagues from Opoku Ware.

With JayRay Ghartey of JayRay Ghartey FashionHauz.

With my brother Kwabena Appiah (second from left), my cousin Bossman Nixon (third from right), former Ghana national track champion Martha Appiah (fourth from right), Baffour-Awuah Manu with their children in Columbus, Ohio.

L-R: Baffour-Awuah Manu, former Kotoko player Joe Mensah, Suzzie Gyamfi, and former Black Stars player Joe Addo in Columbus, Ohio.

With the Black Stars technical team at the Kumasi Sports Stadium.

(L-R): C.K. Akunnor, Stephen Appiah, Ibrahim Tanko and me at the Kumasi Sports Stadium.

In Kumasi for a 2019 AFCON qualifier.

With Ibrahim Tanko.

The Black Stars with His Excellency Nana Akufo-Addo following the team's qualification for AFCON 2019.

· CHAPTER 15 ·

BLACK STARS: THE ROAD TO AFCON 2019

American poet Henry Longfellow once said, "The heights great men reached and kept were not attained by sudden flight, but they, while their companions slept, were toiling upward in the night."

Lifting the 2019 African Cup of Nations (AFCON) trophy was not going to happen simply because we are Ghana, the four-time African champions who have been to the World Cup three out of the last four times. That success would only come with preparation, focus and execution.

The 2019 AFCON was going to be the first major tournament the Black Stars were going to be involved in since the dissolution of the Ghana Football Association following the scandal highlighted by investigative journalist Anas Aremeyaw Anas' undercover movie released a few months earlier. A Normalization Committee (NC) of the GFA had been appointed to handle the affairs of Ghana football. Therefore, the NC was in charge of many of the decisions related to the Black Stars' preparations for the AFCON, including outstanding off-the-field issues.

Meeting with the Stakeholders

In late December 2018, key stakeholders of the national team held a closed-door meeting to address outstanding issues and concerns that could get in the way of the team's success if not resolved. Those present at that meeting included Sports Minister Isaac Asiamah, NC Chairman Dr. Kofi Amoah, Captain Asamoah Gyan and other high-level individuals.

In that very candid meeting, outstanding issues discussed included the renewal of my contract which was due to expire before the start of the AFCON tournament, player bonus amounts, fairness in what each player will receive, as well as allocation of funds for the team's preparation. While some of the issues were addressed in the meeting, the stakeholders made a good-faith commitment to take the necessary steps to ensure that the remaining issues were resolved satisfactorily and in a timely manner.

Contract Discussions and the NC Chairman's Public Statements

My contract was due to expire in April 2019, before the team's appearance at the AFCON. At that time, NC Chairman Dr. Kofi Amoah made public statements on a TV show regarding a six-month contract extension that had been handed to me. But in actual fact, that contract discussion was ongoing and had not been finalized. It was therefore baffling to me that he would go public talking about a decision that had not been finalized yet. Moreover, saying that I would be fired if the Black Stars did not win the trophy was unnecessary.

As the leader of a football association preparing for a tournament, such statements are not helpful. It was not surprising that many people called me to ask why Dr. Amoah went on TV to make such comments. Their guesses were as good as mine as to why he did that. As a clean-up effort, the NC issued a statement, which among other things said, "The GFA has no interest in putting pressure on Coach Appiah, but would rather provide the necessary mechanism to facilitate his role in achieving the nation's quest."

I don't have a problem with my employers having a performance clause in my contract (or in the contract of any national team coach). However, sending a head coach to the scaffold even before the start of a tournament is not a productive preparation tactic for any team.

Dr. Amoah is a very knowledgeable man with good ideas for Ghana football. His business and organizational abilities are important to the development of football in Ghana. However, some his public statements, just like those of any leader in his capacity, can bring about unnecessary confusion.

Again, in an interview with Paul Adom-Otchere on Metro TV in mid-May, Dr. Amoah disclosed a phone call Sulley Muntari had made to him to express how much he (Sulley) wanted to be in the Black Stars' AFCON 2019 squad. While he had the right to disclose conversations that he had with people, I don't think that disclosure was necessary.

Players are fond of lobbying their way into national teams with statements they make in the media or to key influential people. By being the bearer of Sulley's wishes, Dr. Amoah was either allowing himself to be used by the player to lobby his way into the team or he was prejudging my decisions as the team's coach. Paul Adom-Otchere pointed out to Dr. Amoah during the interview that such public statements from someone in his capacity put undue pressure on a coach.

Dr. Amoah explained that he was only making a recommendation. While I didn't have a problem with his recommendations, I didn't think it is appropriate for recommendations made in private to be shared on national TV, especially ahead of the release of a list that naturally could generate a lot of contentious debates.

Sulley is an exceptional player who has served Ghana well. I have no doubt that Sulley is passionate about helping Ghana in any way he can. At 34 years old, Sulley has made just two appearances over a five-month period since joining Spanish second-division side Albacete on loan.

I select players based on their playing form and the team's needs. For the AFCON, Ghana had hundreds of active players to choose from. If I selected a player, I should be able to justify why that player was being selected, and that justification would have to do with performance. I had to select a squad that I believed would give us the best chance of winning now and also in the future.

In the interest of Ghana football, a player should not be contacting the person in charge the national team to express his desire to be invited. That behaviour should not be encouraged. Furthermore, sharing information about such a conversation on national TV could send the wrong signal to other players who would also contact powerful people to lobby for them.

People are free to lobby whichever way they choose but at the end of the day, the people I call to any national team will have earned their spots on merit. I am sure Dr. Amoah meant well but his public comments on these two occasions did not go down well with me.

Inviting Kevin-Prince Boateng to the Team

In late January 2019, Spanish giants FC Barcelona signed Kevin-Prince Boateng on a six-month loan from Italian side Sassoulo. That was a big move for Kevin's career and naturally, that dominated the headlines around the world and particularly in Ghana. The focus of the debate in Ghana was Kevin's possible return to the Black Stars squad for the AFCON. For weeks, the debate went on and various people voiced out their opinions. I was asked several times by the media about inviting Kevin back into the team, and I was as clear as I could be with my answers.

Kevin was suspended from the team in 2014 – five years earlier – in Brazil. The Dzamefe Commission, which the Ghana government constituted to investigate issues related to Brazil and to make recommendations for the future, said that Sulley and Kevin would have to render an apology to the nation before ever playing for the national team. To the best of my knowledge, Kevin had not yet rendered any apology.

When I returned from Sudan, I inquired from the GFA if the two players had apologised and I was told it was only Sulley who had apologised. Kevin's behaviour and the resulting disciplinary action had become a much bigger deal because he had let it drag on for far too long. If Sulley did apologise, then Kevin had no reason not to apologise.

Unless maybe he (Kevin) had no regard for the authority of the Commission. On my part, I didn't have the authority to invite a player who had been sanctioned by a government Commission.

Kevin is a good player, and I welcome his contribution if he can help the team win. However, it is not lost on me that he has a pattern of choosing to play for Ghana when it suits him. A serious national team cannot be built around players who pick and choose when they want to play for the national team. And that is true no matter how big a star the player is or how big a club the player plays for.

If Kevin had met the Commission's condition for reinstatement, and was one of the best options for the team, I would have had no problem inviting him. And if he returned to the team, I would expect him to play when the team needed him – and not when he decided he wanted to play.

Tour of Europe and the Middle East

In March 2019, my assistant Ibrahim Tanko and I set out on a trip to monitor players outside the country. That trip was also used to visit injured Black Stars players. Tanko went to Spain, Germany, Holland, and Belgium while I went to the UK, Italy, Turkey, Qatar, and United Arab Emirates. I also explored options for our pre-tournament camping while in the Middle East.

For some of the players that we were considering inviting, I wanted to be 100% sure about their form and capabilities before extending an invitation to them. That is why it was necessary to observe them in person when they were playing competitive matches.

In the UK, I paid a visit to Daniel Amartey who was recovering from an injury. He had just had the cast removed from his leg, and I spent some time with him in his home. In Turkey, I spent time with Asamoah Gyan and also with Andre Ayew in their respective homes. I spoke on the phone with other players I could not meet in person.

Assistant Coaching Changes

I brought Maxwell Konadu on to the Black Stars as my assistant and worked with him for two years before leaving for Sudan. After I parted ways with the team, he continued to work as an assistant for my replacement, Avram Grant, for another two years. On my return, I retained him as my assistant for another two years, along with Ibrahim Tanko as my second assistant coach.

Having been around as an assistant coach on the Black Stars for six years and having done well at his job, I believed Maxwell needed a new challenge to get him ready for future opportunities. Being given an opportunity to autonomously lead one of the junior national teams to a major tournament was going to be an important means of proving himself further to the Ghanaian public. That way, he would be in a very good position for consideration when the GFA was ready to go in a different direction with the senior national team head coaching job.

Frankly, I will not be the Black Stars' coach forever and there is no guarantee that my assistant will automatically be promoted to take that job whenever I moved on. Even though Maxwell is one of the most qualified Ghanaian coaches who can someday lead the Black Stars, there are many very qualified coaches and prospects waiting impatiently for my job. In my view, and as was the case with my path to becoming the Black Stars' coach, success at leading a junior national team is an important experience that is necessary for earning the senior team head coaching job.

The national Under-23 team was scheduled to play an Olympic Game qualifier on the same day as the Black Stars' final AFCON qualifier, as well as two games in June. With the preparation for both Under-23 games coinciding with the Black Stars' preparation for the AFCON, an assistant coach of the Black Stars could not successfully handle both jobs. One of the options for the NC was to have one of my two assistants be appointed to head the Under-23 team, and that was a decision the NC was going to have to make.

Before heading out for my tour of Europe and the Middle East, I informed the NC of my recommended assistant coaching changes, which would have them consider Maxwell for the Under-23 head coach since he was one of my two assistants with the longer tenure on the senior national team. They welcomed my recommendation and announced the change as part of a coaching reshuffle for all the national teams.

Tanko had been the Under-23 team's step-in coach, tasked with assembling players for the qualifiers and remaining in charge until a substantive coach was appointed. Tanko coached the Under-23 team for their March game in Accra.

Final Qualifying Match against Kenya; Mauritania Friendly

Regardless of the outcome of our final qualifying match, both Ghana and Kenya were going to the AFCON because both had enough points to come out first and second from our qualifying group. However, it was an important match for me and for the team. I wanted to give certain players an opportunity to justify their inclusion in the final AFCON call-up. Several new and returning players, both locally-based and foreign-based, had the opportunity to showcase what they were bringing to the team.

The essence of that Kenya match, and the Mauritania friendly we played three days later, was to assess both old and new players. That was my primary objective since those were the only competitive games we were going to play before I called a squad for the pre-tournament training camp. For the Kenya game, I fielded mainly people who had been on the team for a while. And then for the Mauritania game, I used a squad that featured mainly new players. I wanted to give each of the players a fair chance to prove that they deserved to be on the team for the AFCON.

Before the match, I reminded them that each one of them had been invited because they were the best at their respective positions. Those two matches were their opportunities to show Ghanaians what they (the players) were capable of. Their performances during the matches gave me a clearer picture of who could be most useful to the team, alongside other key players who had not been invited for the Kenya game.

For instance, Caleb Ekuban played two games and scored two goals, which made many Ghanaians happy with him. I had been monitoring him since he was with Leeds United and I knew what he was capable of. He certainly is a good player and added to the potency of our attack. Also, Joseph Aidoo was impressive with his confident decision-making.

During the second half of the Mauritania match, many of the veterans, especially the midfielders, proved why they should be a part of the AFCON squad. After the substitution to bring on several of the veteran players, the pace of the game and the effectiveness of our attack improved drastically.

One of the key differences between a young, inexperienced player and an experienced one is when and how they decide to move the ball forward. As was evident during the game, some of the inexperienced and less confident players had a tendency of sending the ball back into our half even when they should be pressing forward. The experienced players, on the other hand, made decisions with more confidence and that made a significant difference in the game. The inexperienced players were playing the game too cautiously for fear of making mistakes, and that was very obvious. With experience comes confidence and an improved decision-making ability. I have no doubt that the young players will get better and become key members of future squads, even the ones who did not make it to the 2019 AFCON.

Visiting Egypt ahead of the Tournament

The essence of the three-day trip to Egypt in April 2019 was to participate in CAF workshops; take part in the balloting exercise, which would place Ghana in a group for the tournament's group stage; and to visit the locations where the team was going to lodge and play our matches.

I was in Egypt with Normalization Committee Chairman Dr. Kofi Amoah, Black Stars Management Committee Chairman Dr. K.K. Sarpong, and Acting FA General Secretary Alex Asante.

At the CAF workshop, the coaches and the officials discussed issues related to the tournament and football on the continent. We received a special briefing from the nations that participated in the Russia 2018 World Cup. They shared their experiences and passed on their insights for improving Africa's representation in future tournaments.

The balloting exercise was one of the highlights of the trip. It was a spectacular event that took place outdoors in the shadows of the Egyptian pyramids. Each of the 24 teams were represented by a delegation who observed the proceedings.

The teams were separated into four seeding pots based on CAF ranking. They were then drawn, one at a time, into six groups of four. The teams in each group, as well as the fixtures, were picked by random ballots. It was like picking names out of a hat, except that they used a clear plastic bowl instead of a hat. It was a very transparent process. Tony Baffoe, my former teammate and now CAF deputy general secretary, moderated the balloting with a fine display of his multilingual skills. Four African football legends, including Cote d'Ivoire's Yahya Toure and Senegal's El Hadji Diouf were also on hand to help with the process.

Ghana landed in Group F with Benin, Guinea-Bissau and defending champion Cameroon. While our group, on the surface, may not have seemed to be one of the strongest in the tournament, it would be a mistake to underrate any team. I have always maintained that every team that qualified to be at the tournament was a good team. Moreover, our strategy for winning the tournament was more about being prepared to defeat any team rather than hoping to avoid specific teams. African football has come of age and anyone would be in for a surprise for underrating any opponent. So, I was fine with our group.

Apart from our group, Group D, which had three powerhouse teams – Cote d'Ivoire, Morocco, and South Africa – seemed to me the most interesting group. Namibia was the fourth team in that group. Host nation Egypt was in Group A with DR Congo, Uganda and Zimbabwe. Group B comprised Nigeria, Guinea, Madagascar and Burundi. Senegal, Algeria, Kenya and Tanzania made up Group C. Tunisia, Mali, Mauritania and Angola rounded out the groups with Group E.

Our first match was to be against Benin on June 25. Four days later, we were to play Cameroon, and then play Guinea-Bissau three days later. The top two teams from each group would advance to the knockout stage, along with the four third-placed teams with the best ranking (based on total points, and then goal difference, and so on.) The knockout stage would start with the Round of 16, and then the quarter-finals, to the semi-finals, and then the final on July 19. The third-place match was to be played two days before the final.

Following the balloting exercise, the countries in each group were assigned a bus that took them to go and inspect the hosting facilities where the teams were going to lodge for the tournament. We drove for about two hours outside Cairo to Ismailia, where we toured the hotel, the training facilities and the stadium for our matches. The 19,000-capacity Ismailia stadium, where we were going to play two of our three group matches, was the smallest of the six stadiums to be used for the competition.

By comparison, Cairo International Stadium, where the final match was to be played, has a capacity of 74,000. We also travelled to Suez to go see the location of the third of our three group matches.

Even though additional preparations were underway to have the facilities ready for the tournament, I was satisfied with what I saw. That was going to be Egypt's fifth time hosting the tournament, and the most by any country.

Inspection of Pre-Tournament Camping Location

We needed a camping location near Egypt, in order to prepare as close to the AFCON host country as possible. In March, I visited locations in Abu Dhabi and Dubai, both in the United Arab Emirates (UAE), and then Turkey. In selecting a training camp location for a tournament, the important things to consider include the location's similarity to the location of the tournament, the available training facilities, the nature of the accommodation, and the opportunities for good friendly matches.

From what I learned, several of the AFCON teams were to be camped in Dubai and Abu Dhabi. With those two cities located about an hour and a half drive apart, I recommended Dubai. That way, we would have many options when it came to scheduling friendly matches.

When the Black Stars management team and I left Egypt, we went to the UAE for a final inspection and to secure the locations for our camping.

Between June and July when the tournament was to take place, Egypt's hot summer weather was expected to intensify. With an average daytime temperature of 32°C (90°F), we needed to get used to the weather. The AFCON tournaments have typically been played in the cooler, earlier parts of the year, in January and February. But with Egypt's weather expected to be much warmer, our players needed to build up the capacity for a lot more endurance.

Naturally, the body warms up when a person is involved in physical activity. Running up and down the field in a competitive match warms up the body more. Lots of hydration is necessary and a very high level of physical endurance is needed. That is why the three-week camping in such a warm environment was going to be crucial to our preparations.

The Provisional Squad

As at the time of my visit to Egypt, I was very close to having my final list of players I was going to invite to camp. However, I was still monitoring several players. I was certainly going to invite more players than the final 23 we needed for the tournament.

Injuries and sickness happen all the time and you can never know what would happen before the tournament. There had to be other players in mind to step in when others are not going to be available. For example, Harrison Afful, a key member of the team broke his jaw and was going to need a minimum of six weeks to recover, which could exclude him from the tournament. Thankfully, we had other options.

It was also important for me to keep monitoring the players because some of our best players were coming back from injuries and I needed to be confident that all injured players would be back in form to participate in our pre-tournament camping and also the tournament. With all that in mind, releasing the names of players as close to camping as possible always made sense. The 29 players I invited to the training camp included veterans and younger players I believed were the best available for the task ahead.

Richard Ofori (Maritzburg United, South Africa), Lawrence Ati-Zigi (FC Sochaux-Montbéliard, France), and Felix Annan (Kumasi Asante Kotoko, Ghana) were the goalkeepers.

The defenders were John Boye (Metz, France), Andy Yiadom (Reading F.C., England), Abdul Baba Rahman (Stade de Reims, France), Lumor Agbenyenu (Goztepe S.K, Turkey), Kasim Nuhu, (TSG 1899 Hoffenheim, Germany), Jonathan Mensah (Columbus Crew S.C., USA), Joseph Aidoo (Genk, Belgium), Nuhu Musa (St Gallen, Switzerland), Joseph Attamah (İstanbul Başakşehir F.K., Turkey), and Mohammed Alhassan (Accra Hearts of Oak, Ghana).

The midfielders were Mubarak Wakaso (Deportivo Alavés, Spain), Thomas Partey (Atletico Madrid, Spain), Kwadwo Asamoah (Internazionle, Italy), Ebenezer Ofori (New York FC, USA), Afriyie Acquah (Empoli, Italy), Andre Ayew (Fenerbahçe S.K., Turkey), Christian Atsu (Newcastle United, England), Samuel Owusu (Cukaricki, Serbia), Thomas Agyepong (Hibernian F.C., Scotland), Yaw Yeboah (CD Numancia, Spain), Abdul Fatawu (Kumasi Asante Kotoko, Ghana).

The forwards were Asamoah Gyan (Kayserispor, Turkey), Jordan Ayew (Crystal Palace, England), Abdul Majeed Waris (FC Nantes, France), Caleb Ekuban (Trabzonspor, Turkey) and Kwabena Owusu (CD Leganes, Spain).

Before leaving Accra for Dubai, President Nana Akufo-Addo hosted the team at the Jubilee House, the seat of the Presidency. That was an important event for the team. For the players, it reminded them that the whole country was behind them as we set off to go represent the nation. It was also a public demonstration of the President's ongoing and significant support of the team's preparation for the tournament. Most of the team left Accra on June 1 for Dubai. The remaining players and technical team members later joined us there from their respective bases.

The Technical Team

I place as much importance on who is on the field as I do on who is helping me gather the information that I need to make the important decisions before, during and after the game.

Coaches David Duncan, Sellas Tetteh, and Mas-ud Didi Dramani are some of the brilliant football minds we have in Ghana. These are proven professionals who know the African football landscape very well. These men have coached or observed many of the players on the Black Stars, or coached against some of the teams that were going to be at the tournament. They were perfect to serve as scouts. So, shortly after their appointment, they went to work gathering information about our group-stage opponents.

Scouting was a key part of our preparations. As I have always said, we were not going into the tournament underrating any team or making assumptions about any team. Every team at the tournament had earned the right to be there and we would be making a big mistake if we didn't take a close look at their strengths and weaknesses, and prepare accordingly.

We hired Simon Copley as physical trainer. Simon is a youth coach for English Premier League team Arsenal, and his job was to help the players with their physical conditioning before and after games. Dr. Patrick Ofori, Samuel Kwame

Ankomah, and Jermaine Lopia were the other members of the team serving as psychologist, masseur, and video analyst respectively.

The Captain of the Team

A leader is always a leader whether they have a title or not. In my career as a player and as a coach, I have been a leader even when I was not the captain or the one in charge. I have seen others lead even when they didn't have official titles as the ones in charge. So, I expect leadership from each of my players regardless of what role they are assigned on the team.

On a high-profile team like the Black Stars, leadership from the senior players take many forms, including encouraging the entire team ahead of matches, mentoring younger players and showing them the proper way to develop, checking up on other players when the team is not in camp, and helping resolve issues among players or with the team's management.

Asamoah Gyan had been the captain of the team for the previous seven years. I appointed him as the captain to take over from John Mensah. During Gyan's tenure, he discharged his duties well and won the hearts of many players and fans.

Heading into the tournament, it was an open secret that the players on the team were not as united as they should be, all because of what was perceived to be a captaincy issue. When I took over as the coach the team at the beginning of my "second coming," there were whispers that Gyan's tenure as captain should end. Some players publicly questioned the Gyan captaincy (since he was not the most senior player). I maintained him as captain because he was doing the work well and I didn't see a need for a change at that time.

It is unfortunate that sometimes people grumble when someone has a job they think the person has had for too long, and that the person is standing in the way of others. To me, that was the root of the captaincy issue, and that issue had been lingering around the team while I was away and continued upon my return. I reserve the right to appoint a captain for the team depending on what the team needs. Keeping Gyan as the captain for as long as I did was the right thing for the team.

Andre Dede Ayew, who had been the deputy captain, was viewed by many people as next in line because of his seniority and the leadership he had shown on the field. He had been a very influential leader in the team all the time that Gyan had been the captain. Dede had been excellent at checking on his teammates when they were away from camp. He helped to ensure the players were doing what they needed to do when the team was together for camping and matches. Dede's leadership on and off the field was vital to the team. He did what he needed to do to support Gyan in leading the team.

During a conversation with Gyan days before announcing the provisional squad, I told him that I needed him, Dede and Kwadwo Asamoah to be the leaders of the team for the tournament. That arrangement, I told him, was vital to restore the unity and cohesion the team needed for their successful in Egypt. Therefore, I was going to appoint him the general captain and make Dede the substantive captain with Kwadwo Asamoah as the deputy captain.

I could have announced my decision without notifying Gyan in advance but I called him because of the respectful relationship we had maintained over the years. Additionally,

I saw an opportunity to use the captaincy transition to demonstrate unity among the leaders of the playing body, and for that unity to eventually spread through the rest of the team. If Gyan had understood my point and had made it seem to Dede that it was his own decision to hand over the captaincy to him, I believe that would have been a boost for unity in the team.

When we ended our initial conversation, it was clear that Gyan was not happy about the captaincy change but I encouraged him to ponder over it and let's talk again the following day. When we spoke on the phone the following day, Gyan informed me that after consultations with his brothers and family members, he wanted to continue to play on the team as the captain. He insisted that he wouldn't be a part of the team if he couldn't be the captain. I encouraged him to give his concerns more thought, and that we could talk it over after a previously-scheduled meeting I was headed into with the Normalization Committee.

During that meeting with the Normalization Committee, Gyan's letter announcing his decision to be unavailable for selection for the AFCON squad arrived. In that letter, he also announced his retirement from the national team.

With the kind of relationship I've always had with Gyan and his family, and the respect I had shown him throughout the years we had worked together, I was very disappointed with the letter he wrote. The content and the rushed nature of the resignation letter, which he also made available to the general public, did not put Gyan in the best light. But there was nothing I could do about that. In summary, he was so upset about the captaincy change that he would rather resign from the team than be on the team and not be the substantive captain.

The President of the country intervened, seeking to restore what seemed to be an unexpected turn of events that could hurt the team badly. I respectfully explained my decision to the President and emphasised Gyan's importance to the team. I added that he would be welcomed into the squad for the tournament but as the general captain and not the substantive captain. The President subsequently had a talk with Gyan, which led him to rescind his decision to resign and then be a part of the team. I appreciate the President's compassionate approach to helping resolve the issue.

There is no doubt that wearing a captain's armband and leading a team during matches is a very high honour and an important job. For the tournament in Egypt, I had made the decision of who will play that role. I had appointed the official leaders of the playing body and we were going to move forward. Players don't decide what roles they play on a team. That is a coach's job. A coach can seek the input of players but the decision ultimately rests with the coach.

It had been the practice in the Black Stars that substantive captains, in the twilight of their national team careers, are reassigned as general captain of the team. Another player then takes over that leadership mantle. Stephen Appiah, for instance was made general captain when John Mensah was appointed the substantive captain. When I believed the time had come for the team to have a change in leadership, I made John Mensah the general captain and appointed Gyan the substantive captain. All these leadership transitions happened without a hitch. I maintained Gyan as the substantive captain even when other senior players on the team felt they should be captains.

It didn't help matters that people who were speaking publicly on Gyan's behalf made wild claims about why I made the captaincy change. And as is typical of the Ghanaian media, both sports and non-sports stations, everyone had an opinion about the captaincy issue and they were not shy about expressing their opinions. Unfortunately, there were also others who started rumours to keep the story alive for weeks.

There were all kinds of discussions on radio, TV and on the internet about the timing and the rationale for my decision. There were reports that a spiritualist had advised me to change the captain because Gyan was not a lucky person and that he was not destined to lift a trophy. There was no truth to those stories. I do respect the counsel of others, including pastors, but that story was ridiculous.

I chose not to participate in the media hysteria. I had spoken directly to the people involved in the matter and did not need the additional distraction. No matter what I said, there were going to be people who would tear my statements apart and make more sensational stories from them.

When Gyan arrived in Accra ahead of the team's departure to Dubai, we met for a conversation. That was a fruitful discussion. I walked away from that meeting convinced that he was committed to the team and that I could count on him to help ensure the unity that the team needed. Even though Gyan was not in his prime, I knew what he was capable of and was looking forward to having him on the team. Throughout the pre-tournament camping and during the tournament, Gyan showed good leadership, for which I was grateful to him.

Camping in United Arab Emirates (UAE)

The first batch of Black Stars players and officials arrived in the United Arab Emirates (UAE) on Saturday, June 1 and the second batch joined us the following Monday. The team was based at the Jebel Ali Resort Hotel, a five-star beachfront property with excellent accommodation, training facilities, and other logistics.

Prior to the beginning of the camp, most of the players had been enjoying a two-week break following the end of their respective leagues. So, one of the objectives was about conditioning and getting them prepared for competitive action. Also, many of the players were new to the team and I wanted to observe closely how they played individually and collectively as a team.

Physical trainer Paul Maxwell took the players through various fitness and endurance drills to bring them to our desired level of conditioning for the physically-demanding tournament that the AFCON promised to be. The conditioning required a high level of endurance training and core strength training, which kept the players spending a longer time at the gym and on the beach. They also had to get enough rest to allow their bodies adjust well to the physical stress they were putting on their bodies.

To the players' credit, their levels of seriousness were as high as could be expected. Obviously, each of them knowing very well that they could be dropped from the final line-up if they did not meet my expectations, had a lot to do with that high level of seriousness they displayed.

During that first week, I paid particular attention to Samuel Owusu, Kwabena Owusu and Musa Nuhu. Those were good players from the Under-23 team but new to the senior team. I had to observe them closely to know how best I could utilize them. There were other players, like Majeed Waris and Ebenezer Ofori who were competing with others for a striking role and a midfield role respectively. I was closely monitoring them to decide whether to keep them or not.

Musa Nuhu, who was a strong contender for a central defence role for the tournament, sustained an injury in one of the training sessions. The injury robbed the team of a decent young player who had demonstrated his readiness for the big stage. His injury was also a big blow to the team's diversity in defence as he had to leave the camp to get further medical attention with his club's doctors. His injury did not affect the remaining players' intensity during our training sessions.

Practice is vital to the various decisions our players should be making instinctively during matches. While many of the decisions are standard actions that each player should be familiar with, making those decisions in the context of a match requires good memory recall. Memory recall can only be improved through repeating the routines and practicing that in-game decision-making over and over again. It is common knowledge that if a team doesn't practice enough, they will struggle during a match. On the other hand, practicing particular routines again and again increases their chances of successfully executing those routines in an actual match.

At the end of our first week of camping, we played Namibia in an international friendly match where I had a look at the entire team against a good opponent. We had been training among ourselves all along and the test match showed how well our players could fit together against an opposing team.

We divided the team into two, and each player, with the exception of Dede Ayew and Asamoah Gyan, played in that match. By the end of that match, which ended 1-0 in favour of Namibia, I had a much clearer picture of who would be in the final squad.

Comparing notes with my coaching staff, I selected the final 23 guided by each player's technical abilities and playing form during the season and at the time of selection. I gave the final list to the management team, and we were to speak with each player one-on-one and then as a group to announce the final list to the team. The final list, however, found its way into the media before we had our group meeting.

Defender Mohammed Alhassan, midfielders Ebenezer Ofori, Yaw Yeboah and Abdul Fatawu, and forward Abdul Majeed Waris did not make the squad. As could be expected, the players who were dropped seemed disappointed for not making the final cut. Majeed Waris was extremely upset. As a result, he refused to participate in a meeting of the players with the management and technical team.

Leaks of confidential information such as the selection of the final squad or details about internal team decisions or news about a player's health condition are not helpful to any team. While each media practitioner wants to be the first to break any news, actions that interfere with the smooth running of the team may provide a short-term benefit to certain individuals but create both short-term and long-term problems for the team.

And the problem with leaks continue to prevail because it is difficult to say who passed on such information to their friends in the media.

Waris explained later that he was offended by learning about his exclusion from the final squad through the media. While I do not support his decision to not attend the meeting, I can understand how he felt about the whole situation. I was not happy with those leaks either.

With the final squad in place, the focus of our training shifted to the shape of the team and the best ways to use the players in the team's system of play. Which players to pair together in defence or in midfield, for instance, was something we had to assess closely during practice. The key roles in which to deploy Dede Ayew and Kwadwo Asamoah was also an important focus. We were also implementing insights from the scouting reports about the teams we were going to play against at the group stage.

Scouting reports helped the team prepare for what could be expected. However, opposing coaches may choose to use players in non-typical roles and we needed to plan for such surprises by having a response for several scenarios they were likely to throw at us.

We played a second international friendly, which was against South Africa. We fielded the players who were expected to have starting roles at the tournament, and used that game to test the team's shape and tactical abilities. That match ended goalless and I was pleased with how the pieces were fitting together. I was also pleased with the confidence and competence of our players, especially the younger ones.

With the help of my technical team, we had achieved the goals we set out to accomplish three weeks earlier. The team had taken shape and looked ready for the tournament.

Criteria for Selecting the Final 23

In selecting the final 23, there was a conscious effort to balance experience and youth for the tournament, and for the future of the team. Experience matters a lot when it comes to the team's ability to change the pace of the game or when we have to respond to unplanned events. Having younger players in the squad was critical to the lifeblood of the team. Also, exposing these younger players to a high-level international competition was necessary for the team's progress toward developing replacements for our older players.

Each of the 28 players available for the final selection had exhibited competence and proved themselves worthy of the call to the national team. However, there were only 23 spots and I had to make decisions based on the physical, technical, tactical and mental abilities of each player.

For the left- and right-hand side of defence, we looked at the players' speed, endurance, tackling skills, skill at receiving the ball and passing the ball, how well the player ran with the ball, the players' positioning and repositioning, the players' sense of timing and anticipation, the player's involvement in the attack, as well as his aggressiveness and confidence with the ball. Also, we considered the players' height, muscular power and jumping skills, how good they were with intercepting passes, how they used long and short passing, how they covered, supported and directed plays.

For the central defenders, we looked at many of the same characteristics we looked at for the left- and right-hand side defenders. Additionally, we looked at their physical strength, how well they deployed defensive techniques, and their cooperation with the defensive midfielders.

For the midfielders, we looked at both aerobic and anaerobic endurance. Aerobic endurance is the ability of a person's cardiovascular and respiratory systems to sustain intense physical activities over extended periods. Anaerobic endurance refers to the person's ability to sustain intense, short duration activity such as sprinting. Midfielders move around a lot, and midfielders need a high level of both types of endurance to be able to do their jobs as expected. We also looked at the players' speed, how they ran with the ball, dribbled, crossed, or shot the ball; how they moved back to defend, their level of concentration and their willingness to take risks, their ability to use both feet to send the ball to the desired destination, and their ability to make smart decisions quickly.

For the attackers, we looked at their ability to receive and deal with the ball skillfully, their passing and finishing, how they moved without the ball, how well they changed positions, how creative they were with the ball, their willingness to take risks and be able to think clearly. How fast they could run and how well they could cross the ball were also key evaluation points.

For all the players, we looked out for technical abilities such as their spatial awareness, which is a player's ability to see space clearly across the entire pitch and use that to their advantage. Also, communication skills, composure, and the players' receptiveness to direction and feedback were assessed.

A player's ability to play in more than one position was very desirable. We needed at least two players for each position to give us more options for when we had to move players around in response to our opponents' actions, disciplinary actions or due to injuries.

Discipline and Leadership in Camp

While discipline in the Black Stars camp had seen an improvement in recent years, player indiscipline was one area the technical team and management paid particular attention to as we prepared for the tournament. One measure to ensure discipline in camp was that both the technical team and the players agreed on monetary fines as a form of punishment for individuals who went against the team's code of conduct.

Nonetheless, there were few cases of minor indiscipline like lateness to dinning and team meetings, which the technical team resolved per the agreed-upon code of conduct. The team leaders' ability to quickly identify and handle difficult situations within the team was something that needed commendation.

We still need to continue to take proactive measures to ensure an environment for consistency in good behaviour. When team administrators find out about players not doing the right thing, it is important for such information to be shared with the appropriate people in order for the appropriate actions to be taken. In Egypt, that didn't always happen as some leaders shielded players from being reprimanded in a timely manner. There is room for improvement in this area.

Strengthening Relations with Backroom Staff

As the head of the technical team, I was focused on building effective work relationships with all the members of the coaching staff. Each technical team member is an expert in their area of specialization, and I got the benefit of each person's expertise in making decisions for the team.

In addition to encouraging them to develop closer relationships with each other, I also made sure the technical team members did things like eat together at the same table, hold pre-training meetings to discuss, clarify and address any issues bothering the members of the technical team.

Nurturing relationships with colleagues takes time and effort. Therefore, while in Egypt, I sometimes invited members of the technical team to my room or visited them in their rooms for conversation. While some of those visits were brief, I found them helpful in conveying my desire that we worked closely together as a unit. Although we had differing opinions, ideas and work habits, strong working relationships were developed and I hope these relationships are maintained beyond the tournament.

Ready for Egypt 2019

The final 23 represented the best combination of the Black Stars players available, and we were as ready as we could be after the three-week camping session.

The friendly match against South Africa was our final competitive match before the team left for Egypt. The starting line-up for the tournament was fielded as the starting line-up for this match. Though the South Africa match ended goalless, it was a good test as it gave us additional insight on how to set up tactically for future matches.

We left UAE for Egypt feeling confident in the team's composition and ability. We had trained and we had learned. We had gotten to know each other and we had bonded. We had prepared and we had prayed. And we were ready - ready to take on one match at a time and march on to victory.

· CHAPTER 16 ·

BLACK STARS: GOING FOR GLORY AT AFCON 2019

We arrived in Egypt's capital, Cairo, on Friday, June 21, and travelled two hours by road to Ismailia where we were to play our first two matches against Benin and Cameroon. Guinea Bissau is the other team that was in our group. Our first game of the tournament was to be against Benin at the Ismailia Stadium.

A visit from President Nana Akufo-Addo, on the eve of our opening match, was a major morale booster for the team. The President, who had all along been a major force backing the team's preparations, wished the team well and urged them to give their all for themselves and for their country.

Some players were late in catching the team bus, which delayed our departure to the stadium. Coupled with the traffic situation on the route, we arrived late at the stadium and had insufficient warm-up session, which I believe contributed to our slow start in the match. It is worth pointing out that the leaders of the playing body met with their colleagues after the game and rebuked them. The players later came to render an unqualified apology to the technical team for their lateness.

Ghana versus Benin – Summary

The starting line-up had Richard Ofori in goal. Andy Yiadom and Lumor Agbenyenu had the right- and left-back positions respectively. John Boye and Kasim Nuhu were in the central defence positions. Mubarak Wakaso and Thomas Partey were in midfield. For the attack, Christian Atsu, Andre Ayew and Thomas Agyepong were on the right, center and left respectively playing behind Jordan Ayew.

We began the match poorly due to a lack of concentration from the middle, which resulted in an early goal for Benin. Our defensive shape was not the best as the gap between the two central defenders was too wide. We corrected that gap immediately after the goal, kept our composure and stuck to our initial game plan. We responded well through goal by Andre Ayew in the ninth minute.

All was going well until Thomas Agyepong picked up an injury about 35 minutes into the game. Samuel Owusu took his place. Although we had an able replacement, that unexpected substitution affected our overall approach to the game. However, we kept the pressure on Benin and took the lead through a Jordan Ayew goal just before half time. The goal resulted from a direct ball from the defence line to Jordan. That was a weakness we had seen in Benin through our scouting and pre-match analysis.

We continued to dominate in the second half until John Boye received a second yellow card in the 55th minute, which resulted in a red card. That unfortunate turn of events tactically affected the shape of the team, requiring an immediate response to adjust. We needed to fill the huge void created by Boye's absence. It made more sense to pull out a winger, strengthen the midfield and stabilize the defence in order to maintain the slim lead we had.

I reluctantly pulled out Owusu and kept Christian Atsu due to Atsu's higher level of experience and his ability to keep balls high up the pitch. Jonathan Mensah came on and we resumed play. We changed the shape of the team from 4-3-3 to 4-4-1. Even though we were down by a man, our guys continued to play well until fatigue started to set in.

With more than 35 minutes of play left and up by one man, Benin was motivated to take advantage of the situation. They continued to mount pressure on us. Benin equalized from a corner kick around the 65th minute. A momentary lapse in concentration and poor marking by our players brought about the goal.

Generally, the equalizer was more disappointing because we had thoroughly discussed and exhausted the issue of keeping their concentration at the peak throughout. Even though we were one man down, we looked for another goal but could not deliver. An attempt by Thomas Partey from 25 yards away from the goal post was denied by Benin's goalkeeper.

Even though two of our players were signaling possible injuries, we had to manage the situation carefully to avoid putting ourselves at a much greater disadvantage. We kept our last substitution till late in the game so as not to risk going down to nine men should another player sustain an injury.

Ghana versus Benin – Analysis

We set up with a 4-2-3-1 formation while the opponent came with their usual 5-3-2. We were aware of their tactical and technical orientations, the technical abilities and positions of their key players, as well as their general passing pattern and playing tempo.

1. Attack Build-up:

When build-up began with our goalkeeper, we always had the opportunity to start from the back. However, that was usually a slow build-up and both central midfielders came back to pick up the attack, which created a 4-v-1 situation in our build-up.

That situation made our center-backs and midfielders rely on sending long balls behind the opposing defenders, which was not the main game plan.

When building up through the middle third, we experienced a similar situation as both central midfield players were always dropping deep to get the ball. And when we had possession in the middle, the fluidity of the midfield was not very effective as our attacking midfield player was not giving us many options. He was not positioning himself in the "pockets" or the holes between opposition midfield and defence.

We had planned to play out wide most often, and to use our fast wingers to exploit our opponent's weakness at their full-back positions. Instead of our planned 4-1-4-1 system when attacking (to create more width and numbers in attack), our players were attacking with 4-2-3-1, which had the central midfield dropping deep. That made it difficult for our wingers to get on the ball. The second half was better as Partey played his assigned role of staying higher to receive the balls, leaving Wakaso as the defensive midfielder to initiate the attack together with the two central defenders.

2. Playing in the Attacking Third:

When you think of the field as divided into three parts in the direction of play, there is the defensive third, the middle third and the attacking third.

To build our attack, our midfielders distributed balls forward into the attacking third, where we created few opportunities from open play. That was due to the long balls we were sending in behind the opposing defenders. On the few occasions that we stuck to our game plan of building up to use the wide areas, we almost always created goal-scoring opportunities.

With fast wingers like Thomas Agyepong, Christian Atsu and Samuel Owusu, we knew from the start that we could always create opportunities from the wings. Our first option of attack was to link well from defence to attack through the wide areas, and also to combine the striker with two midfielders supporting the attack to make more numbers in the attacking third.

The second half was much better with our build-up and also with the fluidity and phases of attack, even though we played most of it with 10 men. We dominated the game in terms of possession and chances created.

BALL POSSESSION MAP

	Ghana		Benin
TOTAL	**53%**		**47%**

1
1 - 15min	56%	44%
16 - 30min	63%	37%
31 - 45min	50%	50%

2
1 - 15min	39%	61%
16 - 30min	54%	46%
31 - 45min	51%	49%

3. Set Pieces:

I was very disappointed in how we executed our set pieces as most of what we practiced were not put to use when it mattered. Free kicks and corner kicks are good opportunities for the team to reset and creatively attempt to score. In the regular course of a game, it is not very easy to get a goal against a well-organised team through the regular attack build-up. Set pieces are good opportunities to get goals, and our players knew not to waste such opportunities.

For example, England's 2018 World Cup team spent about half of their preparations practicing corners and free kicks, and they scored nine of their tournament goals from set pieces. Likewise, we practiced and practiced our corners and free kicks, and also various tactics that would allow us to take advantage of such situations when the moment arrived.

We had practiced set pieces extensively because we wanted to take advantage of them as much as possible. And because we had very good players who had proven to be very effective with set pieces, we put a great deal of emphasis on set pieces during our training sessions.

Unfortunately, we were not effective in that area during the match and could not create goals out of any of the set pieces we had.

4. Defending:

The first phase of our defending was our attackers stopping Benin from building up from the back, which we executed well. We pressed well and set traps in the middle to counter-attack immediately when we won the ball.

The understanding between Andre and Jordan was impressive when defending. Our attackers pressuring high up the field forced the opposing team to kick long balls.

In the second half, the effectiveness of our defending declined a bit as we lost balance due to the red card shown to John Boye. On a few occasions, we could not stop their crosses into our penalty box. Sending crosses into our box was one of Benin's main strengths and we were nearly punished late in the game, which would have been an unfortunate price to pay for our numerical disadvantage.

5. Defending Set Pieces:

We defended set pieces well in the first half, especially with the way we set up with three of our players pushing up to contain four of their players. By doing that, we made the opponent bring only a few players into the attack.

In the second half, the numerical disadvantage put our backs against the wall. Just one switch off from a corner resulted in their second goal.

Ghana versus Benin – Overall Assessment

By the final whistle, the score was 2-2. That was a match we could have won comfortably but for the unfortunate red card. Benin's output against Ghana, and in their subsequent matches, proved that the ten-man Black Stars matching them for nearly half of the game was a commendable effort.

Ghana versus Cameroon – Summary

Cameroon, the defending champion, had beaten Guinea Bissau 2-0 in their first group match. We made two forced changes to our starting line-up. Kwadwo Asamoah started in place of the injured Thomas Agyepong and Jonathan Mensah started in place of the suspended John Boye. Baba Rahman replaced Lumor Agbenyenu for tactical reasons.

The complete line-up had Richard Ofori in goal. Andy Yiadom and Baba Rahman had the right- and left-back positions respectively. Jonathan Mensah and Kasim Nuhu were in the central defence positions. Mubarak Wakaso and Thomas Partey were in midfield. For the attack, Christian Atsu, Andre Ayew and Kwadwo Asamoah were on the right, center and left respectively playing behind Jordan Ayew. Cameroon played a 5-3-2 system and we maintained our 4-2-3-1 system.

Based on our scouting report and our analysis of Cameroon's first match against Guinea Bissau, we changed our game plan. For the first half, we decided to soak the pressure, invite them to attack, and then strike on the counter. We changed our approach during the second half due to their general passing pattern and high playing tempo within the first 45 minutes.

Christian Atsu had to be pulled out 15 minutes into the match due to an injury that effectively ruled him out of the tournament. That was another huge setback for the team as a lot of our wing play depended on him. Samuel Owusu replaced Atsu.

Jonathan Mensah stood tall in the match with his timely clearance that foiled a Toko Ekambi attempt at goal. That was one of the many vital decisions Jonathan Mensah made to keep Ghana in the match. Goalkeeper Richard Ofori proved equal to threats thrown at him by Bassogog and Ekambi.

Baba Rahman started ahead of Lumor because of Lumor's fondness for attacking close to the line before crossing, which exposed our back against Benin. With Cameroon, we could have been punished for decisions like that. Additionally, Rahman's experience and efficiency in crossing the ball was also pivotal to the team's shape, especially when attacking.

Kwadwo Asamoah had a specific role in the midfield. Normally, we need a defensive midfielder and an attacking midfielder to create balance in the team. That was what Wakaso and Partey were assigned to do respectively.

I had realised that their right-back, Bassegog, overlapped deep and brought a lot of crosses from the right. Kwadwo Asamoah's introduction was to stop Bassegog, who was very pacey and known to operate from the right wing. He was Cameroon's target man from defence through to attack. I put him there so that any time we lost the ball and Bassegog was going for the ball Kwadwo would track him down. He executed that role perfectly.

Additionally, Kwadwo was supposed to attack deep when we had the ball but he was often found in the middle supporting the attack. I was satisfied with Kwadwo Asamoah's performance in the match even though getting more out of him in the attack could have resulted in a more favourable outcome.

Asamoah Gyan came on as a substitute in the 78th minute in place of Kwadwo Asamoah. He provided an additional bite in attack and kept the Cameroon defence busy. Gyan's presence kept the Cameroon defence from joining their attack as they felt threatened.

Introducing Kwabena Owusu in place of Andre Ayew in the 86th minute was to provide additional pace for the attack and provide a scoring threat with the team's shape moving to 4-4-2. With his first touch of the ball, Owusu was unlucky to hit the bar after an explosive run on the counter in the dying minutes of the match.

Even though Cameroon had the bulk of the ball possession, our performance was an improvement over the first match. We made 15 shots at goal, compared to seven by Cameroon. With about twice as many shots at goal and our players continuing to attack even late into the game, I was pleased with their performance.

		Cameroon	TOTAL	Ghana	
		58%		**42%**	
1	1 - 15min	53%			47%
	16 - 30min	61%			39%
	31 - 45min	49%			51%
2	1 - 15min	61%			39%
	16 - 30min	54%			46%
	31 - 45min	65%			35%

BALL POSSESSION MAP

Ghana versus Cameroon – Analysis

Even though Kwadwo Asamoah was not as fast as Thomas Agyepong, I put him in place of the injured Agyepong. I also gave him the role to drift in as a midfield option in order to give us a numerical advantage in the middle third of the pitch.

1. Attack Build-Up:

Our build-up was good in its setup with our attacking midfielder, Partey, pushing higher to create space for the defensive midfielder, Wakaso, to operate. That setup was also to give confidence to our center-backs to step in with the ball, and for our full-backs to also push higher to engage the opposition wingers. Unfortunately, in the first half, our center-backs did not show enough confidence to carry the ball forward and to break the lines with decisive passes. Instead, they played long balls, which caused us to lose possession of the ball.

When we had possession of the ball, our midfielders combined passes and switched swiftly to the wide areas for either Christian Atsu or an overlapping full-back to deliver crosses. Jordan Ayew, as the lone striker, combined effectively with Andre Ayew and the attacking players to create chances for the team.

Our setup pushed the opponent to defend deep and rely mostly on counter attacks. Having our full-backs high up the field, our attacking midfielders did not have to drop deep to receive the ball but rather stayed high to look for spaces in between the lines. We were really effective at that, especially in the first 30 minutes of the first half.

Our midfielders also supported the attack really well and had some shots at the end of most attacks. We could not turn any of those chances into goals.

2. Set Pieces:

When we did what we had practiced, we were dangerous with set pieces. We had several of such opportunities and we should have made something out of them. Unfortunately, we could not score from those even though we got some decent attempts out of them.

3. Defending:

We did more of a medium press with our plan to contain the opponent and to win the ball quickly in the middle third. When the need arose, we switched to a high press and that resulted in a few chances. Our team was compact in the middle, leaving the opposition to go through the wide areas.

Due to our compactness and how well we defended, the opposition created only a few chances. The chances they created were in instances where we switched off or lost possession cheaply.

4. *Defending Set Pieces:*
We did not defend the set pieces well. We lived on the edge with most of the set pieces, and got away with most as well. That was where the opponent created most of their chances.

Ghana versus Cameroon – Overall Assessment
Generally, our performance against Cameroon was an improvement over the first game. Still, there were aspects of our performance that could have been better.

Ghana versus Guinea Bissau – Summary
The team travelled about an hour and forty-five minutes to Suez for the final group match against Guinea Bissau. We made four changes to our line-up from the previous match: Kwabena Owusu started in place of Kwadwo Asamoah, Samuel Owusu in place of the injured Christian Atsu, John Boye came back from suspension to replace the injured Jonathan Mensah, and Joseph Aidoo took the place of suspended Kasim Nuhu.

Samuel Owusu and Kwabena Owusu were both impressive against Cameroon, which earned them spots in the Starting 11 against Guinea Bissau. That decision was to also create more attacking strength with their speed.

The complete lineup had Richard Ofori in goal. Andy Yiadom and Baba Rahman had the right- and left-back positions respectively. John Boye and Joseph Aidoo were in the central defence positions. Mubarak Wakaso and Thomas Partey were in midfield. For the attack, Samuel Owusu, Andre Ayew and Kwabena Owusu were on the right, center and left respectively playing behind Jordan Ayew.

We controlled the match both defensively and offensively. Our first opportunity came from Baba Rahman, who attacked from the left side and delivered a good cross into the penalty area. Unfortunately, the opportunity was wasted. Rahman stood out by playing according to instructions. His effort contributed to the two goals that ensured our qualification to the next stage.

Afriyie Acquah's introduction was to stabilize the defence and further free Partey to push up-field and increase our attacking options. Partey did in fact push up-field. Mubarak Wakaso, Kwabena Owusu and Samuel Owusu all came close to sending Ghana ahead but none of those efforts turned into goals in the opening half.

Jordan Ayew put Ghana ahead a few seconds into the second half after connecting to a pass from Baba Rahman and fending off a challenge from the opposing defender and goalkeeper.

Afriyie Acquah provided a shield to help protect our lead, and also to allow Partey space to join the attack. Partey added the second goal in the 72nd minute. That was from another cross by Baba Rahman. We held on to win the game convincingly.

Ghana versus Guinea Bissau – Analysis

We continued with our 4-2-3-1 system purposely to push high and press the opposition high up the field, to prevent them from building their attack from the back.

1. Attack Build-up:

Play from the back was always to start with full backs high and center backs wide open to give space to the defensive midfielder to come in to receive the ball. There were occasions where we should have been more confident to carry the ball forward and keep the ball but we lost possession cheaply by going for long passes from defence.

We controlled possession well in the middle third, and stuck to the game plan of using the width and the pace of Samuel Owusu and Kwabena Owusu to give the opponents lots of threats in our attack. The movement of our wide players drifting inside to create spaces for the fullbacks to attack was also very effective. That created more chances for us, especially with the swift crosses of Baba Rahman from the left side.

In the middle and final third, there was good support in all areas of the field with good combination play among Jordan, Andre, Kwabena Owusu and Samuel Owusu. Jordan was really a threat with his runs behind the defenders and also with link-up plays. He was rewarded with a goal from a good move to receive a pass from Baba Rahman.

In the second half, we maintained possession and remained patient with our play switching from side to side to wait for the right opening since the opposition was deep and compact. Our second goal was a result of that patience. Rahman was at his best with his attacking and crossings to deliver the assist, which saw Partey make a deep run from midfield to finish off with a beautiful goal.

2. Set Pieces:

We had a few set pieces but, again, we were wasteful and could not use them well.

3. Defending:

We did not defend as much since we had possession during most of the game. The opposition was set up to defend and counter-attack, and our loophole in the game was defensive transition. On one occasion, we did not get our balance right and that gave an opportunity for the opponent to create their chances through their attacking transition. We were sometimes slow to react in such situations and could have conceded on two occasions.

In our defensive third, we defended solidly apart from two moments where we did not stop crosses from wide areas, and that almost cost us. Once again, we gifted our opponent chances by losing the ball cheaply. We were lucky not to have been punished.

4. Defending Set Pieces:

We defended well and the opponent did not cause much of a threat with set pieces except with the last free kick..

They went for a direct kick, and Goalkeeper Richard Ofori did well to prevent them from scoring.

Ghana versus Guinea Bissau – Overall Assessment
With the aim of winning at all cost, our players stepped up their game in the second half to defuse the first-half defensive tactics deployed by the opponent. That effort paid off with us finishing the group stage at the top of our group.

Ghana versus Tunisia – Summary
We returned to Ismailia for the Round of 16 match against Tunisia. Afriyie Acquah started his first game. Nuhu Kassim returned from suspension to partner with John Boye. Thomas Partey was deployed to play deeper with Jordan Ayew playing in front of him and pushing Andre Ayew to the left wing. The reason was to make Partey and Dede advance more upfield to prevent the Tunisian defence and midfield from advancing forward regularly.

Andre Ayew scored a perfect goal in the first half, which was disallowed for a perceived hand ball by Partey. Replays suggested the ball only touched Partey's chin on the build-up to the goal.

The referee, Victor Gomes, had accepted the goal initially but his assistant had his flag up. At that stage of the competition, there was no VAR to consult. The VAR was to be deployed at the quarter-final stage and beyond.

Both teams approached the match particularly cautiously. Kassim Nuhu's header from a corner in the 15th minute came off the bar and Mubarak Wakaso struck the bottom of the post later on.

We went all out to win during the 90 minutes in order to progress in the tournament. The Tunisians came with a defensive mentality and stuck to it. The introduction of Ekuban for Afriyie Acquah was to re-inject additional pace and bite to support our attack and track back to help the defence whenever needed.

Taha Yassine Khenissi scored 17 minutes to the end of regulation time. That lone goal for Tunisia separated both sides until a late own goal (from the Tunisians) sent the match into extra time. With no goals in the extra time, penalty shoot-out was inevitable.

Mubarak Wakaso, Jordan Ayew, Thomas Partey and Lumor converted for Ghana. Caleb Ekuban who had the best conversion rate at training, surprisingly missed his. The selection of the penalty takers was based on the players' success at shoot-outs during training.

With Tunisia converting all their penalties, the game ended with Ghana's elimination from the tournament.

Ghana versus Tunisia – Analysis

We went in knowing it was a do-or-die affair. We maintained the same format from our previous games with a slight variation. We played with two holding midfielders – Wakaso and Acquah – and with Partey playing on top of them. That was to win the middle tussle and also stop their wide players who usually came inside to pick the spaces in between the lines.

1. *Attack Build-up:*

We started well by keeping to our game plan, attacking with a patient build-up from the back and using the wide areas when there were spaces. Tunisia was also very tactical and kept their shape really well. We tried to be quick in switching play from side to side. Thomas Partey, who played behind Jordan Ayew, gave a good balance in attack and defence as well.

Andre Ayew on the far left was tasked with drifting inside more to create the space for Baba Rahman. While Andre drifted inside, Samuel Owusu was instructed to stay out wide and utilize the 1-v-1 situations to either go wide to cross or cut inside to shoot. Chances were created in the first half from our play but, unfortunately, we could not make them count.

When we conceded a goal in the second half, we had to make changes with the players and also the system. Gyan came on to allow us to go directly towards the goal because of his good physical presence and ability to win aerial duels. That paid off with our equalizer and the creation of many chances, which could have won us the game.

In extra time, the players still had good energy. We dominated and created more chances, but finishing those chances all the way was the problem.

2. *Set Pieces:*

We had so many set pieces but we could not utilize any of them. We often went direct to look for attacking runners and forgot most of the well-rehearsed ones we had practiced over and over and discussed many times.

3. Defending:

We defended more in a 4-5-1 format but sometimes during the game switched to 4-4-2. We adopted both the high and the medium press due to the style of Tunisia's individual players. That worked for us on more occasions, especially with the medium press.

During open play, the opposition created few chances on mostly the left side. Having Andre on the left did not give Rahman enough defensive back up.

4. Defending Set Pieces:

We were vulnerable in defending as the chances created by the opponent were from set pieces. We gave the opponents free headers and switched off when it mattered most. I expected more from the team regarding how we made use of our set pieces and also how well we defended when the set piece was against us.

Ghana versus Tunisia – Overall Analysis

Generally, our team looked compact in every department of the game, which made us create goal-scoring opportunities. But for the near misses, Ghana would have progressed into the next stage of the competition.

Ekuban's missed penalty kick was unfortunate. The moment proved too big for him but I encouraged him not to be too hard on himself. He is a good player and will do well if he keeps working hard. The rest of the team was equally disappointed. They had worked really hard but we didn't get the results we wanted.

End of the Road

While it was our objective to go deep in the tournament and even win it, we fell short. Like all the players and most Ghanaians, I was disappointed that we were eliminated in the Round of 16 on penalties. Even though the team had room for improvement, I was satisfied with the performance of key players and the prospects of the team in the coming years.

Below is a snapshot of the team's strengths and areas needing improvement:

Strengths:	Areas Needing Improvement:
• *Attacking from wide areas*	• *Two midfielders, instead of one, dropping deep to initiate build-up*
• *Midfield supporting attack*	
• *Full-backs pushing high to deliver crosses*	• *Defensive line pushing high when in possession*
• *Dominating play most of the times when calm with possession*	• *Set pieces*
	• *Defensive transitions*

On purpose, the team for the tournament was a blend of experience and youth to provide results for now and for the future. The plan was also to begin phasing out of some of the older generation of players, while at the same time providing the platform for the younger players to benefit from the experience of their seniors. That plan proved to be a good idea.

We have a lot of work to do as a nation and as a team to put us in the best position to win an AFCON as well as a World Cup in the near future.

Based on everything I've learned about the Black Stars in previous years through to the recent AFCON, I believe such achievements are possible. However, that possibility can only become a reality if we are committed to the required player and team development process, and if we give the process the necessary time to materialize.

That, to me, is how the Black Stars will regain its place of dominance in international football.

· CHAPTER 17 ·

BLACK STARS: BIGGEST LESSONS FROM AFCON 2019

The 2019 AFCON tournament proved that modern football has very few underdogs. Once upon a time across Africa, football dominance was in the hands of a few countries, including Egypt, Nigeria, Ivory Coast, Cameroon and Ghana. While some countries depended on the presence of one or two stars, other countries across the continent were making serious investments in long-term planning.

While talent abounds in Ghana, we slipped back into the idea of relying on a few stars and not building a serious talent pipeline. The 2019 AFCON was a moment of truth. We had not done a very good job of planning for the future.

History points to the impact of long-term planning in achieving national team goals. Nations that have been successful in the past decade have been beneficiaries of long-term planning. They developed a plan, became committed to the plan, and gave the plan enough time to materialize.

The core of the Black Stars team that qualified for the World Cup in Germany in 2006, in South Africa in 2010, and in Brazil in 2014 were beneficiaries of such a development plan that birthed the likes of Asamoah Gyan, Sulley Muntari, Michael Essien, Derek Boateng, Addoquaye Pappoe, John Mensah, Laryea Kingston, Razak Pimpong, Yussif Chibsah, Baffour Gyan and the likes.

In 2001, Ghana won the silver medal at the FIFA U20 World Cup in Argentina. The core of that team became the core of the Black Meteors team that qualified and participated in Athens 2004 Olympics. That core group later became the Black Stars team which qualified Ghana to our first-ever World Cup in Germany. That same group of players formed the core of the Black Stars team which won the bronze medal in the 2008 AFCON hosted by Ghana.

Even though placing third in the 2008 AFCON was seen by some people as a failure, the core of that team was solid and we stayed on course with our long-term plan. The emerging young players who won the FIFA U20 World Cup in 2009 were promoted to the senior team. Players such as Andre Ayew, Emmanuel Agyemang Badu, Dominic Adiyiah, Rabiu Mohammed, and Samuel Inkoom strengthened the Black Stars to place second in the 2010 AFCON in Angola, and went on to reach the quarter finals of 2010 FIFA World Cup in South Africa.

The success in that era was the result of long-term planning.

Madagascar's success at the 2019 AFCON surprised many but that success did not happen overnight. Following year after year of failed qualification attempts and problems with the football infrastructure in their country, they eventually got their acts together. They did the work needed to turn things around. Of course, they benefited from the money and expertise that FIFA invested in developing football in their country. They also benefited from many of their players who joined the team from France and other competitive leagues. The bottom line, however, was that their success was not an accident.

For them, it took many years to create a national team capable of qualifying to the AFCON, let alone win a game at the tournament. Finishing at the top of their group and exiting the tournament at the quarter-final was impressive. Watching Madagascar's success, it was evident that commitment to a long-term plan was needed in order to achieve success.

Nigeria had its share of difficulties but it was another recent example of planning and sticking with the plan. After failing to qualify for the 2015 and 2017 AFCON tournaments – despite winning the 2013 edition – they came back strong, placing third in the 2019 tournament. For a nation that made it to the Round of 16 at the 2014 World Cup not to qualify for two successive AFCONs, rethinking their national team's long-term future was necessary. The work they did is what is bringing them back to prominence. It has not been all that rosy for them and they still have more work to do. But they, at least, seem to be on the right path doing the right things to make them successful.

There are many stories of such long-term planning going on around the continent, including Aliou Cisse being given five years to build a winning team for Senegal and Mali's effort at building for the future. Ghana, therefore, cannot afford to bury our head in the sand and pretend we are one of the best national teams on the continent.

Dismissing coaches without much thought about how that affects the long-term plan is a short-sighted action that may satisfy fans but hurt the team in the long run. While a coach has ultimate responsibility for the team's success, the quickness with which African national teams get rid of coaches is a problem that affects the continuity of long-term planning. Nearly a third of the coaches at the 2019 AFCON were either fired or ended their relationships with their respective FAs at the end of the tournament.

In Ghana, the facts show that between 2014 and my eventual return to the team in 2016, the nation put all her eggs in the win-now basket and neglected long-term planning.

While no coach wants to be fired, I would have walked away from the Black Stars job if I failed to pull together a team that had a good chance at advancing deeper into the AFCON 2019 tournament. Also, I would have resigned from the job if my prospects of making the team successful were slim.

For various reasons, certain individuals in the media and in the general public have made it their mission to have me fired. Such people give no regard to my competence, my record, and the progress the team continues to make. When you read some of these headlines about me, it becomes very obvious that their publishers have an agenda to make me look incompetent and to get me fired.

For such people, there will always be something to criticise even if I coach the Black Stars to win the next World Cup. That is why I ignore many of such people, take constructive criticism of objective people, and focus on doing my work. It is wise to ignore the noise of the detractors.

Speaking of detractors, that is a real problem and something I have to contend with all the time. Sometimes, I get criticised severely and publicly by people in the media and others in high places for no other reason than the fact that I did not select their preferred player. I understand that some of these individuals have a financial interest in certain players being in the squad but my job is to select players who will give us the best chance of winning our matches. If the idea of forcing players on coaches prevails, we will be heading nowhere as a nation as far as football is concerned.

Even if, for argument sake, I allow every media house to choose one player for the team, there will certainly be some people who will still not be satisfied. Some will still complain about who starts or who plays for how long. Others will even criticise me for allowing them (the media houses) to chose the players in the first place.

If a surgeon was to perform surgery on a journalist's family member, it would be unheard of for that journalist to tell the surgeon who to include on his team. Unfortunately, my job is done mostly in public and it naturally lends itself to many opinions. As appropriate, people are free to suggest players that I should consider. However, insisting that a player becomes a part of the team simply because of who recommended him is a recipe for disaster.

Ghana is bigger than any one individual, and it is my greatest hope that all national team coaches at all levels in the present and in the future are strong enough to resist those kinds of player-selection pressures. If a player is good and will be useful to the team, I will give him an opportunity. If he is not, it is a disservice to the team and to the nation to select him.

Our success in the 2013 and 2015 AFCON tournaments, reaching the semi-finals and finals respectively, were the results of building around a core team and infusing the team with a younger batch of players from our talent pipeline. We can achieve future success by doing the things that made us successful in the past.

The Way Forward

On the evidence of the historical background, it is clear that it takes a deliberate effort off the field to win on the field. The current Black Stars team has many young players with enough talent to propel the nation to the top of the world stage.

We have a lot of work to do – building a solid team around the present core by phasing out veteran players and integrating the next generation of champions into the team. That will be the best next step on our journey to winning the cup in one of the next two AFCONs. My confidence in the team has been boosted by the combine performances of our young players and the experience of the team's core of veteran players.

Placing a special focus on strengthening the Black Meteors is going to be critical to our immediate and long-term success as a nation. It is very unfortunate that the Black Meteors could not qualify for the Tokyo 2020 Olympic Games. That would have offered our young players tremendous tournament experience ahead of AFCON 2021 and World Cup 2022 campaigns, giving the Black Stars a large pool of talented and capable players to choose from. I look forward to the growth development of the Under 23, Under 20 and Under 16 players as we continue on the Black Stars' journey back to prominence.

I thank Ibrahim Tanko, Stephen Appiah, Richard Kingson and the entire technical team for their services to the nation, specifically for their contributions at AFCON 2019. I look forward to what C.K. Akunnor will bring to the team, now and in the future, to help us build on what we've already started.

Bringing Back the Love

We began the 2021 AFCON campaign in November 2019 with a 2-0 win against South Africa and a 1-0 win against São Tomé and Príncipe. Those victories were key to ensuring a smooth qualification as well as for reviving the passion most Ghanaians have for the Black Stars.

The "Bring Back the Love" campaign, started by the GFA to rally support for the Black Stars and Ghana football in general, is a very good step in the right direction. The many people who came out to greet us when we were on our way to Cape Coast for the South Africa match, the tremendous reception we received from University of Cape Coast students, the stadium attendance for the match, the goodwill displayed by members of the media, and the fans showing up in their numbers at our training sessions proved that Ghanaians love the Black Stars. I'm very hopeful that future victories will help strengthen the love.

For the South Africa match, we started with a 4-4-2 formation because we were playing at home and I wanted to put early pressure on the opposing team. Throughout the match, we varied our formation to respond to situations on the field of play. For example, one of the two strikers was to fall back to help the midfielders whenever we lost the ball, changing the formation to a 4-5-1 at that point in time.

Formations are important but a rigid thinking about formations does not leave much room for creativity. I certainly don't believe in sticking to a single formation and drilling that into the heads of my players. As a team, we practice many scenarios and deploy our best tactical option a situation calls for. It is more important to me that my players know their respective roles and perform those efficiently. Formations are useless if players don't play their roles. Thankfully, many of our players performed their roles well and we were able to secure the three maximum points in each game.

We still have work to do to be ready to win AFCON 2021. We need to correct our weaknesses, improve on the things we do well, and have all our best players well integrated into the team. Winning our remaining matches and qualifying convincingly for the tournament will provide a momentum that could help end our nearly forty years drought for an AFCON title, and sustain the love Ghanaians have for our national teams.

We are on a journey, once again, to become one of the best football nations in the world. We have our work cut out for us and I will continue to do my part, working closely with my players and technical team. And with all things being equal, we will wave Ghana's flag from victory to victory in the years ahead.

AFCON 2019: With Afriyie Acquah. Baba Rahman, Samuel Owusu and Ibrahim Tanko behind me.

AFCON 2019: With Afriyie Acquah. Christian Atsu, Caleb Ekuban and Mubarak Wakaso looking on.

AFCON 2019: With Dede Ayew.

AFCON 2019: With Andy Boakye Yiadom.

AFCON 2019: With Jonathan Mensah.

AFCON 2019: With Nuhu Adams and Jonathan Mensah.

AFCON 2019: With Lumor Agbenyenu.

AFCON 2019: Looking on as Thomas Partey, Jordan Ayew, Baba Rahman and Nuhu Kassim go in for a ball.

AFCON 2019: With Coach Ibrahim Sunday.

AFCON 2019: With Coach Sellas Tetteh.

AFCON 2019: During the press conference (with Jonathan Mensah) ahead of the Tunisia match.

AFCON 2019: (L-R): Stephen Appiah, Richard Kingson, Ibrahim Tanko, and me.

AFCON 2019: Starting line-up against Cameroon; **Top (L-R)**: Baba Rahman, Jonathan Mensah, Richard Ofori, Kasim Nuhu, Thomas Partey, and Jordan Ayew; **Bottom (L-R)**: Mubarak Wakaso, Christian Atsu, Andre Ayew, Kwadwo Asamoah, and Andy Yiadom.

AFCON 2019: Starting line-up against Tunisia; **Top (L-R)**: Jordan Ayew, Baba Rahman, John Boye, Richard Ofori, Kasim Nuhu, and Thomas Partey; **Bottom (L-R)**: Mubarak Wakaso, Afriyie Acquah, Samuel Owusu, Andre Ayew, and Andy Yiadom.

AFCON 2019: Conferring with Dede Ayew during a group-stage match.

AFCON 2019: Looking on as Samuel Owusu prepares to get the ball past an opponent.

AFCON 2019: Calling out instructions to my players as Kwabena Owusu presses on with the ball.

AFCON 2019: Team lines up as we watch the penalty shoot-out with Tunisia.

With Kwabena Yeboah at the Accra Sports Stadium.

With Kwabena Yeboah (third from left), Dede Ayew (fourth from left), Jordan Ayew (fourth from right) and the Black Stars technical team preparing for the 2021 AFCON qualifier against South Africa.

With Torric Jibril.

With Black Stars players and Assistant Coach C.K. Akunnor at the Cape Coast Sports Stadium preparing to play against South Africa in the 2021 AFCON qualifier.

With GFA President Kurt E.S. Okraku at the Cape Coast Sports Stadium when he visited the team ahead of our 2021 AFCON qualifier against South Africa.

With Black Stars players and technical team at the Cape Coast Sports Stadium saying a prayer as we prepared to play the 2021 AFCON qualifier against South Africa.

With Black Stars players during a training session ahead of the South Africa match.

With Kassim Nuhu during a training session ahead of the South Africa match.

In a discussion with Dede Ayew during the South Africa match.

Giving instructions to Mohammed Kudus during the South Africa match in which he scored the second goal that gave us a 2-0 victory. Thomas Partey scored the first goal.

Celebrating with technical team members after the South Africa match.

With South Africa Head Coach Molefi Ntseki following the South Africa match.

PART IV: LEAVING A LEGACY

· CHAPTER 18 ·

MAKING MONEY AND INVESTING WISELY

The reason many parents, including my father, historically discouraged their children from becoming professional footballers was because of the lack of financial benefits that came with that career. It used to be, and it still is the case in some families, that parents insisted that their children complete the highest level of education possible and become employable in something other than sports. That was the case even if the child was extremely talented in sports. That was the case because in the 1980s through the 1990s, only a handful of Ghanaian footballers were rich or financially secure.

Historically, the most talented footballers were kids we referred to as "kobolo boys" – boys who just roamed around from one neighbourhood to another playing football from sunrise till sunset. Many of such boys grew up without much education and might not have learned any trade. They might have made it into the highest levels of the local league and even to got called into the national team. That success didn't always translate into financial benefits, especially when the player did not get to play in a foreign league or suffered a career-threatening injury.

The negative perception about football changed significantly when many players started making so much money that they became some of the richest people in Ghana overnight. With many young Ghanaian players doing well at international tournaments, beginning from the 2000s, people's perceptions started shifting from the mindset that playing football was only for kobolo boys or people who did not have any other career options.

Even though the perception began to shift and has largely shifted, it is a fact that not every player makes a lot of money. It is also a fact that earning millions of dollars does not guarantee long-term financial success for a player. Injury can prematurely end a player's career. With all these facts in mind, making money and investing wisely is an important topic that every serious footballer should pay close attention to.

It worth noting the perception that playing football was for kobolo boys changed not only because the footballers made money but also because many of the players did not abandon their education. Some of the very successful footballers the country has produced completed secondary school.

In the course of my career, both as a player and as a coach, I have been a part of an era where players barely made any money from their football career, as well as a part of an era where players make millions of dollars in a month. I have seen players raising families and living decent lives even though they did not make a lot of money. I have also seen players who made a lot of money and made choices that did not preserve their wealth.

My father was not in favour of my playing football as a professional because he didn't know any professional footballer at that time who owned a house or a car. My father feared that if I took football seriously, I was going to end up with the same future as the kobolo boys in the neighbourhood.

While my father's fears were coming from a good heart, that fear was made greater because he never took the time to assess whether I was good enough to have a successful football career. If I wasn't good at football, I myself would have abandoned it a long time ago.

It was when I started making money from playing for Mine Stars that my father warmed up to the idea that playing football as a professional may not be such a bad thing. Even though the money I made then wasn't that much money, that was enough money to take care of my living expenses and help out my parents.

I built my first house during the middle part of my years at Kotoko. That was around 1989 and it was situated in Sunyani. I bought the land earlier and, over time, was able to build a boys' quarters on part of the land. As modest as that was, I considered that a major accomplishment because it required a great deal of future-thinking on my part to invest in land and build a house.

It has always been true in the Ghanaian culture that if a person does not build a house of their own, no amount of financial success is respected by the community. Apart from a building being a tangible evidence of the fruits of a person's labour, there is a practical reason for owning one's own house.

Making Money and Investing Wisely

Shelter is one of the basic human needs and nobody wants to rent a place forever.

In those days, the money I was making from playing for Kotoko and the national team was not enough to put up a two-storey building. Additionally, my wife and children did not live in Sunyani. They lived in Kumasi and subsequently in Tema, near Accra. With that, my approach was to build gradually over time. By 2008, I completed the main house in my Sunyani residence.

My first car was a Toyota Corolla, which I later turned into a taxi after I bought a Mercedes Benz. I also bought a VW Golf. I grew my fleet of taxis to three and then to five. Five taxis were a lot to manage since I was travelling most of the time. Not being at home for the drivers to render daily accounts to me made it easy for the drivers to keep significant portions of the daily sales to themselves. One of my drivers bought his own taxi out of money that I believed was mine. I eventually sold all the taxis and got out of the taxi business.

I invested in an Urvan minibus, which plied an Accra-Kumasi route. I did that for a while. However, when the bus went to Accra and did not return on schedule, I became stressed out thinking about what might have happened to the bus and the driver. During those days, cell phones were rare so I could not simply call to check on the driver. I had to wait, sometimes for days, to hear from my driver. The stress of that transportation business was too much for me so I sold that business.

With my football career, I successfully took care of my wife and children, helped my parents and siblings, and retired from playing football with a respectable amount of money to my name. Respectable meant I could afford the standard lifestyle that most middle-class Ghanaians enjoyed. With the same career, I was able to send my children to a private school like most middle-class Ghanaians did.

At that time, my wife and children lived in her parents' home in Tema because I was always away travelling for matches or in camp for Kotoko and the Black Stars. Thus, I preferred the stability my children experienced being around their mother and my in-laws. That support system was key to my ability to do the kind of work I did and also to raise my family.

Abdul Razak was one of the first people I knew who made significant earnings from playing football. After he left Kotoko to join Cosmos in the US, he built a house and established a transport company, Golden Boy Transport. That kind of success was rare until the era of Nii Odartey Lamptey and his colleagues from the Starlets championship team. It was around that era that professionalism in football took on a whole new meaning for most of us in Ghana. Until then, most footballers were not exposed to life-changing sums of money like current footballers are expected to.

When I retired from playing, I knew I was going to have to work in order to take care of my family. There was no question in my mind about that. While I preferred to work in football, because of my experience and passion for the game, I was open to using my other skills to earn a living.

Serving as an assistant coach with Kumasi Asante Kotoko, immediately following my retirement, did not come with a significant amount of money. It was, however, a good job to have. It was an opportunity to learn under a respected coach and put myself in a position for a better-paying opportunity in the years ahead.

Before my better-paying opportunity as an assistant coach of the Black Stars and later as the head coach, I had to take on regular jobs like most people. Decent work was never a bother to me. In London, I worked for several years as a control room analyst for Barclays Bank. Even though coaching was my first-choice career, I was open to doing other regular jobs like several of my colleagues did and continue to do.

Fortunately for me, my coaching career took off and I have been blessed with the opportunity to earn a competitive salary over the past 10 years. Many of the significant investments I currently own, including a hotel, an apartment complex and guest houses, were all acquired over the course of the last 10 years.

Unlike many young players, I was in my 50s when I began earning significant amount of money and my perspective on life was different. If you have a wife and children, you think differently about how you spend money.

Many young players today, make huge amounts of money before they become experienced enough to make long-term decisions. And if such players are not surrounded by good people who have real financial management expertise, the fortunes that the players earn may be spent on flashy cars, overpriced clothes, on women, and on ill-advised business ventures.

Even though my job as a coach is to help players win on the field, I care enough about my players to want to see them succeed in life. Sadly, I know of too many players who have mismanaged their finances though I do my part to sound a note of caution and offer pieces of advice whenever I have the opportunity. But knowing that I am not their father or their uncle, they can choose to take or ignore my advice.

I am not saying that a player should not wear nice clothes or drive nice cars or buy a nice house if he is making enough money and can afford those things. What I am saying is that spending all your money before sitting with a qualified financial management professional to match your expected career earnings with your expenses is like building a house without a floor plan. You can certainly do that but that is never a good idea.

While travelling for matches with the team, we have sometimes gone out as a group to shopping malls in Europe. Knowing how lavishly some of our players spend, I hesitate to go shopping with many of them otherwise I become the boring older person who keeps complaining about how ridiculously expensive some items are priced. While on some of these shopping trips, I see players pay $1,500 for a pair of jeans that should cost $100 at the most. And they proudly explain to me that such clothes are designer brands reserved exclusively for rich people like them. I smile at such remarks and hope that they're not buying into a hype.

The fact is, many players buy into the hype of the media and the people around them. The stardom gets into their heads and overspending becomes a norm for them. And for some players, they stretch themselves to buy things, such as cars that they cannot afford, simply because another player had bought that car, and they want to do the same.

With the kind of money most of our young players make these days, it is better for them to have credible and experienced financial advisors. The players could meet with their advisors at least once a year to take stock of all their assets and liabilities, and help them plan for future income and expenses.

One of the difficulties with having our salaries in the public domain is that anyone can know how much money we make, and assume we should be able to give them whatever they want. Such people do not take into account the fact that we have to pay taxes and most players have to pay their agents. While most players are left with significant amount of money after these payments have been made, some players assume that they will be earning that kind of money year after year, for many years to come. However, that is not always the case for many players. That is why planning for a player's financial life ought to start with the first significant amount of money a player makes.

Many players, with the best of intentions, venture into business. However, not everyone has that business acumen. Moreover, investing in a business you do not fully understand is often an opportunity for someone else to take advantage of you. There are many bad people out there looking for ways to take advantage of rich people, and footballers are often an easy target.

Many players spend a fortune on girlfriends and other women. Shopping sprees, expensive trips and nights out at the clubs are some of the ways many players spend their money. Those are the common ways some players say they wasted money earned during their playing days. Some players are willing to spend a significant amount of money to keep expensive girlfriends whom they would otherwise not have been able to date.

Unfortunately, I cannot tell a player who to date or fall in love with. What I can do is to give my younger players an opportunity to hear from their senior colleagues about the good and bad decisions they made with money. Hopefully, such conversations will encourage the younger players to make smart financial decisions.

Stephen Appiah is one of the most successful and respected former Black Stars players I believe could drive home the message about making money and investing wisely. So, I invited him to give a talk to the players during one of our camping sessions. He spoke candidly about the good and bad decisions he made with his money, the things he did not pay enough attention to, and the bad people who targeted players no matter how much precaution they took. He offered his insights like an older brother who genuinely wanted his younger brothers to be successful.

I was not the only person in the room that day who was moved by what Stephen Appiah had to say. The players listened attentively as he spoke and gave him a standing ovation when he was done. I can only hope that the lessons he shared stay with our young players for a long time because becoming broke after earning so much money is the last thing I will ever wish for any player.

Safe investments like treasury bills and real estate are some of the popular options available to most people looking for safe investments. I am sure qualified professional financial planners know of more ways that a player can manage his money so he lives comfortably, enjoys the fine things in life, and also prepare for life after football.

Just like my players, I realise that a coach can lose his job at a moment's notice and there is no guarantee that I will always have a job at the same salary level for the rest of my career. Therefore, I take my own advice and invest wisely.

I understand real estate so I have invested my money there. In Sunyani, I put up a nine-unit apartment building with six three-bedroom and three two-bedroom units. The building is currently occupied by Sunyani Central Hospital doctors. In Kumasi, I put up a building with sixteen one-bedroom and four two-bedroom units. Originally intended as a student hostel, that property located near Kwame Nkrumah University of Science and Technology (KNUST) is now rented out as regular apartments.

Royal Baron Hotel is the 22-room hotel I recently completed. It is uniquely designed to meet every traveller's needs, whether they are travelling to Kumasi for business or for pleasure. Staffed with well-trained professionals, our people seek to deliver excellent and personalized services to guests. It is located in the same vicinity as the hostel in the Ayigya suburb of Kumasi, minutes away from KNUST Hospital, KNUST Police Station, KNUST Botanical Gardens, and the Kumasi-Accra Road.

Obviously, the investments are intended to generate income for me and to leave an inheritance for my children. Much more than that, investing in the kinds of real estate that I have invested in helps address a major need in my community – affordable and decent accommodation. With these investments, I also offer employment to people who work at the hotel and those who manage the hostel and the apartment building.

Many years ago, Ghanaian footballers played the game purely for the love of it and often relied on the benevolence of their club's supporters to help them acquire lands, build homes and leave a legacy for their family. Those days are gone. As long as clubs and national teams are making money from the services of the players, there is every reason that the players must be paid fairly for their work.

Most Ghanaian players take up football early in life and give up the opportunity to learn a trade. So, for many players, the only trade they know is football. When such a person retires and does not get an opportunity to coach or work in a professional capacity for a team, that person is often left with the business of buying and selling items as their main source of income. Many times, such businesses do not last, leaving the player desperately looking for something else to do.

Even though every individual is responsible for planning for their own future, many footballers would benefit from a pension plan, especially in their older years.

Many footballers from the pre-2000 era did not earn much during their playing days. Some earned decent money but did not plan for their old age. Some planned but things did not work well for them when they became older.

Several people and I have done our part to financially support those that we can support. Some of the current and old players belong to associations that seek to look out for their welfare. There is the Professional Players Association of Ghana (PPAG) and also the Retired National Footballers Association of Ghana (RENFAG). These associations are great but they are not a substitute for an individual player planning for his own future.

My foundation, the Kwasi Appiah Foundation, has been set up to contribute my quota to the welfare of older, former players who need support. Other initiatives exist to help look out for the elderly. However, that will never be a sufficient substitute for a professional footballer's preparation for retirement, especially for a player who earns a good living during his active playing years.

There is a Bible verse that says money is the answer to all things. That's in Ecclesiastes 10:19. Daddy Lumba cites that verse in his song "Sika" where he says, *"Wiase mu ohia yɛ ya; sika ne nipa nkwa."* That translates into "Poverty is painful; money sustains life."

Money can be the answer to many things and players who earn huge sums of money can have answers to many of life's problems. That same money can come and go quickly if not handled carefully with a plan.

Money is important in life but managing money well is more important. I hope that our players will surround themselves with good people and make careful decisions when it comes to how they manage their money. Ultimately, the decision about what a player does with their career and with their money rests with them.

LEADERS DON'T HAVE TO YELL

The 22-room hotel is located in the Ayigya suburb of Kumasi.

Making Money and Investing Wisely

The Kumasi Apartments located near KNUST include sixteen one-bedroom and four two-bedroom units; each comes with a kitchen and a hall.

Nine three-bedroom apartments for Sunyani Central Hospital Doctors.

· CHAPTER 19 ·

GHANA'S BEST XI

Ghana has a long tradition of producing very talented players, some of the best in the world. As a player and as a coach at the club and national team levels, I have had the pleasure of working with many of Ghana's best players both locally and internationally. Whether playing with them on the same team or playing against them, I have always had a great admiration for professionals who demonstrated a dedication to the game. Such players played with consistency at a very high level, and contributed to the success of their teams.

Ghana's Best XI is my selection of past and present players that I can confidently lead to victory against any team in the world. These players, who played between the 1980s and now, have excellent individual skills, often "killed themselves" for the game by playing with a sense of purpose, and consistently made their teams better.

Considering their complete body of work over the course of their careers, below is my selection of the eleven starters, along with five reserves, and seven additional players who did not make my team but deserve a special recognition.

1. **Richard Kingson**

Whether playing for local club Accra Great Olympics or international clubs or for the national team at various levels, Kingson's ability to command his defence made him a first-class goalkeeper. He had a good vision of the field, read the game well and had good anticipation skills. No wonder he played consistently on the national team at various levels over a long period of time.

2. **Ernest Appau**

Ernest Appau played for Kumasi Asante Kotoko in the 1980s. His seriousness with everything, whether at training or playing a match, made him an excellent teammate. During the 1980s when most of us were incorporating overlapping runs into our style of play, he was one of the best I ever saw. He defended well and was always attack-conscious, making him a very reliable member of any team.

3. **Offei Ansah**

Offei Ansah spent most of his career playing for Accra Hearts of Oak and was a member of the Black Stars in the 1980s. He was a versatile defender known for his aggressive tactics. He was good at intimidating opponents and frustrating wingers. He was the kind of player we referred to as a "hard guy" due to how difficult it was to compete against him. He was tactically disciplined and always had a winning mentality.

4. **Samuel Osei Kuffour**

Osei Kuffuor came to the attention of most football fans as a member of the 1991 Starlets team that won the Under-17

World Cup. From his early career in Kumasi through his years in Italy and Germany, he was one of the young players who blossomed very nicely into a world-class player. He successfully played at a very high level for a very long time. Tactically disciplined, he had a commanding presence at the back. His aggressiveness and his winning mentality made him a first-choice defender most of the time.

5. **John Mensah**

From his early days on Ghana's Under-20 national team, it was evident that John Mensah was going to have a long, successful career as a footballer. His height and physical build made him stand out. Because of his speed, he was able to cover many areas of the defence. He was very good in the air and used his strength very well to dominate opponents. As a defender, he didn't just clear the ball but often controlled the ball and passed it to the right person to build the attack. Whenever he was part of the team, his discipline and leadership inspired my confidence in the defence.

6. **Papa Arko**

Papa Arko was Kumasi Asante Kotoko's midfield commander for many years and also the team's captain. He was very good at putting himself in good positions to receive the ball. He always played with an attacking mindset and was very good about switching the pace of the game as needed. One of his unique qualities is his ability to control and shoot the ball very well with both his left and his right feet. That made him unpredictable on most occasions. His leadership and skills were key to Kotoko's 1983 success.

7. Michael Essien

Michael Essien's success as one of the best Ghanaian footballers of all time was due to his strength, his high work rate, and his unique ability to play well at several positions. While Essien traditionally plays as a midfielder, I selected him for this position on this team because he can play it well and switch smoothly if I needed to move him into another position. He attacks, he defends and he scores. He knows how to make himself available for the ball, and he is very good at controlling the pace of the game.

8. Stephen Appiah

Whether playing for local and international clubs or for Ghana's national teams, Stephen is a natural leader who played a true captain's role. He was technically skillful, had a good vision of the field, and covered a lot of ground in the midfield. In one-on-one situations, he used his physical dominance to his advantage. He led by example and controlled what was happening on the field with his ball handling and his motivation of other players. He had a winning mentality and inspired confidence in his teammates. For this Best XI team, he is the captain.

9. Asamoah Gyan

Gyan is a powerful weapon in a team's attack. With his unique ability at creating spaces for himself and also making use of scoring opportunities, he is able to score goals regularly. He has great speed and knows how to get around defenders. In the air, he is competent at using his head and demonstrates a lot of passion for the game. It is no surprise that he is the player with the most caps for the senior national team and the record holder for the most goals scored for the Black Stars. Of course, his special dancing after he scores goals and his love of gyama (cheer songs) makes him a big inspiration to his colleagues.

10. Abedi Ayew Pele

Abedi Pele's passion and technical skillfulness was the centerpiece of his illustrious career, which made him one of the best African footballers of all time. From his days with Real Tamale United, to his time in Europe where he won the UEFA Champions League with Marseille, and also as a member of the Black Stars for many years, his high work rate and his aggressiveness with the ball made him a very effective attacker. A natural leader, his tendency to always want the ball and his ability to create scoring opportunities for himself or other players made him an energizing part of the attack.

11. Samuel Opoku Nti

Opoku Nti, one of the best forwards in the history of Ghana football, had a distinguished career with Kumasi Asante Kotoko before he moved to Switzerland and played there for many years. His high work rate and his intelligence on the field made him extremely successful at both the club and national team levels. His ball-handling skills were superior and he knew how to smoothly get away from defenders. As a good scorer who could shoot from a distance, he gave his teams multiple scoring options. He earned the nickname Zico for how similarly his playing reflected that of the Brazilian legend with the same name.

The following players make up the reserves:

12. Sulley Muntari

Sulley is one of the most passionate people I know. Definitely very outspoken, he often says what's on his mind. He is extremely talented and very aggressive on the pitch, and he hates to lose. Since his days as a member of the national Under-20 team or at the club level in Ghana or in Europe, he has been playing almost every game passionately until the final whistle. He plays different positions, attacks when necessary and defends when necessary. His left foot is his weapon and he's used it in scoring some very crucial goals.

13. Anthony Yeboah

Anthony Yeboah earned the nickname Yegoala for his goal-scoring reputation. From Kumasi Asante Kotoko to Kumasi Cornerstones and to Okwahu United, Yeboah established himself as Ghana's leading striker of his era. In Germany and in England, he made a name for himself as a fan favourite with goals scored from powerful, long-range shots. Yeboah was good in the air and handled crosses well. With speed and strength, he would often find a way to bulldoze his way through defenders.

14. Harrison Afful

Harisson is an intelligent full-back who can play on the left and on the right. From playing for Kumasi Asante Kotoko, for international clubs and for the national teams, he established himself as a reliable defender. He doesn't just clear the ball but looks for the right person to pass the ball to. He has good ball-handling skills, defends very well and is efficient at overlapping.

15. Frimpong Manso

He played for Kumasi Conerstones but made a name for himself while playing for Kumasi Asante Kotoko and the Black Stars in the 1990s. He was very strong and would not allow an attacker to have their way with him. He was a nice guy who could be ruthless. He defended well and passed well. Even though he was very good in the air, he preferred to keep the ball on the ground and pass to his midfielders.

16. Sam Ampeh

Known for his amazing ability to dive really wide – like a cat – Ampeh spent most of his career with Kumasi Asante Kotoko career and was considered one of the safest hands in the team's history. He had a good view of the pitch and could command his defenders well.

The following list of Honourable Mentions includes players who would be a part of my team if this was a 23-man squad for a tournament:

17. Nketia Yawson

Nketia Yawson played for Accra Hearts of Oak in the late 1970s and in the 1980s, and was voted Ghana's best player by the Sport Writers Association of Ghana in 1979. A really fast midfielder who was good at the wings, he had a very high work rate, and was a good crosser of the ball. When his team lost the ball, he was very good about falling back to defend.

Ghana's Best XI

18. Kofi Badu

Kofi Badu is one of Ghana's greatest midfielders and he always played with an attacking mindset. He had a successful career with Kumasi Asante Kotoko in the early 1980s and then moved to the Ivory Coast. He was always serious with his game and didn't hesitate to yell at his own teammate if he thought the teammate was not doing his job. He preferred to control the ball for as long as possible. He was a very good passer who regularly assisted with goal scoring.

19. Kwadwo Asamoah

Kwadwo Asamoah is a midfield dynamo with a fantastic work rate. He defends well, he is a very good dribbler with excellent ball-control skills, and very good passer. His ability to play multiple positions to perfection makes him a great resource on the field. He is good at changing the pace of a game and can be counted on to lead the team to execute a game plan. His consistency and high level of play both at club level and with the Black Stars make him one of the best all-round players I know.

20. Andre Dede Ayew

Dede has lived up to the huge expectation that comes with being the son of a successful international football star. Even though his style of play is very similar to that of his father, his eagerness to make a name for himself has always been evident. At the youth level and beyond, for both club and national teams, his enthusiasm for the game is unmistakable. A very good passer, he plays several positions and is a good scorer with his head. He is good at motivating his colleagues on the pitch. His high work rate and his leadership qualities make him an excellent player to have on a team.

21. John Paintsil

Paintsil was a very good defender who played with an attacking mindset. He was a very passionate player who found ways to make his teammates play better on the field. Whether playing for his clubs or for the national team, he demonstrated great confidence in his role as a defender and was always committed to winning. His good leadership qualities made him a great guy to have in any dressing room.

22. John Boye

From his time as a youth international, John Boye has shown immense potential as one of the toughest defenders of his generation. Since becoming a consistent member of the Black Stars, his physical toughness has been a great asset to the team. He has proven himself to be a reliable ball passer who is also very dominant in the air. He is very good at switching between his defensive and his offensive mindset. He is an inspirational teammate with a good sense of humour.

23. Edward Ansah

Edward Ansah was a goalkeeper for Kumasi Asante Kotoko in the 1980s before leaving for Nigeria. Ansah had a long career at both club and national team levels including being in the post for the Black Stars at the Senegal 1992 AFCON. He was quick on his feet and had good instincts regarding when to get off his line. He made critical saves during his career, including his Senegal '92 final game performance.

Special Recognition

Any conversation about the best players in Ghana football cannot be complete without a recognition of the legendary careers of people like C.K. Gyamfi, Robert Mensah, Malik Jabir, Ibrahim Sunday, Abdul Razak, Mohammed Polo, George Arthur, Opoku Afriyie, Addae Kyenkyenhene, Sam Johnson, Kofi Abbrey, George Alhassan, Tony Baffoe, Prince Opoku Polley, Albert Asaase, Joe Addo, Emmanuel Armah "Senegal," Joe Debrah, Shamo Quaye, and many other legends that I only heard about but did not see play.

Additionally, many young players are currently building impressive careers for themselves and I look forward to their accomplishments both at the club and national team level. It goes without saying that Ghana has enough legendary talents to create multiple Best XI teams to successfully face the best teams in the world.

I am honoured to have played alongside or against many of these great players. I am equally honoured to have coached several of these amazing players.

Just as the great careers of people who came before me motivated me to be the best I could be, it is my prayer that current and future crop of players will also be motivated by the accomplishments of the players who came before them.

· CHAPTER 20 ·

THE FUTURE OF GHANA FOOTBALL

Ghana football has seen some glorious days, some very low points, as well as some hopeful moments. We have celebrated the glorious days, we have mourned the low points, and have been inspired by the hopeful moments.

In spite of the overwhelming abundance of talents in the country, Ghana football had been slowly slipping into a decline over the past few years. That decline was swept under the carpet because the Black Stars were doing fairly well and more Ghanaian players than ever were playing professionally outside the country. With that, the slow death of our local league was going on unnoticed.

It took the undercover work of journalist Anas Aremeyaw Anas to wake the nation up to some of the problems that were causing the decline of football in Ghana.

In the undercover video recorded by Anas, former GFA President Kwasi Nyantakyi's statements drew the nation's President into the scandal and the government took a court action to dissolve the GFA and remove Mr. Nyantakyi from office. That court action, in the eyes of FIFA, amounted to an undue influence by the Ghana government in the affairs of the GFA. FIFA threatened the GFA with a suspension. A FIFA suspension of the GFA would have meant that all our national teams were no longer going to take part in FIFA-related international competitions until the suspension was lifted.

Following a meeting between FIFA and Government of Ghana officials, FIFA in August 2018 appointed a normalization committee for the GFA. The normalization committee's mandate, according to a FIFA press release, included the following:

- To run the GFA's daily affairs and cooperate with the special task force once it had been set up by FIFA, CAF and the Government of Ghana;
- To review the GFA statutes to ensure compliance with the requirements of FIFA and CAF, particularly Article 15 of the FIFA Statutes, and;
- Once the GFA statutes met the requirements of FIFA and CAF, to organise and conduct elections of a GFA executive committee on the basis of the revised GFA statutes.

The Normalization Committee, chaired by businessman Dr. Kofi Amoah, had three other members: former Airtel Ghana CEO Lucy Quist, lawyer and former Kotoko Board member Dua Adonten, and a Board member of the Attorney General's Department Naa Odofoley Nortey. Several others were subsequently appointed to lead sub-committees to help with the Normalization Committees' work. The Normalization Committee was to complete its work by not later than the end of March 2019. They were granted an extension to continue their work of normalizing Ghana football.

While events of the last couple of years in the administration of Ghana football have been filled with uncertainty, I saw the period of normalization as a period of huge opportunity. The nation had an opportunity to assess where we were, how we got there, and how to create the most sustainable future for Ghana football.

The Anas movie, Number 12, exposed several referees and football administrators involved in corrupt practices that were affecting football in Ghana. The biggest casualty of Anas' movie was GFA President Kwasi Nyantakyi, who eventually resigned from his post at the GFA. He also resigned from his roles as a member of the FIFA Council, a member of the FIFA Associations Committee, First Vice President of CAF and President of Zone B of the West African Football Union (WAFU). FIFA also banned him from the sport for life.

Kwasi Nyantakyi is a banker and lawyer by training, and he became the GFA president in December 2005. Under his leadership, Ghana qualified for the 2006 World Cup. That was Ghana's first-ever qualification to the tournament. During Nyantakyi's tenure, Ghana again qualified for the 2010 World Cup and the 2014 World Cup. The national Under-20 team also won Africa's first and only U20 World Cup in 2009.

While Nyantakyi may forever be known as the man on tape allegedly taking bribes, it is important that we do not forget to acknowledge his significant contributions to Ghana football.

As a Ghanaian proverb states, "Sɛ wo tan ɔkwaduo a, ɛnyɛ n'amrika tuo," which translates into, "Even if you hate the antelope, you must give it credit for how fast it runs."

The Future of Ghana Football

I met Kwasi Nyantakyi in 2008 when I applied for the assistant coach job with the Black Stars. He was always respectful towards me when I worked in his administration as an assistant coach and later as the head coach. Even when we disagreed, we related to each other with respect and tried to focus on what was in the best interest of the team. One of the things I liked about Kwasi Nyantakyi was that when he gave me a job to do, he made sure the team had the resources we needed to be successful, and he rarely interfered in how I did my work.

Kwasi Nyantakyi is a very intelligent man and he was competent at his job. When I discussed an issue with him, I got the sense that he was thoughtful and was not afraid to think big. The fact that he rose through the ranks to become the CAF vice president and a member of the FIFA Council said a lot about his competence.

I first heard about the Anas video while in Japan with the Black Stars for a friendly match. My assistant Ibrahim Tanko told me after he heard the initial reports that there was a video about the GFA president. He checked with a personal contact in Accra to see if there was indeed such a video or if it was just a rumour. The person confirmed that there was such a video and that it implicated the GFA president as well as many football officials.

Our players had heard about the tape as well and were talking about it among themselves. Even though he sometimes travelled with the team, Mr. Nyantakyi was not with us on that trip to Japan. Understandably, everyone was anxious to see the video and to know the facts for themselves. During our team meeting that day, I confirmed the news about the tape and advised the players to focus on the match we had ahead of us. We won that match 2-0.

In the months that followed, almost anyone who wanted to see the movie saw it. It became the hot topic across the country with many people offering their opinions on the movie and on the future of Ghana football. As deeply involved as Mr. Nyantakyi was in running the affairs of Ghana football, his departure from the GFA left a big question of what was going to happen next.

It was unclear what FIFA or the Government of Ghana was going to do and how any fallout from the scandal was going to affect Ghana football, our AFCON qualifiers and our eventual participation in AFCON 2019. Much of that uncertainty was addressed when the Normalization Committee was put in place.

The local league was suspended indefinitely due to the rampant match-fixing issues that involved referees taking money to influence the outcome of the matches. As a national team coach, I was very worried about that suspension because the local league is one of our strongest talent pipelines which I rely on to identify new talent for the Black Stars. Also, keeping our local teams idle for too long could further diminish fans' interest in the local league.

While bringing back the local league as quickly as possible was needed, I was also well aware that rushing the process without the necessary clean-up of the system was not a wise option.

After about nine months of no local Premier League football, the Normalization Committee's special competition was a step in the right direction for returning normalcy to the local football scene. The special competition was also necessary because Ghana's representatives to the 2019/20 CAF Champions League had not been decided since the 2018 Ghana Premier League was not concluded before the suspension. Fifteen teams participated and Kumasi Asante Kotoko emerged as the winners.

At the GFA Extraordinary Congress in early September 2019, the members of the Association voted unanimously to adopt the proposed statutes presented by the Normalization Committee. The adoption of the new statutes also paved the way for elections for a new president and Board for the GFA. The rule changes appeared to address some of the biggest issues for which the Normalization Committee was put in place.

In late October 2019, Kurt E.S. Okraku, an accomplished football administrator and CEO of Dreams F.C. was elected as the President of the GFA. That was after two rounds of voting and followed by George Afriyie's honourable decision to concede the elections to Kurt in the interest of unity in the football community.

With Kurt's experience and with the support of the newly-elected Executive Council and all stakeholders, I am hopeful that Ghana's football will be back on track soon.

As was made evident in the Anas movie, a big part of the problem with the local league was referees and how easily corruptible they appeared to be. The Referees' Association of Ghana launched an investigation into the allegations and handed down severe penalties to the referees found guilty as accused. More than forty match officials were punished, each banned for ten years. Others were banned for life. CAF also banned two of these referees for life.

While the bans tell us that the necessary clean-up is happening in the system to ensure fair officiating, there are probably other corruptible people in the system who are still there because they were not caught on tape. Therefore, the Referees' Association of Ghana's work is not done yet. They will need to continue to keep an eye on the referees and linesmen to make sure they're acting with the highest form of integrity. Ongoing refresher courses should emphasise the responsible use of the power they have over matches. FIFA and CAF organizing a five-day integrity course for 150 referees was a commendable step to help the referees do the right things and to restore the public's confidence in match officials. That type of training should happen periodically.

Another reason referees become soft targets for corruption is obviously about money. Referees only get paid allowances. For some of the referees, that allowance may be the only source of regular income. Increasing how much referees make in allowances could also minimise their tendency to fall for bribery temptations. It was a good move by the Normalization Committee to increase allowances for referees during the Special Competition. Timely payment of such allowances would also go a long way to keep the referees' hands clean.

It is worth noting that the Anas movie did not incriminate only referees from Ghana. Referees from other African countries were also implicated in match-fixing allegations, and they were also sanctioned. One of them was a Kenyan referee who was scheduled to officiate at the 2018 World Cup in Russia. He resigned from the World Cup, was banned for life by CAF, and was under investigation by FIFA. I'm not sure what happened in that FIFA investigation but it is likely it ended up in a severe penalty like a ban, based on the video evidence against him.

Obviously, some people were not happy with the work Anas did. There was a perception that Anas was trying to destroy people, and that opinion was also shared by some people outside Ghana. We were in Ethiopia for a match when a non-Ghanaian referee said to me, "You Ghana people, you want to destroy African referees o!" I smiled and carried on.

While I don't want anyone to lose his or her job, or be destroyed, as the non-Ghanaian referee said to me, Ghana football is bigger than any individual. Much of the debate about Anas' methods calmed down eventually and we seemed to have taken steps to improve Ghana football. I hope we continue on this path of keeping Ghana football clean so that the next investigative journalist who sets out to do an undercover movie would find nothing incriminating to report.

Speaking of journalists and the media, they are important stakeholders in Ghana football. Their work is greatly needed to grow the public's interest in the sport and to hold people accountable for their actions. However, a journalist cannot throw professionalism out of the window simply because he or she is trying to create sensational headlines.

With Ghana's thousands of journalists and bloggers, hundreds of radio stations and TV stations, and how easily anyone can set up a YouTube channel, there should be competition for good quality content to keep the public informed and entertained.

Unfortunately, some media personalities choose to take "short-cuts" and throw professionalism out of the window. When people take short-cuts, that is when criticisms turn into personal insults, or people make up and publish false stories, or spread rumours as facts. When that happens, it is difficult for any serious person to take such journalists and the media seriously.

Of course, there are very good journalists in Ghana and I salute them for their great work. I've known Kwabena Yeboah for a long time and I will point to him as the model of personal integrity that I will recommend Ghanaian journalists emulate. Kwabena is firm and fair, knows his stuff and will never trade his integrity for a cheap headline. No wonder he's respected across Ghana and around the world. Kwame Sefa Kayi is another good example of a media personality who takes the trouble to present facts and holds respectful conversations. He is not a sports journalist but he is professional that all journalists in Ghana can learn something from. He is known for being firm and fair. Majority of Ghanaians listen to him not only because he discusses politics and can speak multiple languages but also because he is a respected professional.

There are many professionals in the media, whether on air or behind the scenes, who are doing a great job. I appreciate all of them and their contributions to developing football and Ghana. Unfortunately, there are more noisemakers than there are professionals. Therefore, I limit how much media I consume. And I do that on purpose.

People are free to share their opinions but I don't have enough time to listen to everyone's opinion. Frankly, when people make constructive contributions that could be useful to me, people find and share those with me. And I appreciate such respectful contributions.

While I don't listen to Ghanaian sports radio most of the time, my wife does. I have advised her against that many times but she can't help it. She spends a great deal of time listening and then gets upset when rude people on some of the shows speak disrespectfully about me. When she complains about how disrespectful some of the people can be, I smile and remind her about why I stay away from many of the arguments on radio or TV.

I hope the owners and administrators of the media stations make it a priority to demand professionalism from the people they put on air. Criticisms are fair and I have no problem people criticizing me or any player fairly. However, there is a line that should not be crossed. When the criticisms become personal insults or based on false reporting, that behaviour has crossed the line. That behaviour should be unacceptable anywhere.

The future of Ghana football is bright. However, we have to put in the needed resources and the necessary time in order to realise that bright future. In addition to the improvements discussed above, here is what Ghana needs to do to take full advantage of the talents and passions that the nation is blessed with:

1. Improve Community-Level Infrastructure
2. Create Sustainable Funding for Local Clubs
3. Establish Continuity in Coaching for the Black Stars

1. Improve Community-Level Infrastructure

In many places in Ghana, community pitches have been encroached on by people who have built their houses on them. The pitches have been squeezed into a small piece of space or have been eliminated entirely. As a result, children in some communities across Ghana have nowhere to play football. If children have nowhere to play football, they are unlikely to develop their talents, and that could be the end of the road for them. Investing in community-level infrastructure will create the necessary environment for young talents to develop.

Not only should we create spaces for young people, but we should also find a means to restore the infrastructure for the entire community. Football in communities have a lot of benefits that include bringing the community closer together. There is a direct benefit from such an investment because most young people actively participating in football activities are less likely to participate in criminal activities in the community. Another direct benefit is that people coming out to watch the matches will buy food or drinks from the traders in the neighbourhood, helping those traders earn a living.

At the regional level, in this day and age, it should be possible for every region to have two or three synthetic pitches where young people can play competitive matches. Understandably, the national stadium and other key stadiums should be reserved for higher-level matches. However, making the investment in our regions to help young talents develop their skills will go a long way to help develop new talents for our leagues. Synthetic pitches are very good for developing dribbling and passing techniques. They are also more manageable than grass, and they last for years.

Because of the long-term benefits such investments will bring to the nation, building such infrastructure should be part of our long-term national agenda for community infrastructure. While we wait for the government to come in, private individuals and companies can invest in such infrastructure by creating partnerships with local communities.

The local communities and their leaders can take the lead by identifying the land they would like to use for such infrastructure and then putting a plan together to recruit investors.

And once we have the community infrastructure, it is very important that we maintain them well. Fixing things in a timely manner when things break is a major problem in Ghana.

People destroy property by doing what they're not supposed to do there. Examples include pasting posters on walls everywhere, throwing rubbish about or using the synthetic pitches for events that have nothing to do with football. If you cast your mind around, you can find many examples of things most of us can do to maintain our football infrastructure and use it for our own benefit. If we can take good care of our infrastructure, that will go a long way to help our football future.

2. Create Sustainable Funding for Local Clubs

Several clubs in Ghana are owned by one individual and the funding for that club depends on the resources of that individual. When that person's business is not doing well or if that person dies, the team often struggles to stay alive. There have been legendary teams that raised many young talents but are no longer in existence, simply because there is no financier.

While a local professional team may make a lot of money from transferring a player to a foreign league, that funding option is not available to every club. As a matter of fact, some teams rush their players out of the country before the player is ready, all because they need the money badly. Some players, who could otherwise have had successful careers, have flopped because they were rushed outside in exchange for transfer fees to help their local clubs survive.

It is a good idea for groups of people to come together to run a team like they will run a company. I know that Accra Hearts of Oak adopted that model. Even though they have not been as successful as they would like to be with that funding model, they took a step in the right direction. When they figure out a way to make that model work, that will be a model which many local clubs can follow.

In past years, we have had companies in Ghana adopting and sponsoring local teams, where the companies were not only sponsors but were also part owners. That is a model that could be revived.

With Ghanaians being as passionate as we are about football, we need to find more ways for companies and local clubs to partner beyond just sponsorships. That way, the companies would have a vested interest as owners and it would make more sense to them as to why they should invest more and more money into the teams to ensure their sustainability and advancement.

A solid fan base for any team is very important. Fans who come to the stadium whether the team is doing well or not are fans clubs need to survive. Those are the fans whose passion and constructive criticisms help teams to be successful. When teams are built around a community, the team has the community as its core fans. They will support the team because they associate their community pride with the team, and will want the team to do well. Wealthy people who are connected to that community could pool resources together to invest in their local teams.

Every region in the nation can be encouraged to have at least one Division 1 team. Each team could be given an incentive based on a partnership with their community and not just based on personal interests of an individual or a small group of individuals. The teams in Ghana that have been around for many years have been sustained largely by the existence of their loyal, do-or-die fan base.

The government can help by giving tax incentives to investors who agree to own teams in specific towns and be in partnership with the people in that region. If the people have a vested interest in the team, their hearts will follow the team. If done properly, individuals, companies, communities and the government can all benefit from the outcome of proper, sustainable funding model for local clubs.

3. Establish Continuity in Coaching for the Black Stars

There are many opinions among Ghanaians about who should coach the Black Stars. No matter who is appointed to be the Black Stars head coach at any point in time, it is essential that the appointment is made with continuity in mind. Continuity means we don't hire and fire just based on short-term public opinion but rather operate within a thoughtful plan. That will ensure we build on what have learned and not tear down to start afresh every two years.

The debate among many Ghanaians often come down to a choice between a foreign coach or an indigenous coach. There is more to selecting a coach for a national team than where the person comes from.

For many years, Ghana and most African countries have relied on foreign coaches for their national teams. Ghana has had no fewer than 20 foreign coaches since independence in 1957. In that same period, we've had about 10 Ghanaian coaches in the job. Many of the appointments of Ghanaian coaches have been as caretaker coaches while we were looking for a foreign coach. Other times, a Ghanaian coach was appointed because we didn't have enough money to afford a foreign coach.

Needless to say, foreign coaches have always worked under better conditions in terms of salary and professional courtesies from the GFA. The GFA, historically, have not extended the same salaries and professional courtesy to Ghanaian coaches. In spite of that, most of Ghana's successes at the senior or junior national teams have come about under Ghanaian coaches. Based on these facts, there is no question that Ghanaian coaches are capable of coaching the Black Stars.

It is an open secret that a section of the Ghanaian population is obsessed with foreigners. It is that same kind of obsession which makes a trader in the marketplace promote the value of their product by convincing the prospective buyer that the product is from outside the country so it is good. It is very common to hear, *"Wei diɛ efiri aburokyire enti ɛyɛ papa!"* which translates into, "This item is from abroad so it is good!"

Unfortunately, that mindset makes many Ghanaians' think that made-in-Ghana products or services are inferior. That same mindset is what makes rich people and politicians choose to go abroad for medical treatment even though Ghana has good doctors who will do a great job if they are provided with the needed infrastructure right here in Ghana.

The mindset of preferring foreign products and services over our own can also be seen in how willingly a Ghanaian will pay a foreigner for a service rendered but will do everything possible to undercut a Ghanaian providing the same service. Most Ghanaian business people, whether they live in Ghana or abroad, can tell you stories upon stories that display the predominant Ghanaian thinking that a foreigner's service is better than that of the Ghanaian.

So, I know the debate about a foreign coach or a local coach for the Black Stars is not necessarily about me. It's about a fundamental problem of some Ghanaians' desire to be led by a white man, like it was in the colonial days. It's about a lack of confidence in the expertise of our own people. It is also about a lack of appreciation for good things when they are made in Ghana or services provided by Ghanaians.

As a society, Ghanaians have come a long way from our preference for foreign products and services but we still have a long way to go. I hope the awareness that I have raised about this issue causes each of us to be mindful of the words we use when comparing foreigners to Ghanaians or assessing the quality of a product or service made in Ghana.

I wholeheartedly believe in developing indigenous coaches for Ghana's national teams. That is not because I have benefited from that approach but because it is extremely important for raising the standard of coaching across the country. That is also important for ensuring continuity in the leadership philosophy for the national teams. Appointing a foreign coach for the Black Stars at this point in our history is a step backward.

I want to be very clear about my position that the color of a person's skin or a person's country of origin should never be a basis for assessing the person's competency. In fact, denying someone an opportunity because of the color of their skin, or because of their country of origin, or because of their tribe, or because of their religion is a sign of backward thinking and should be avoided at all cost. Coaches should be appointed based on competence, and many Ghanaian coaches can be highly successful when given the opportunity and the appropriate support.

I am not saying that if a made-in-Ghana product or service is bad, we should not speak up. No, we should. We should, however, not tarnish the Ghanaian identity because we're unhappy with the product or service or behavior of one Ghanaian.

With the appointment of coaches for Ghana's national teams, we have historically taken a step forward and then taken a step backward because we've not made continuity a priority. We have often made many knee-jerk reactions with the hiring and firing of coaches, and those decisions have had consequences on the national team.

As a nation, we cannot go down the path of "fire-the-coach" every time something doesn't go well with the national team. Even with the most expensive, experienced and accomplished coach in charge, we cannot be successful if we do not commit to long-term planning and continuity.

Partnerships with foreign coaches should be encouraged. Ghanaian coaches need to be consistently exposed to the technical and leadership expertise of experienced coaches from around the world. Coaching involves continuous learning and Ghanaian coaches can benefit from the expertise of accomplished coaches, foreign or local.

Just as many Ghanaians have become world-class surgeons, engineers and experts in many professions around the world, Ghanaian coaches can become the world's best if given the opportunity, the resources and the support.

To be fair, the problem of the lack of continuity is not limited to just Ghana. It is an African problem. After the 2019 AFCON, eight out of the 24 teams parted ways with their coaches. Egypt sacked their coach. Cameroon fired their coach. Guinea fired their coach. Namibia's coach's contract was not renewed. The Ugandan FA and their coach mutually parted ways. Tanzania terminated their coach's contract. Morocco's coach quit. South Africa's coach resigned. That is just one third of the teams who are starting over. These countries perceived it is mostly the coach's fault that their teams didn't do as well as they wanted. Unfortunately, that sort of thing happens at least every two years with African national teams.

While each situation is different and the firing of some coaches may be justified, that trend suggests the lack of thoughtful long-term planning on the part of the FAs when they hired these coaches. Also, the short-term nature of coaching tenures in many African national teams suggest an impatience on the part of the FAs.

What is interesting is that the same person that one African national team fires for being incapable gets hired soon after by another African national team.

A good example is French coach Herve Renard. He led Zambia to win the AFCON in 2012. They fired him in 2013 and Ivory Coast hired him in 2014. He led Ivory Coast to win the AFCON in 2015. He left to coach French club Lille. Morocco hired him in 2016 and he qualified them to the 2018

World Cup. After his Moroccan team, who were one of the favourites to win the tournament, was eliminated in the Round of 16 at AFCON 2019, he quit. About two months later, Saudi Arabia hired him.

One of the things this example shows us is that while one nation cannot wait to get rid of their coach, there is usually someone who is willing to pay good money for that coach's services. Another thing the example shows us is the absence of patience on the part of these national teams to stick with a long-term plan that is focused on continued success.

By the way, 12 indigenous coaches have won 16 times in the last 32 AFCONS. The 2019 AFCON final was between two teams coached by African coaches - Djamel Belmadi with Algeria and Aliou Cisse with Senegal. Coach Belmadi's team won.

With the recent change in leadership at the GFA, the new leaders have an opportunity to take stock and determine the areas where Ghana football falls short. I hope the new GFA will seriously prioritize long-term planning with a continuity in coaching for the Black Stars in mind, and have the patience required to see the building process through.

If we focus on these three things – improving our community-level infrastructure, providing a system of sustainable funding for local clubs, and ensuring continuity in coaching for the Black Stars – we will be setting ourselves up for success for many years to come.

Additionally, a serious focus on the development of youth leagues is absolutely necessary. It is a widely-known fact that many of the legends of Ghana's football history came through the colts football system. Organised, juvenile football that offers consistent competitive action for the youth across the country is essential to discovering and developing football talents in a place like Ghana.

When I think of the success of Ghana football, I think of the success of all the national teams as well as the success of Ghana's local league. Our national teams would bring us international recognition and a strong local league is vital for the continued success of our national teams. The future is promising for our national teams and our local league. However, we have a lot of work to do. If we don't do the work, we will continue to see the "Promise Land" but may never set foot there. If we do the work, we will reap the benefits.

I trust that we – the GFA and all stakeholders of Ghana football – will do the right thing for Ghana, and sincerely do the necessary work. That will be the only way to restore Ghana's glorious football history.

· CHAPTER 21 ·

CLOSING THOUGHTS

In August 2019, I turned 60 years old. That milestone birthday gave me a reason to pause and reflect on what I have done with my time on Earth. I also thought about my impact on the world and what I needed to do with the years ahead.

As I went about my day, gratitude filled my thoughts. I spent most of my birthday thanking God for everything that I have been blessed with in my personal and professional life.

I have a lot to be thankful for, and I do not take anything for granted. I have enjoyed good health, great family and friends, dependable mentors and advocates, as well as supportive colleagues and associates. God gave me the football talent, and also gave me amazing opportunities to play and coach the game at the highest levels. I am very grateful to God for the life I've lived.

NBA basketball coach Phil Jackson has been quoted as saying, "The strength of the team is each individual member, and the strength of each member is the team."

Closing Thoughts

Throughout most of my adult life, I have been a part of one team or another. My teams, whether personally or professionally, have been a big part of everything that I have done. For that reason, I will take a moment to say thank you.

I am very grateful to my wife, Angela Tuffour Kwarteng, for her immense love and support throughout our years together. My children, Peggy, Audrey, MaryPearl, and Diamond, are blessings to me. I am thankful for my son-in-law Eric Nketia, my grandchildren Jirah and Nissi, brothers, sisters, my nephews, nieces, uncles, aunts and all other relatives.

Many of the people who played key roles to help me become successful in my profession have also become significant parts of my professional life.

My sincere gratitude goes to Asantehene Otumfour Osei Tutu II, President John Agyekum Kufour, President John Dramani Mahama, President Nana Addo Dankwa Akufo-Addo, and President Jerry John Rawlings for their leadership.

I am also grateful to Coach Malik Jabir, Kwabena Yeboah, Anthony Yeboah, Rajevac Milovan, Ambassador Ayisi Boateng, Kwabena Aidoo, and Maxwell Brobbey for the important roles they've played in my life.

I greatly appreciate all my teammates and coaches from Kumasi Asante Kotoko, the Black Stars, Prestea Mine Stars, and Rainbow Stars; the players, technical team members and administrators I've worked with in the Black Meteors and the Black Stars.

My sincere thanks to the pastors and imams who have shown their support through their prayers and advice; government officials who have been instrumental in the affairs of Ghana football; my friends and colleagues from Opoku Ware;

the fans for the passion they invest in supporting Ghana football; and the media for promoting Ghana football.

My sincere thanks to Kyei Amoako for helping to write this book. It was a great pleasure working with him to produce this book that will serve many generations. Also, my thanks to all those who helped in diverse ways. Your contributions are greatly appreciated.

For a coach or the leader of a team, I cannot say enough about how important self-respect is. In my line of work, it is helpful to be friendly towards the people I work with. It is also important that the same people take me seriously when I need them to do what they are supposed to do. Therefore, I have to maintain a certain level of conduct that dictates how people behave towards me.

To me, that is where self-respect plays a big role. By having respect for myself, it is easier to treat others with respect; and in return, people will usually treat me the way I treat them. On a team, that means treating people fairly and consistently acting with integrity.

I set out to become a coach because I love football and I love to develop people. I have come this far in my career because I have committed myself to mastering the technical and non-technical aspects of my job. I have also committed myself to always getting better at how to work with people. It has not always been easy, whether with the people I work with directly or those I work with indirectly. But not everything will be easy when you lead people. That is even more so the case when you have a high-profile job or a job that's very public.

I am not in the profession I am in because it is supposed to be easy. I am in my profession because I have skills and

Closing Thoughts

ideas that I believe can help others become the best at what they do. I am in my line of work because I have developed my technical and non-technical abilities to a level that I can use it to deliver value for others. Nevertheless, each day, I have to earn the opportunity to keep the job I have. I also have to frequently navigate complex situations that can be annoying, and can cause headaches or sleepless nights.

Living under the constant scrutiny of fans and the media, managing the egos of players and leaders, and handling unnecessary political influences are all examples of the occupational hazards that add complexities to my job as a coach. For every leader, there are unique complexities that may get in the way of doing your job well, and it is absolutely necessary to find a way to overcome such impediments.

At the end of the day, my professional training and professional experiences set me on the right path to navigate the hurdles. Above all, the decisions I make daily are what keep me moving forward.

I have tried to manage through situations by being firm and fair, and not by how loudly I yelled or screamed at people. I don't expect every leader to have the same approach to leadership as I have. However, I believe that if we treat people with respect, we are likely to get the best out of them.

I thank God immensely for the gifts I have been blessed with. I am honoured to have shared my life with so many people. I look forward to more great experiences in the future.

When all is said and done, I hope that my life has been an example and an inspiration to the people I encountered, both directly and indirectly.

At the Accra Sports Stadium in late 2019.

With Baffour-Awuah Manu in Kumasi in 2018.

AFTERWORD

by Baffour-Awuah Manu
Executive Publisher

This book started as a suggestion - a suggestion to Coach Kwasi Appiah to document his experiences so that other people could learn from him. The suggestion led to several conversations and eventually into a book for the world to read.

I am grateful to Coach for making the time to share his story with Ghanaians, Africans and people around the world. While many people have amazing stories that will inspire others, finding the time and committing to such a project is often difficult. As a result, many stories go untold.

Kwasi Appiah's career as a player and as a coach is a success story made in Ghana. His story reminds me of the great things Ghanaian footballers and coaches can do if they commit to playing or coaching to the best of their abilities. His story also reminds me of how well every Ghanaian or African in any profession can perform if we are very determined, if we

Afterword

are committed to excellence, and if we display a high level of personal integrity.

Kwasi Appiah became the first Ghanaian coach to qualify the Black Stars for a World Cup, and that historic moment also became a ground-breaking moment that inspired many Ghanaians. That was a shining example of a Ghanaian rubbing shoulders globally with the very best professionals in his field. In my mind, that was an African story that needed to be told to the present and future generations so that they could be inspired to dream big.

Having known Coach Kwasi Appiah since his early days as a Kotoko player up until now, I have been impressed by his belief in teamwork. I have been impressed by his leadership qualities. I have also been impressed by his humility. I have learnt many things from observing him from far and near, and I hope this book gives all readers an opportunity to have a conversation with Kwasi Appiah.

I am very thankful to all the people who contributed to making this book a reality. To the journalists who covered and continue to cover the activities Kotoko and the Black Stars; to the players who make it possible for us to enjoy the game; to the fans who cheer the team on. I cannot thank you enough for your support of Ghana football.

Eric Amankwah, thank you for your great ideas, your support, and your directions on how to think globally about this project. Kwabena Yeboah, thank you for your guidance. Kyei Amoako, thank you for your commitment to excellence.

To my wife Martha Appiah, thank you for your support and your counsel throughout this project. To Kwasi Appiah's family, thank you for your friendship throughout the years.

And to the many people who helped in diverse ways, you have helped to document and present a very important aspect of Ghana's history.

So, thank you Maxwell Brobbey, Kwabena Appiah, Audrey Appiah, Papa Arko, Francis Agyeman, Hon. Martin Obeng, Anthony Osei Kwadwo, Nana Kwasi Adinkrah, Fiifi Anaman, Maurice Quansah, Okyeame Kwame, Abeiku Santana Aggrey, JayRay Ghartey, Gideon Bugli N., Kennedy Adom Asamoah, Charles Teye, Sam Stephens, Alex Asante, Emmanuel Offei, Kwabena Fokuo, Veronica Commey, Jonathan Mensah, Eric Kwame Appiah, Duncan Ablordeppey, Debbie Boampong, Ben Boampong, Tony Hammond, Ben Opoku, Alex Okyere, Obeng Amoako, Mrs. Charlotte Akyeampong, Stevenson Manu, William Ampadu, Emmanuel Adu, Barbara Amoako, Kwacy Koranteng, Felix Quachey, Kojo Pumpuni Asante, Ransford Antwi, Kwame Adinkra, Frank Takyi Appau, and all the contributors to the Ghana Football Legacy Facebook page.

And to you who are reading this book, thank you for doing so. I hope it has been a blessing to you. To those who haven't read it yet, I highly recommend that they do so. I'm sure they will be glad they did.

Until next time, God richly bless you us all.

APPENDIX

i. Career Timeline and Highlights

1959	*Born in Sunyani*
1964 – 1969	*Attended Roman Catholic Primary School*
1969 – 1974	*Attended Ridge Experimental School*
1974 – 1979	*Attended Opoku Ware Secondary School*
1979	*Played for Rainbow Stars, Tomacan Stars* *Played in Middle League for Tomacan Stars*
1979	*Played for Black Meteors (National Under 23)* *Competed in WAFU Championship*
1979	*Joined Prestea Mine Stars*
1981	*Called to Black Stars (National Senior Team)*
1982	*Joined Kumasi Asante Kotoko*
1982	*Black Stars at Libya '82* *Ghana wins fourth AFCON title*
1983	*Kotoko wins African Clubs Championship*
1985	*Appointed Kotoko Vice Captain*
1988	*Appointed Kotoko Captain*
1988	*Appointed Black Stars Captain*
1992	*Black Stars at Senegal '92*
1992	*Retired from playing for the Black Stars*
1993	*Retired from Kumasi Asante Kotoko; appointed Kotoko Assistant Coach*
1996	*Appointed Kotoko Interim Head Coach*

i. Career Timeline and Highlights (continued)

1996	Attended Coaching Course in the UK
1999	Appointed Black Stars Assistant Coach
2008	Received State Award (Grand Medal for Sports)
2008	Appointed Black Stars Assistant Coach
2011	Appointed Interim Black Stars Head Coach
2011	Appointed Black Stars Assistant Coach
2011	Appointed Black Meteors Head Coach (Won gold medal at All-Africa Games in Mozambique)
2012	Appointed Black Stars Coach

- Qualified Ghana for the 2013 AFCON

- Qualified Ghana for the 2014 FIFA World Cup (eliminated in group stage; match against Germany voted by FIFA as the Best Match of the Tournament)

- Ranked 32nd Best Coach in the World (FIFA)

- Honourary Doctorate in Psychology (Day Spring University, Mississippi, USA)

- Coach of The Year (SWAG)

- Sports Personality of The Year (SWAG)

- Most Influential Person in Ghana (Global Media Alliance)

2014 – 2017	Appointed Al Khartoum Head Coach
2017	Appointed Black Stars Head Coach

ii. Ghana Black Stars Coaches since 1958

Name	Nationality	Tenure
George Ainsley	Great Britain	1958-59
Andreas Sjolberg	Sweden	1959-62
Josef Ember	Hungary	1963
C.K. Gyamfi	Ghana	1963-65
Carlos Perreira	Brazil	1967
Karl Heinz Marotzke	Germany	1968-70
Karl Weigang	Germany	1974-75
Oswaldo Carlos Sampaio	Brazil	1977-78
Fred Osam-Duodu	Ghana	1978-81
C.K. Gyamfi	Ghana	1982-83
Emmanuel Kwasi Afranie	Ghana	1984
Herbert Addo	Ghana	1984
Rudi Gutendorf	Germany	1986-87
Fred Osam-Duodu	Ghana	1988-89
Bukhard Ziese	Germany	1990-92
Otto Pfister	Germany	1993
Fred Osam-Duodu	Ghana	1993
E.J. Aggrey-Fynn	Ghana	1994
Jorgen Larsen	Denmark	1995

ii. Ghana Black Stars Coaches since 1958 (continued)

Name	Nationality	Tenure
Petr Gavrilla	Romania	1995
Ishmael Kurtz	Brazil	1996
Rinus Israel	The Netherlands	1997-98
Giuseppe Dossenna	Italy	1999-2000
Fred Osam-Duodu	Ghana	2000
Jones Attuquayefio	Ghana	2001
Fred Osam-Duodu	Ghana	2001
Milan Zivodinovic	Yugoslavia	2002
Emmanuel Afranie	Ghana	2002
Bukhard Ziese	Germany	2003-
Ralf Zumdick	Germany	2003-2004
Mariano Barreto	Portugal	2004
Ratomir Dujkovic	Serbia	2004-2006
Milovan Rajevac	Serbia	2006-2010
Goran Stevanovic	Serbia	2010-2011
James Kwasi Appiah	Ghana	2011 - 2014
Avram Grant	Israel	2014-2017
James Kwasi Appiah	Ghana	2017-2019

Source: Ghanaweb.com

INDEX

A

Abdul Baba Rahman 257, 280, 281, 286, 287, 288, 291, 292, 303, 306, 309
Abdul Fatawu 105, 108, 257, 266
Abdul Karim Zito 46, 142
Abdul Majeed Waris 108, 257, 266
Abedi Pele 2, 39, 40, 74, 153, 155, 158, 333
Accra Great Olympics 39, 133, 330
Accra Hearts of Oak 46, 50, 55, 87, 154, 257, 330, 335, 351
Addae Kyenkyehene 46, 66
Adolph Armah 40
AFCON viii, 96, 101, 102, 104, 105, 106, 107, 111, 112, 116, 118, 121, 134, 140, 180, 201, 212, 215, 241, 242, 243, 244, 245, 246, 247, 248, 250, 251, 252, 254, 255, 256, 258, 260, 261, 262, 264, 266, 268, 270, 273, 274, 276, 278, 280, 282, 284, 286, 288, 290, 292, 293, 294, 295, 296, 297, 298, 300, 301, 302, 303, 304, 305, 306, 307, 308, 309, 310, 311, 337, 343, 356, 357, 372
African Cup Championship 46, 144
African Cup of Nations 133
Afriyie Acquah 257, 286, 289, 290, 303, 309
Ahmed Adams 177, 179
Ahmed Rockson 46, 66, 142, 235

Akatakyie 21
Akwettey Quaye 46
Akye Erzuah 52, 66, 142
Alan Kyeremateng 224
Albert Asaase 28, 41, 46, 48, 49, 135, 141, 149, 338
Alex Asante 252, 367
Alhaji Sanie 178
Al Khartoum Al Watani 117, 206
All-Africa Games 175
Anas Aremeyaw Anas 243, 339
Andre Ayew 108, 109, 110, 111, 196, 249, 257, 274, 280, 282, 284, 286, 289, 291, 296, 309
Andy Yiadom 257, 274, 280, 286, 309
Anthony Yeboah 73, 80, 81, 153, 158, 159, 161, 334, 360
Appiah Glory Hostel 324
Asamoah Gyan 95, 105, 108, 109, 110, 125, 127, 171, 198, 236, 244, 249, 257, 259, 266, 282, 296, 332
Asantehene 19, 21, 44, 49, 50, 58, 150, 220, 360
Augustine Sefa 177

B

Baffour-Awuah Manu 51, 227, 239, 365
Benin 119, 154, 167, 207, 253, 254, 273, 274, 275, 276, 279, 280, 281
Benjamin Acheampong 178
Ben Kayode 39, 135
Ben Koufie 218
Brazil 115, 183
Brendan Rogers 223

INDEX

Brong-Ahafo Region 11, 12, 17, 33, 45, 51, 97

C

CAF 60, 141, 150, 211, 217, 236, 252, 253, 340, 341, 342, 344, 345
CAF Champions League 141
Caleb Ekuban 251, 257, 290, 303
Cameroon 119, 135, 167, 170, 177, 179, 187, 253, 254, 273, 280, 281, 282, 283, 285, 286, 295, 309, 356
Cape Coast 16, 33
Captain 2, 6, 36, 47, 49, 50, 53, 71, 79, 84, 91, 105, 108, 135, 138, 142, 154, 155, 156, 157, 159, 160, 162, 198, 199, 259, 260, 261, 262, 263, 331, 332
Charles Allen Gyimah 49, 143
Charles Oppong 46
Christian Atsu 105, 109, 257, 274, 275, 277, 280, 281, 284, 285, 303, 309
C.K. Akunnor 301
Coach Abdul Razak 225
Coach Abubakari Ouattara 59
Coach Adabie 46, 142
Coach Aliou Cisse 297, 357
Coach Avram Grant 118
Coach Burkhard Ziese 59, 154
Coach Claude Le Roy 89, 114
Coach David Duncan 258
Coach Djamel Belmadi 357
Coach E.K. Afranie 29, 36
Coach Goran (Plavi) Stevanovic 96
Coach Herve Renard 91, 356
Coach Howard Wilkinson 80
Coach Ibrahim Sunday 142, 235, 307, 338
Coach Jones Attuquayefio 85
Coach Malik Jabir 59, 142
Coach Mas-ud Didi Dramani 258
Coach Milovan (Milo) Rajevac 27, 92, 93, 94, 95, 96, 98, 122, 123, 165, 168, 169, 181, 196
Coach Otto Pfister 154
Coach Sellas Tetteh 92, 258, 307
Coach Stephen Keshi 222
Collins Addo 177

D

Daddy Lumba 326
Daniel Adjei 177
Dede Ayew 125, 127, 260, 266, 267, 304, 310, 336
Dekyemso 51
Dr. Hilla Limann 134
Dr. K.K. Sarpong 252
Dr. Kofi Amoah 244, 252, 340
Dr. Kwame Kyei 224
Dr. Patrick Ofori 258
Dua Adonten 340
Dzamefe Commission 199, 247

E

Ebenezer Ofori 257, 265, 266
Ebo Mends 52, 66, 142, 149
Edward Ansah 73, 74, 154, 160, 337
Edward Kpodo 177
Egypt 48, 67, 94, 106, 107, 108, 109, 110, 114, 126, 146, 147, 148, 157, 158, 169,

INDEX

177, 183, 207, 215, 252, 254, 255, 256, 260, 262, 270, 271, 273, 295, 356
El Ahly 48, 52, 65, 141, 144, 147, 148, 149, 150
Emba Owusu Sekyere 38
Emmanuel Agyeman Badu 109, 110, 127, 177, 196
Emmanuel Armah viii, 102, 104, 107, 109, 110, 115, 116, 117, 125, 126, 140, 162, 180, 183, 184, 185, 186, 187, 188, 190, 191, 192, 194, 196, 197, 198, 199, 200, 202, 203, 247, 296, 373, 374
Ernest Appau 52, 66, 142, 234, 235, 330

F

Felix Annan 257
FIFA 105, 109, 154, 185, 186, 188, 206, 296, 297, 301, 340, 341, 342, 343, 345, 372
Fiifi Anaman 114, 367
Flt. Lt. J.J. Rawlings 71, 134, 136, 138
Francis Agyeman 52, 225, 234, 367
Francis Kumi 41, 46, 48, 142
Francis Morton 177
Frimpong Manso 70, 71, 72, 73, 74, 154, 161, 217, 335

G

George Adusei Poku 60
George Afriyie 217, 219, 344
George Alhassan 40

George Arthur 51, 66, 67, 68, 72, 338
GFA 45, 89, 90, 91, 92, 95, 96, 97, 98, 113, 115, 154, 155, 156, 157, 158, 169, 175, 184, 185, 188, 189, 192, 193, 196, 199, 200, 201, 202, 212, 213, 214, 217, 219, 243, 245, 247, 249, 340, 341, 342, 343, 344, 353, 357, 358
Ghana Best XI viii, 329, 330, 332, 334, 336, 338
Ghana Black Meteors vii, 29, 36, 37, 38, 123, 124, 175, 176, 178, 180, 182, 229, 296, 300, 301, 360, 371, 372
Ghana Black Stars 58, 101, 116, 134, 153, 163, 373, 374
Ghana Black Stars Coaches 114
Ghana Football Association 89, 184
Gilbert Fiamenyo 178, 179
Godfred Graham 26, 201
Guinea Bissau 119, 273, 280, 281, 285, 286, 287, 289

H

Harrison Afful 105, 110, 256, 334
Haruna Yusif 46, 135
Honourary Doctorate in Psychology 228

I

Ibrahim Tanko 70, 240, 241, 248, 249, 301, 303, 308, 342
Isaac Asiamah 219, 244

INDEX

J

Jermaine Lopia 259
John Bannerman 46, 66, 71, 72, 135, 142, 149, 235
John Boye 105, 257, 274, 279, 280, 285, 286, 289, 309, 337
John Mensah 125, 171, 172, 259, 262, 296, 331
John Paintsil 105, 236, 337
Jonathan Mensah 105, 127, 128, 233, 257, 275, 280, 281, 285, 305, 309, 367
Jordan Ayew 111, 257, 274, 280, 284, 286, 289, 290, 291, 306, 309
Joseph Addo 177
Joseph Aidoo 251, 257, 285, 286
Joseph Attamah 257
Joseph Carr 46, 135
Justice Senyo Dzamefe 184

K

Kasim Nuhu 257, 274, 280, 285, 309
Kevin-Prince Boateng 112, 193, 247
Kobolo 315, 316, 317
Kofi Anokye Owusu-Darko 184
Kofi Badu 28, 41, 46, 47, 48, 49, 135, 141, 234, 336
Kolo Toure 223
Kumasi 19, 20, 51
Kumasi Asante Kotoko vii, 1, 2, 6, 28, 36, 38, 43, 44, 46, 48, 50, 52, 54, 56, 58, 59, 60, 61, 84, 89, 102, 133, 141, 142, 144, 146, 148, 150, 152, 154, 224, 257, 319, 330, 331, 333, 334, 335, 336, 337, 344, 360, 371
Kurt E.S. Okraku 344
Kwabena Owusu 257, 264, 282, 285, 286, 287, 311
Kwabena Yeboah 1, 80, 347, 360, 366
Kwadwo Asamoah 105, 108, 127, 257, 260, 267, 280, 281, 282, 283, 285, 309, 336
Kwame Sampson 52, 66, 135, 142
Kwame Sefa Kayi 347
Kwasi Appiah Foundation 325
Kwesi Nyantakyi 96, 97, 190, 200, 219, 339, 340, 341, 342, 343

L

Lawrence Ati-Zigi 257
Lawrence Lartey 177
Leeds United 81
Lesotho 106, 166, 196
Libya 40, 133
Lucy Quist 340
Luis Suarez 95, 170
Lumor Agbenyenu 257, 274, 280, 306

M

Mahatma Otoo 178, 179
Malik Akowuah 177
Maxwell Konadu 102, 124, 176, 222, 249
Michael Essien 108, 111, 112, 127, 192, 296, 332
Ministry of Youth and Sports 184, 186, 189

INDEX

Mohammed Alhassan 257, 266
Mohammed Sabato 177
Money viii, 316, 318, 320, 322, 324, 326, 328
Moses Foh-Amoaning 184, 202
Mubarak Wakaso 105, 109, 110, 127, 257, 274, 280, 286, 290, 303, 309
Mumuni Abubakar 177

N

Naa Odofoley Nortey 340
Netherlands 169, 172, 185, 374
Nigeria 87, 88, 105, 151, 154, 158, 167, 169, 175, 176, 207, 223, 254, 295, 297, 337
Nketia Yawson 335
Normalization Committee 243, 340
Nuhu Musa 257

O

Offei Ansah 40, 55, 330
Opoku Afriyie 41, 46, 47, 49, 50, 51, 135, 137, 142, 338
Opoku Nti 28, 41, 46, 50, 52, 53, 65, 66, 67, 68, 72, 73, 74, 75, 135, 136, 142, 149, 150, 153, 160, 227, 234, 235, 333
Opoku Ware School vii, 18, 19, 20, 22, 24, 26, 28
Osei Kuffour 330
Otto Addo 195
Owusu Mensah 72, 135, 138

P

Papa Arko 41, 46, 49, 50, 52, 53, 66, 142, 149, 234, 235, 331, 367
Paul Maxwell 264
Pius Hadzide 219
President John Agyekum Kufuor 53, 89, 90, 91, 221
President John Mahama 139, 219
President Kutu Acheampong 139
President Nana Akufo-Addo 242, 257, 273
Prestea Mine Stars 6, 37, 38, 41, 45, 52, 371
Prince Baffoe 178, 179

R

Rainbow Stars 28, 33, 34, 35, 36, 37, 360, 371
Rashid Sumaila 108, 177
Real Tamale United Tamale 56
Richard Kingson 301, 308, 330
Richard Mpong 177
Richard Ofori 257
Royal Baron Hotel 324

S

Sabaah Quaye 124, 176, 192
Sam Ampeh 335
Samuel Kwame Ankomah 258
Samuel Owusu 257, 264, 274, 277, 281, 285, 286, 287, 291, 303, 309, 310
Sarfo Gyamfi 66, 67, 68, 71, 72, 74, 75, 159, 178
Senegal vii, 2, 73, 74, 75, 91, 153, 154, 156, 157, 158, 160, 162, 163, 170, 177, 253, 254, 297, 337, 338, 357, 371

INDEX

Serbia 92, 94, 169, 170, 257, 374
Seth Ampadu 46, 66, 135, 142, 149
Simon Copley 258
Sims Kofi Mensah 45, 49
South Africa vii, 94, 122, 166, 167, 168, 169, 170, 172, 177, 178, 179, 254, 257, 267, 271, 296, 356
Stephen Appiah 171, 198, 232, 240, 262, 301, 308, 323, 332
Sudan viii, 106, 117, 128, 129, 167, 180, 205, 206, 207, 208, 210, 211, 212, 213, 214, 215, 247, 249
Sulley Muntari 108, 109, 110, 170, 192, 245, 296, 334
Sunyani 11, 13, 14, 16, 17, 18, 19, 20, 21, 24, 27, 28, 32, 33, 35, 38, 45, 317, 318, 323, 324, 328, 371
Sunyani Ridge Experimental School 14

T

Thomas Agyepong 257, 274, 277, 280, 283
Thomas Partey 257, 274, 275, 280, 286, 289, 290, 291, 306, 309
Tomacan Stars 28, 29, 36, 38, 371
Tony Baffoe 159, 253
Tunisia 119, 135, 254, 289, 290, 291, 292, 309, 311

U

United Arab Emirates (UAE) 255, 264
Uriah Asante 178

V

VAR 289
Victor Gomes 289
Victor Moses 223

W

World Cup vii, viii, 3, 87, 92, 94, 95, 101, 102, 104, 106, 107, 110, 111, 113, 114, 118, 122, 125, 126, 154, 155, 165, 166, 167, 168, 169, 170, 171, 172, 173, 183, 184, 185, 186, 187, 188, 190, 191, 192, 194, 196, 197, 198, 200, 202, 203, 209, 212, 215, 243, 253, 278, 293, 296, 297, 298, 301, 331, 341, 345, 356, 366, 372
Wyscout 103

Y

Yahya Kassum 52, 66, 142, 147, 235
Yaw Bawuah 49, 50, 53, 143
Yaw Yeboah 257, 266, 301

Z

Zambia 92, 96, 106, 113, 135, 136, 157, 158, 356

www.ingramcontent.com/pod-product-compliance
Lightning Source LLC
Chambersburg PA
CBHW030429010526
44118CB00011B/560